Scotland on a Shoestring

Scotland's Best for Less

Anna Fenge

MAINSTREAM
PUBLISHING

EDINBURGH AND LONDON

First published in Great Britain in 1997 by
MAINSTREAM PUBLISHING COMPANY (EDINBURGH) LTD
7 Albany Street
Edinburgh EH1 3UG

ISBN 1 85158 937 6

A catalogue record for this book is available from the British Library

Designed by Jenny Haig
Typeset in Sabon
Printed and bound in Finland by WSOY

SCOTLAND ON A SHOESTRING

ACKNOWLEDGEMENTS

There are a number of people who need particular thanks for their help. An enormous thank you to: Prue Borthwick, Ruth Buckingham, Dr Grace Matchett, Joanna Mattinson, Sheila McQueen, Clare O'Connor and Clare Shand, for their detailed checking and work on the text. Absolutely everyone I have spoken to and corresponded with at Tourist Information Centres around the country has been helpful and enthusiastic. People in the recreation departments of local authorities around the country have also kindly given of their time and expertise. There are a large number of individuals in museums, galleries, visitor centres and various other venues around Scotland, without whose help the book would have come to nothing. Many other bodies, including the National Trust for Scotland, Historic Scotland, the Association of Scottish Visitor Attractions and the Scottish Youth Hostel Association have all helped with information.

Above all, thanks to my long-suffering husband, Davie, and my kids – Jess and Alfie. This book is dedicated to you.

CONTENTS

INTRODUCTION

Free, cheap or a real bargain. You should find that everything in this book is one of these three.

Free things are everywhere, and the whole idea of the value of something as precious as leisure time is an intriguing one. Where does it start, and where does it end? It is free to walk along the road. It is also free to walk up Ben A'an or along the Southern Upland Way. It costs nothing to see the sea at Portobello, Durness or Machrihanish. The experience itself is as full of value as the effort and the openness that you give to it. If you want to have a good time, and you aren't worried about the cost, then the chances are that you will have fun. That is the real strength of this book. If you go out somewhere and it costs you nothing, or very little, then you have *always* had your money's worth! You actually can't lose.

Free fun adds a little bit of zest to an everyday activity. You can go to a garden centre, *or* you can visit a garden centre for free. There is a subtle difference; but the second one is definitely a lot more fun! (Please don't panic, dear reader, and shut the book and run screaming from the library, or bookshop, or your friends' house or wherever. I promise I will not list garden centres in any shape or form. I was just trying to illustrate a point.) There are plenty of other places, completely overlooked, which can give you a few minutes' entertainment for nothing. What about pet shops, particularly ones with tropical fish? A visit to a good pet shop is the equivalent of a free half-hour's aromatherapy session. All you have to remember is that you don't need to buy the doggie chews.

There are places which could have been included in this book, but which have been omitted because they would have made the strands of the book too unmanageable. I am thinking primarily of libraries, which dot the country from north to south. Libraries are full of beautiful books, which you can read for free! My strongest recommendation is that you take a library book with you at all times, and go into as many of these temples as you can. You can always find a local paper in the library, which, in turn, might give you another idea to follow up. Libraries are also full of leaflets and 'bumf' about local authority events, the sports halls and leisure centres that usually charge for their facilities, but deliver some great wave pools. Many libraries have events throughout the year for people of all ages. Bookshop events, too, have a powerful pull when the evening draws in and crowds form around the signed bookpiles and the refreshments.

So what about all the things that are included? This is just an introduction, so you need to dip into the book to answer that question. Roughly speaking, the material is split into sections: Days Out, Historical Sites, Museums, Galleries, Festivals, Sports, Accommodation and Travel; entries in each section are arranged by town under local authority headings.

Parks and gardens are featured in the Days Out section; they vary from formal, flowery places to wild forest parks where heather and rock give colour to the landscape. There is such a vibrant variety of Scotland represented that it makes me want to travel on and on. Just around the corner could be the most awesome view, or the happiest, most friendly visitor centre in the country.

The unusual pops up again and again. There are an incredible number of things to do with fish, such as fishmarkets to visit in the early morning, and fish festivals as far afield as Stornoway, Buckie and Eyemouth. It isn't that I'm obsessed with fish (although I am obsessed with rangers), it is simply that fish are a hugely important part of everyday life in many parts of the country. I have tried to give you a feel for the extremes as well as the everyday. You could watch a clog-maker, or get down on your hands and knees and rub brasses.

Festivals and celebrations are truly a part of the Scottish way of life. There are a number of ancient, traditional festivals with an element of the mystic and dark about them. Think of the Up-Helly-Aa celebrations in Shetland, or the Burning of the Clavie at Burghead. The more commercial city festivals, with events in 'venues' won't always be free, but there will be elements that are great value, and good spin-offs. If you go to the Edinburgh Festival, don't miss the Cavalcade on the first Sunday, or Fringe Sunday in Holyrood Park. The fireworks on the final Thursday of the Edinburgh Festival are a spectacular treat, and all of these are utterly free.

Accommodation will cost you about as much as you want to pay. In the cities and towns there isn't much hope of a free pitch for your tent at night, although you will surely find a hostel or a campsite to make your home. The places mentioned include as many hostels and campsites as possible, with just a few sample bed and breakfast places or guest houses, to give an idea what kind of price you would expect to pay, as well as somewhere to start. Hell, have toothbrush will travel.

Travelling will not be free unless you are cycling or walking. The next cheapest is inevitably the bus, which can be a good means of access to tricky places. Even trickier places can be reached by postbus! Route planning should be a little easier with the hints given.

As you wander, be sure to clutch this book and the 'free is fun' attitude to your heart. If you come across places which you think ought to be included (provided they aren't garden centres or car showrooms), then please let me know! God knows whether the publishers will ever let me attempt to update this first edition, but if they do I would like to fit in as many of your suggestions as I can. I am particularly interested in those places that shine in your memory, because they are the ones that make up Scotland's best for less. Write to me c/o Mainstream Publishing, 7 Albany Street, Edinburgh, EH1 3UG. I look forward to hearing from you!

DAYS OUT

Being skint is a challenge. (Being canny, of course, is another.) Being skint and going off and having a great day out is more than just a challenge – it's more like a dare. At the end of the day, you have not only had a great time, but you've also proved something to yourself. Making the most of everything and anything that is available is a large part of it, but creating opportunities where there seem to be none is the key.

I get a real thrill out of going along somewhere for free that other people would pay for – even if only a little extra. A good example here are the Open Door Days, a scheme which allows free access to buildings all over Scotland, including historical sites which can be really expensive at other times of the year. If you are out and about in September, keep a look-out for interesting buildings, from the oldest castles to the most modern of conference centres, and you could enjoy a look inside for nothing.

For some real peace and quiet, and an interesting ramble through the centuries, Scotland has some quite outstanding graveyards. Tombs are the most human form of architecture, particularly in the cities, where, whilst contemplating one's mortality over a sandwich and slug of juice, you can play 'spot the famous gravestone'. Often overlooked, but graveyards can be quietly entertaining.

Then there are the really obvious places, which reek of

the joy of the Scots at play. Parks and beaches of all kinds are glorious, often lively and loud, peopled with folk who have been freed from the *need* to enjoy themselves. When you aren't paying, the fun just comes, or doesn't, as the case may be. At least with a free or cheap afternoon out, there aren't any misery demons in the back of your mind, whingeing, 'They'd better be having a good time, this is costing a fortune.'

As well as the traditional, formal city parks, there are a wealth of country parks, which feature long, rambling walks and give visitors the chance to experience nature in a safe, guided (if you are a ranger fanatic) environment. Country parks are a wonderful resource, usually run by the 'Recreation Department' of the local council.

The further away from the cities and the central belt you travel, the less there is a need for arranged and organised parks. The wilderness that makes up so much of this beautiful country takes over. There is no taming these places! There is so much space, mountain, loch and sky that no book can really do it justice.

THE WEST

Argyll and Bute

Argyll Forest Park extends from Loch Long to Loch Fyne, incorporating three forests – Benmore, Glenbranter and Ardgartan. There are lots of rambles and hikes throughout the area. The Forest Enterprise district office is at Kilmun, near Dunoon. Tel: 01369 840666

Arrochar has a Tourist Information Centre to fill you with ideas, at Ardgartan. Open April to October. Tel: 01301 702432

Cove is the place to see the *Linn Garden*, which covers moorland and glen. No pandas in the bamboo garden, however. Give a donation, please. Open March to October, daily from dawn to dusk. Tel: 01436 842242

Dunoon isn't merely the place you take the ferry. Get to the bottom of some local ancient history by following the *Ardnadam Heritage Trail*. The starting-point is the Ardnadam carpark, two miles from Dunoon, just off the A885 Strachur road (see Historical Sites).

Or you could visit *Dunoon Ceramics*, the famous pottery factory on Hamilton Street in the centre of town. I challenge you to come away without a mug! Factory tours are available from 10 a.m. to 4 p.m. (till 3 p.m. on Friday). The factory shop, with associated bargains, is nearby. Tel: 01369 704360

The Tourist Information Centre (open all year) is at 7 Alexandra Parade. Tel: 01369 703785

Helensburgh has *Hermitage Park* on Sinclair Street. Just the place to go for tennis, putting, or a quiet rest while the kids whirl around their play area. Tourist information is available from April to October at The Clock Tower, East Clyde Street. Tel: 01436 672642

Inveraray, the ancient capital of Argyll, is on the shores of picturesque Loch Fyne. There are many facilities here, from places to stay to some quite expensive visitor attractions. Tourist information can be obtained from the office at Front Street. Open all year. Tel: 01499 302063.

Kilmory Woodland Park is at Lochgilphead. The woodland and gardens are open all year from dawn to dusk. The rhododendrons are really special in late spring/early summer and there are lots of small speciality witch-hazel trees too. Tel: 01546 604227

Kintyre is glorious, a peninsula with a distinctly 'island' feel to it. Head for the southernmost point of the Mull, following St Columba's Footprints to the viewpoint. From here you can see right across to Ireland, only 12 miles away. Look north-west for views of Islay, Jura and Gigha. There is also a lighthouse, which is now automatic, so can no longer be visited.

Beaches are in plentiful supply. Try the sweeping sands of Machrihanish on the west coast, or the sandy coves around Dunaverty on the south coast. The Gulf Stream keeps the sea warm (honest!) and gives the whole peninsula a dry, sunny climate – in summer anyway. To see seals, take a trip to Ronachan Point – the name means 'place of the seals' – between Tarbert and Tayinloan. You might even catch a glimpse of an otter!

Carradale was once a popular holiday spot for Scots. Carradale House is the home of author Naomi Mitchison, whose gardens you can visit.

Campbeltown used to have 30 whisky distilleries. No wonder, in the words of a famous song, they wished the loch was whisky! A working harbour that catches some delicious seafood, Campbeltown is also the centre of the peninsula in terms of activities and facilities, including a museum and a cinema.

Caves to visit include *St Kiaran's Cave* at Kildalloig, near Campbeltown. Remember to go at low tide! Don't get stuck. You could try *Keil Cave* at Garvald, which is also near Campbeltown. You can almost feel the breath of that hairy prehistoric cave-dweller on the back of your neck . . .

Davaar Island lies off the east coast of Kintyre, near Campbeltown. At low tide you can walk across the causeway to the island and visit the cave with a painting of the Crucifixion on the wall, done in 1887. (Presumably by some poor soul who got trapped here by the tide.)

Forest Walks – there are certainly lots of places to go walking on Kintyre. From Ben Ghuilean (south of Campbeltown) to Kildonan (on the east coast), Forestry Enterprise has some spectacular waymarked walks awaiting you.

Glenbarr, down the coast from Tayinloan, is the home of Angus and Jeanne Macalister, appropriately enough the Laird and Lady who run the *Macalister Clan Visitor Centre*. Snatch a glimpse of family life in an eighteenth-century house, and be shown round by the Laird himself to boot! Glenbarr Abbey and the Clan Visitor Centre are open daily except Tuesday, from 10 a.m. to 5.30 p.m. There is a small charge. Tel: 01583 421247

To get to Kintyre, follow the A83 via Inveraray and Lochgilphead, stopping in Tarbert to view the harbour and get a feel of this unique place. There are two local Tourist Information Centres: Campbeltown (open all year) at Mackinnon House, The Pier, Tel: 01586 552056; and Tarbert (open Easter to October) at Harbour Street, Tel: 01880 820429.

Loch Awe has a secret: *Ben Cruachan*, on its northern shore, has a power station hidden in its hollowed-out interior. This is a great family day out – and quite a surprise to those who have driven past the mountain before in all innocence. A tour of the station starts at the visitor centre, which has exhibitions and video. You can pay for a guided tour if you want one. Open from end March to late October, daily from 9 a.m. to 4.30 p.m. Cruachan is on the A85, 15 miles east of Oban. Tel: 01866 822673

Lochgilphead has a Tourist Information Centre at Lochnell Street. Open April to October. Tel: 01546 602344

Luss is not only the home of the Loch Lomond Park visitor centre, it is a beautiful conservation village in its own right. For a really hilarious Scottish visit, pop into the *Thistle Bagpipe Works*. (See also West Dunbartonshire: Loch Lomond Park.)

Oban has a *Caithness Glass* factory shop and exhibition right in the centre of the town, on Railway Pier, by the ferry terminal for the islands. You can view an 'audio-visual and interpretative display', then watch an engraver at work, or see glass being blown. Open all year, Monday to Saturday from 9 a.m. to 5 p.m.; also Sunday from Easter to November, from 11 a.m. to 5 p.m. Tel: 01631 563386

There is plenty to do in and around Oban. If you get stuck try the Tourist Information Centre on Argyll Square. Open all year. Tel: 01631 563122

BUTE

Rothesay is the main town on the Isle of Bute. Here you'll find the charm of *Ardencraig Gardens* hard to resist. They have exotic birds and fish as well as the most glorious gardens for miles, with greenhouse collections too. Open May to September, Monday to Friday from 9 a.m. to 4.30 p.m., Saturday and Sunday from 1 p.m. to 4.30 p.m. Tel: 01700 504225

Scottish Pride Creameries, at Townhead, is the ideal attraction for dairy freaks. You can watch Scottish Cheddar being made, from a special viewing gallery. Open all year, daily except Wednesday. Tel: 01700 503186

Rothesay Tourist Information Centre (open all year) is at 15 Victoria Street. Tel: 01700 502151

East Ayrshire

Cumnock has *Woodroad Park*, with amenities that include an outdoor swimming pool, tennis and putting. These are available only from Easter to mid-September. Well, would you swim outdoors in January?

Kilmarnock. Aim for *Dean Park*; the castle has an admission charge, but you can take a wander round the gardens for free. An adventure playground, an aviary and a fistful of rare sheep can't be bad.

Kay Park is less spacious, but has extras (at an extra charge) such as pitch and putt and trampolining, as well as boats for hire. It is open from dawn to dusk, although the extras are available only in summer. Nod knowingly at the Burns monument in passing. Tel: 01563 521140. There is also a Burns Museum in the park if you haven't had your fill.

Along similar lines try *Annanhill Gardens* for their pitch and putt, golf and a walled garden (presumably to protect joggers and snoggers from low-flying balls).

If you get hungry, try *Dino's*, opposite the Laigh Kirk in the town centre. This is one of those rare chippies where you can sit in with your cholesterol choice. Wonderful as a kind of hot-oil experience for undernourished and dry hair.

You could go along to the helpful people at the Tourist Information Centre (open all year) at 62 Bank Street. Tel: 01563 539090

Loch Doon, with castle ruins which were actually rebuilt this century by the Power People (see Historical Sites), offers walks into the hills, and also free fishing.

Mauchline has a Tourist Information Centre to serve the surrounding areas. Find it at the National Burns Memorial Tower on Kilmarnock Road. Tel: 01290 551916

East Dunbartonshire

Kirkintilloch has an excellent park called *Woodhead Park* which you will find on Lenzie Road. Although the facilities are best in summer, there is an aviary as well as a putting green and trampolines. Tel: 0141 776 2151

Milngavie is, surprisingly, home to the 550-acre *Mugdock Country Park*. A programme of countryside events (frightening things with indigenous species) is organised by the resident ranger service. Excellent facilities also include children's play areas, barbecue sites, mobility equipment for the less able-bodied and, above all, great walks. The park is at Craigallan Road, on the West Highland Way, between the A809 and A81. Open all year; the visitor centre is open from 10 a.m. to 5 p.m. (later in summer). Tel: 0141 956 6100

East Renfrewshire

Giffnock has a huge park. *Rouken Glen Park* is picturesque, with swathes of grass and trees parting to reveal the crags of a Highland glen. They even have a 'walkaboutabit' trail. (Perfect for less sensible footwear!) If you don't believe me, you'll have to go yourself. Tel: 0141 620 2084

City of Glasgow

When you count up all the parks and green spaces in Glasgow, it's easy to see how the city got its name – Glasgow in Gaelic means 'dear, green place'.

Alexandra Park is on Alexandra Parade. This is one of those large, studied parks, with everything in its place, including the lake and the golf course!

Bellahouston Park is on Dumbreck Road, and is mainly a sporty park, with wide open spaces. The daffodils in spring are spectacular. Open all year, daily from 8 a.m. to 9 p.m. Tel: 0141 649 2100

The Botanic Gardens are wonderful – in good or bad weather! Find them at 730 Great Western Road at the end of Byres Road, and head for the shelter of the glasshouses if it rains or the day is cold. The plants and shrubs, as you would imagine, are from all over the world. What better way to imagine yourself into another climate! There is also a herb garden, for cooking and aromatherapy enthusiasts. Open all year, daily from dawn to dusk. The glasshouses are open from 10 a.m. to 4.45 p.m. (till 4.15 p.m. in winter). Tel: 0141 334 2422

Glasgow Green is perhaps best known to non-Glaswegians for big events and concerts that are occasionally held there. This is a city-centre park on the banks of the Clyde, which you can reach from Greendyke Street. Wander to the People's Palace Museum and take a rest in the Winter Gardens, with their towering glasshouse. Open all year, daily from 8 a.m. to 9 p.m. Tel: 0141 771 6372

Kelvingrove Park is on the gentle slopes around the River Kelvin, close to the University and the famous Art Gallery. This is a lovely park, with some excellent views and open spaces as well as secluded spots. There is even putting, a bowling green and tennis for those who feel inclined. Find Kelvingrove Park via Kelvin Way. It is open all year, daily from dawn to dusk. Tel: 0141 287 5064

Linn Park is between Clarkston Road and Carmunnock Road in Cathcart. There are great spaces for sports and play here, and even a children's zoo. If you are completely potty, you could try the assault course.

The Necropolis, on Castle Street, is one of the best graveyards you'll visit in this lifetime! Spectacularly situated on a hill beside Glasgow Cathedral, this is a glorious place for gravewatchers. Beautifully carved tombs with John Knox's statue looking down on them all.

Pollok Country Park is at 2060 Pollokshaws Road, and is the home of the wonderful Pollok House and the splendid Burrell Collection (see Museums and Galleries). With a visitor centre, great nature trail and resident Highland cattle, what more could a body want? Open all the time, anytime. Tel: 0141 632 9299

Queens Park is on Langside Road, and is open daily from 8 a.m. to 9 p.m. Greenhouses galore and woody retreats are the hallmarks of this park. You'll also find one of the most impressive views of Glasgow, from its highest point. Tel: 0141 649 0331

Tollcross Park is on Tollcross Road, Parkhead. There is a pets' corner, fish tanks and even exotic birds. All this and a woodland trail. I'm delirious.

Tourist information in Glasgow can be found all year at 35 St Vincent Place. Tel: 0141 204 4400 or at Glasgow Airport. Tel: 0141 848 4440

Victoria Park and Fossil Grove will set your spirits soaring. An arboretum and some truly lovely trees such as Cornish elms and lime trees; and, within the park is Fossil Grove, the famous home of the best rock gardens in the city. Even model boating, too. Victoria Park is open all year, Monday to Saturday from 8 a.m. to dusk, Sunday from 10 a.m. to dusk; Fossil Grove is open from April to the end of September, from 12 noon to 5 p.m. Tel: 0141 950 1448

Inverclyde

Clyde-Muirshiel Regional Park actually straddles three local authorities – Inverclyde, North Ayrshire and Renfrewshire. There are wonderful opportunities here for all kinds of recreation, from a gentle walk to archery and canoeing. There are a number of different centres in the park to visit, although not all of them are free. Try Muirshiel Centre and Country Park, Tel: 01505 842803. Another one to visit is *Cornalees Bridge Centre and Nature Trail* (see Greenock).

For more information about the regional park itself, contact Clyde-Muirshiel Park Authority, which is based at Barnbrock Farm, near Kilbarchan. Tel: 01505 614791

Gourock has an excellent park at Broomberry Drive. A walled flower garden, pets' corner (including my favourites – guinea-pigs) and even a toddlers' playground add to the sporty attractions of tennis, bowling and pitch and putt.

If in doubt, try the Tourist Information Centre (open April to September) at Pierhead. Tel: 01475 639467

Greenock. About three miles outside town is the *Cornalees Bridge Centre*, overlooking the Firth of Clyde. Of course, there is a nature trail, but more entertaining is the opportunity to walk along a nineteenth-century aqueduct towards the old reservoir of Loch Thom. What better moment to ponder the marvels of the modern age. Aqueduct, viaduct . . . Internet. We're all just part of one huge network and my head is spinning. Tel: 01475 521458

Inverclyde Environmental Project is at Hole Farm Glen, behind the Overton housing scheme. The farm includes a nature trail, rare breeds and friendly farm animals. Open Monday to Friday from 9 a.m. to 5 p.m., Saturday from 12 noon to 2 p.m.

Lunderston Bay, near Gourock, has a picnic site and children's play areas beside a beach with gorgeous views. Not all sand on the beach, but rock pools too. Tel: 01475 521458

North Ayrshire

Eglinton Country Park, two miles north of Irvine, has enough to occupy a whole day, as long as the weather is good. There are an assortment of ancient buildings, and all the accoutrements (see Historical Sites), but best of all, there are sheep, horses, even pigs. Designed to entertain the people of Irvine, there are cycle paths, walled gardens, a tea-room with home-made scoff, and your friendly local rangers. There is an events programme running throughout the year, which promises hands-on fun for those with a burning desire to 'paint pebbles' or take 'a leisurely look at Fruits, Fungi and Fallen Leaves'. Tel: 01294 551776

Fairlie. *Hunterston B*, the nuclear power station, is to the south of town, off the A78 Ardrossan–Largs road. I don't know how you feel about it, but for me all this power gives me a feeling of power*less*ness. It certainly offers an informative day out and the size of it all is incredible. Open all year, daily from 9.30 a.m. to 4.30 p.m. Tel: 0800 838557

Fencebay Fisheries in Fairlie itself offers the chance to see trout in the fish ponds, live crabs and lobsters too – and then eat your new friends . . . Tel: 01475 568918

Irvine might not seem that attractive at first glance, but take a second look at what's on offer. The Harbourfront is charming, and the adjacent *Beach Park* beyond the Magnum Leisure Centre will keep you going for hours. The trim track (a jogging paradise with free-standing parallel bars) is enough to send me scurrying for chocolate. A maze and a dragon statue should ensure the kids are entertained for a while.

The Tourist Information Centre is in an unlikely site: it seems to be next to one of the biggest carparks in the history of the combustion engine, but boy, are they helpful! The lady stayed open at lunchtime for me! Find it at New Street. Tel: 01294 313886

Largs is a coastal resort with a beach and promenade and an annual Viking festival. On the A78 coast road between Greenock and Ayr, this might be just the place to get an ice-cream. Try Nardini's on the Esplanade – I know it isn't free, but sometimes a price has to be paid!

Parks in Largs include *Douglas Park*, which has views of the Clyde from its hilly walks, as well as tennis courts. Or go to *Anderson Park*, which has a playground for the kids. Look for more at the Tourist Information Centre (open all year) on the Promenade. Tel: 01475 673765

ARRAN
Brodick is the place where the ferry arrives (from Ardrossan), and here you will find a Tourist Information Centre, appropriately enough at the Pier. Open all year. Tel: 01770 302140. There is also a Tourist Information Desk on the MV *Caledonian Isles* ferry, which runs between Ardrossan and Arran. Open Easter to October.

Lochranza is a beautiful part of Arran, with a Tourist Information Centre. Open May to mid-October. Tel: 01770 830320

The *Isle of Arran Distillers* offer free guided tours of their distillery, one of Scotland's newest, and a free dram! Open Monday to Sunday from 10 a.m. to 6 p.m. Tel: 01770 830264

CUMBRAE
Millport, the largest town on the Isle of Cumbrae, has a Tourist Information Centre at 28 Stuart Street. Open from Easter to October. Tel: 01475 530753

North Lanarkshire

Carfin Pilgrimage Centre could be the place you have been waiting all your life to visit. The 'Spirit of Pilgrimage' exhibition will stretch your understanding of spiritual journeys. If you feel truly contemplative, spend some time in the Carfin Grotto, a shrine and place of pilgrimage itself, which was inspired by Lourdes. There is a café and shop, and a small admission fee to the exhibition. Open May to October, from 10 a.m. to 7 p.m., November to April from 10 a.m. to 5 p.m. Carfin is 17 miles from Glasgow and 25 miles from Stirling, on the B7066 to the south-west of Newarthill. Tel: 01698 268941

Coatbridge is the site of an excellent country park – *Drumpellier*. With a pets' corner, birdwatching, a butterfly house in the summer, playgrounds and formal gardens, there will be something for all and sundry. Rangers also tiptoe around saving rare stuff and telling you what sex frogs are. Find the A752 to Uddingston (near the M73) and you are almost there. Drumpellier is on Townhead Road, Coatbridge. Tel: 01236 422257

There is a Tourist Information Centre (open April to end October) at the Time Capsule on Buchanan Street in Monklands. Tel: 01236 431133

Cumbernauld is one of Scotland's new towns. Don't be deterred, this can mean that more effort is made in areas such as recreation than in other towns of a similar size. Enjoy the variety of things available at *Palaceriggs Country Park*, just two miles south of town on the A8011. A wonderful variety of Scottish and European animals can be seen, from Przewalski's horses (sorry?) to wolves and wildcats. Lots more besides (see Museums). Open all year during daylight hours; the visitor centre is open from April to September, from 10 a.m. to 6 p.m. (till 4.30 p.m. in winter). Tel: 01236 720047

Kilsyth has the *Dumbreck Marsh Local Nature Reserve*. Get along there and see some water-loving birds and wildlife. Tel: 01236 720047

You could try *Burngreen Park*, which is a large park with many extras, such as trampolines and table-tennis and even a mini road system for bikes. You will have to pay for some of these activities.

Motherwell. On the outskirts of town is the impressive *Dalzell Country Park*, a glorious woodland sanctuary to wildlife and rangers alike. You might even meet one of several colourful ghosts – watch for the 'Green Lady', the 'White Lady' or even the 'Grey Lady'. Surely they must all be the same lady in differing moods? The grounds include a spectacular Japanese garden, arboretum, the Covenanter's Oak and a fairy ring. Contact the ranger service, Tel: 01698 269696. Get to the country park from the Civic Centre in Motherwell, taking Adele Street past Motherwell College; the RSPB/Dalzell carpark are on your right.

Close to Dalzell you will find the RSPB *Baron's Haugh Reserve*, where you can while away the hours watching birds, from a hide. Tel: 01555 770941

For a conventional park try *Viewpark* at Juniper Road. It is open daily from 9 a.m. to 5.30 p.m. and features great play equipment for kids from three to 13.

The Tourist Information Centre (open all year) is at the Library in Hamilton Road. Tel: 01698 267676

Shotts has an enthralling *Heritage Centre*, which is situated in the Library on the High Street. Scenes from the past have been recreated, in a quite uncanny way! The Covenanters and miners are well represented, as they are so key to the past of the town. Why not go down the pit at Shotts Library? Open weekdays from 9.30 a.m. to 7 p.m. (till 12 noon on Wednesday), Saturday from 9.30 a.m. to 5 p.m. Tel: 01501 821556

Strathclyde Country Park makes you tired just thinking of the number of available activites. Rangers are on hand to guide walkers and rescue small mammals. There is so much here – from watersports to camping, putting to curling – that the park has become a leading recreational resource for the West

Coast. At times during the year the park becomes the venue for fairs and concerts. A visitor centre gives full details of all on offer. There are even a number of interesting historical sites if you are that way inclined. Tel: 01698 266155

Uddingston has a treasure in *Viewpark Gardens*. The relaxing ornamental gardens, particularly the Japanese gardens, are well worth a stroll. In the summer there is a flower festival when the park comes alive with activity. The park is on New Edinburgh Road. Tel: 01698 818269

Wishaw has *Houldsworth Park*, which has particularly good facilities for children, including toddlers. Open daily from 9 a.m. to 11 p.m.

Renfrewshire

Erskine has the *Lamont City Farm* on Barrhill Road. This is a community project farm, with some farm animals and small pets. Kids will love the donkey and pony rides (there may be a charge for these), and there are good picnic and play areas for a sunny day. Open daily from 10.30 a.m. to 5 p.m. There is a donation box for you to show your appreciation. Tel: 0141 812 5335

Lochwinnoch is a charming village. You can also dip your toe in the water at *Castle Semple Country Park*, off Largs Road, signposted from Lochwinnoch off the A737. Watersports and wetsuits abound. A part of the Clyde-Muirshiel Regional Park, I expect there are rangers lurking. Tel: 01505 842882

Muirshiel Visitor Centre is on the B786 between Bridge of Weir and Lochwinnoch. Rangers are at work here, with moorland walks to be sampled to Windy Hill and Calder River waterfalls. For people with sensible shoes. Tel: 01505 842803

Paisley is trying hard to change its hard-man reputation. The town has great facilities of all kinds, with a central park (*Barshaw Park* on Glasgow Road) that packs in a boating pond, model railway and a kids' nature corner with goats and ponies as well as the usual attractions. Tel: 0141 889 2908

Gleniffer Braes Country Park, further out of town on Glenfield Road (where the visitor centre is), is the place for stunning views away to the Clyde, and moorland and woodland strolling. There are adventure play places for children. Keep a look-out during the year for events being held in the park (such as motocross championships, sheepdog trials and model aeroplane flying). Countryside rangers are ever vigilant. Tel: 0141 884 3794

The *Sma' Shot Cottages* will fill in the facts about weaver life in the eighteenth and nineteenth centuries. Kept open by the Old Paisley Society, they are open from May to end September, Wednesday and Saturday from 1 p.m. to 5 p.m. Take a guided tour through the 'lived in' feeling of Sma' Shot, which is found on Shuttle Street, in Paisley town centre. There is no charge, but donations are welcome. Tel: 0141 889 1708

Another unusual place to visit in Paisley is *Coats Observatory and Weather Station*. Here you can see meteorology at work! There is a satellite picture receiver and plenty of high-tech stuff to stare at. Open Monday, Tuesday and Thursday from 2 p.m. to 8 p.m., Wednesday, Friday and

Saturday from 10 a.m. to 5 p.m. Find it at Oakshaw Street. Tel: 0141 889 2013

If you are still stuck for something to do, then look in at the Tourist Information Centre, at the Town Hall, Abbey Close. Open April to September. Tel: 0141 889 0711

Renfrew has *Robertson Park* (on Inchinnan Road and Paisley Road) with the traditional floral business as well as a cycle track for those keen to sport their shorts. Youngsters can hire bikes to try out the model traffic area. There is also a pets' corner. Tel: 0141 886 2807

South Ayrshire

Ayr has plenty of great outdoor spaces. Try the *Seafront Play Park*, particularly if you have kids who would benefit from the activity play gear, sandpit and paddling pool. Why not have a stroll along the front while you're at it?

Craigie Park offers a riverside walk, with flowers and the added attraction of pitch and putt.

Craigie Horticultural Centre boasts a tropical glasshouse and a floral hall for true flower children. The centre is in an attractive woody area, beside the River Ayr Walk, on the Craigie Estate. Tel: 01292 263275

Get your tourist information from the centre at Burns House, Burns Statue Square. Tel: 01292 288688

Electric Brae, nine miles south of Ayr on the A719, is a famous weird hang-out. An optical illusion makes you think you're going down the hill, when you are in fact going up! (Local tip – try pouring your juice on the road.)

Girvan has a boating lake by the promenade. This is a great place for bringing back childhood memories; there are trampolines, a bouncy castle, crazy golf and a fun fair. In summer, of course!

Bargany Gardens is near Girvan, north on the B734. For a small donation you can visit this spectacle of azaleas, rhododendrons and the rest. Open end of March to end of October. Tel: 01465 871249

There is a Tourist Information Centre at Girvan, at Bridge Street. Open April to October. Tel: 01465 714950

Prestwick has the *Airport*! Let me guess: you never thought of an airport as the ideal place to visit . . . Well, think again! Tel: 01292 479822

You could head instead to *The Wee Glass Works* to see stained glass craftspeople at work. Go to 176 Main Street or Tel: 01292 476312

South Lanarkshire

Biggar is not merely a place with an inappropriate name; it is the home to five (yes, five) museums (see Historical Sites and Museums). Clearly a historical haunt with a turbulent past, Biggar is on the A702 about 38 miles from Glasgow and 28 miles from Edinburgh. The kids will enjoy the freedom of *Burn Braes*, a park with room to run as well as play equipment. The *Greenhill*

Covenanters Museum is on the edge of Burn Braes too. Check out the Victorian puppet theatre, home to Purves Puppets (Tel: 01899 20631).

Another large park is *Biggar Public Park* on Broughton Road. There is golf, swingball, tennis, putting, even a boating pond and bikes for hire. Open all year. Tel: 01899 20319

For tourist information on Biggar itself from Easter to October you can call their Tourist Information Centre at 155 High Street. Tel: 01899 21066

Chatelherault is an outstandingly ornate William Adam eighteenth-century hunting lodge. A former ruin, the building is now restored and the kennels house a museum, with a country park occupying the spacious grounds. The park actually covers over 500 acres! That's a pretty long woodland walk by anyone's standards! Rangers, too, if you'll let them guide you. On a less tiring note, why not encourage any children in the direction of the adventure playground whilst you sip tea or pause to wonder 'why here?' about the rare white cattle. Reach the park via Ferniegair, off the A72 south of Hamilton. The visitor centre is open all year from 10 a.m. to 5 p.m. Tel: 01698 426213

East Kilbride is a Scottish 'new town'. It isn't all modern estates linked by one-way systems, though; just to the south of town, on the A726 to Strathaven, you will find the peaceful haven of *Calderglen Country Park*. The children's zoo is a special feature of the park, with wallabies, goats, owls and even guinea-pigs for those who like their life a little less wild. The kids will be well amused here, as there is an adventure playpark as well as some sedate riverside walks for the older contingent. Look out for special events here during the summer – everything from sheep to classic cars. Rangers on call, too. The park is open Monday to Friday from 10.30 a.m. to 5 p.m. (till 4 p.m. in winter), weekends from 11.30 a.m. to 4 p.m. Tel: 01355 236644

For a park in the midst of it all, the town-centre park is off Westmains Road, near the railway station and the Dollan Aqua Centre. The special attraction here is the boating pond. Tel: 01355 271200

Serious watersports enthusiasts will want to experience the newly created *James Hamilton Heritage Park,* which features a nature sanctuary, excellent children's play areas and a picnic area, as well as a serious watersports centre. Tel: 01355 276611

Hamilton. The local Tourist Information Centre is at the Road Chef Services on the northbound M74. Open all year. Tel: 01698 285590

Lanark was home to the first meeting of the Scots parliament in 978. Look out for the William 'Braveheart' Wallace statue on the inspiring *St Nicholas Church.*

Parks to try include *Biggar Park* and *Lanark Loch,* which are off Hyndford Road. Some great open spaces here, with all the extras – boating on the loch, tennis, pitch and putt, even fishing. Tel: 01555 661331. *Castlebank Park* is a large Victorian-style park, with woodland walks and proper gardens. *Hazlebank Park* is on the A72 at Hazlebank near Lanark, and features play and picnic areas on the banks of the Clyde.

Lanark Market is a place to visit with a difference. The market is open on Mondays and sale days from 10 a.m. to 3 p.m. Phone ahead to find out the date of the next market. Lawrie and Symington run the markets, at Muirglen, Hyndford Road. Tel: 01555 662281

There is a Tourist Information Centre (open all year) in Lanark at Horsemarket, Ladyacre Road. Tel: 01555 661661

Stonehouse is a conservation village, which can be found on the A71, about 17 miles from Glasgow and only six miles south of Hamilton. The *Alexander Hamilton Memorial Park* has one of those typical Victorian bandstands last seen on *Trumpton*. Find the park on the Larkhall road, near the River Avon. There is a wealth of history associated with this old weaving town, including tales of witches and pagan myths. Look for *St Patrick's Well*, a sulphurous spring that is said to have cured tuberculosis and skin diseases. A couple of miles south of the village, heading out on the Sidehead Road, you will come across the beautiful E'e Falls, which are signposted at Sandford. If you are very observant, you will even spot the remains of a Roman road on the way.

Strathaven, nearby in the Avon valley, is a small market town with farming and weaving roots. Visit Gilmour's sweet shop to taste the famous Strathaven toffee, and take yourself to the park to see the miniature railway (a sit-on one for the little kids out there), boating pond and other delights. The park is between the Glasgow Road, Three Stanes Road and Lethame Road.

West Dunbartonshire

Antartex Village is an Edinburgh Woollen Mill factory, on an industrial estate in Alexandria, but hang on in there! You can watch the workers at their benches, producing leather and sheepskin coats and jackets. Other crafts can be seen in workshops under the same roof. For the flush there is also a factory shop and, naturally, a coffee shop. Lomond Industrial Estate is off the A82 and A811 in Alexandria. Tel: 01389 54263

Balloch is the scenic home of *Balloch Castle Country Park*, with wide green expanses and cosy walled gardens. The park is open daily from sunrise to sunset; the visitor centre is open from Easter to October, daily from 10 a.m. to 6 p.m. The southern waterfront of Loch Lomond is a good place to start on any trip to the Loch. Tel: 01389 758216

There is a Tourist Information Centre (open March to November) at Balloch Road. Tel: 01389 753533

Dumbarton has a glorious park too, at *Overtoun Estate*. This is one of those ranger places, but with a twist, as there are sculptures in the woods around you. You can walk up to the *Spardie Linn Waterfall* from here, too. The park is off Milton Brae on the outskirts of the town. Another Dumbarton park is *Levengrove Park* which has lovely spaces to sit and ponder life's weird mysteries by the banks of the River Clyde and the River Leven. If that gets too boring, try out the putting or the crazy golf. The *River Leven Towpath* will take you for a stroll along to Loch Lomond if the fancy takes you.

Tourist information is available all year at Milton, on the northbound A82. Tel: 01389 742306

Loch Lomond Park is 170 square miles of spectacular natural beauty. The local ranger service is based at Balloch Castle (Tel: 01389 758216), and there are a series of events in the park throughout the year. These events vary from day walks, experiencing the nature of the landscape and environments around the Loch, to meeting local experts on different aspects of the park itself. The *West Highland Way* skirts the east shores of the loch. Stations at Balloch, Tarbet and Ardlui on the west side of the loch give easy access; there are Tourist Information Centres at Balloch and Tarbet, and the Park Centre itself is also on the west shore of the Loch, at Luss (Tel: 01436 860601) on the A82. (See Argyll: Luss.)

The Tarbet Tourist Information Centre is on Main Street. Open April to October. Tel: 01301 702260

THE EAST

East Lothian

Belhaven, near Dunbar, has a beautiful beach. Clear, clean water has won the bay a seaside award. There are many great beaches on this stretch of coast; beware of parking charges though, for example at *Yellowcraig*.

Dunbar is the place for the sun. According to legend it has been the sunniest and driest town in Scotland for 30 years. Perhaps not the achievement of the century. A great view across the Firth of Forth though, from the busy little twin-harboured town full of history. It is well worth a stroll.

Lauderdale Park has skittles and giant draughts in summer, as well as table-tennis, trampolines, swingball, putting and crazy golf. You will have to pay a small charge for the more exciting of these activities, but the paddling pool is gratis.

Visit the *John Muir Country Park* outside the town for spectacular nature walks in memory of Scots philanthropist John Muir (see Historical Sites). Rangers abound. The park is to the west of Dunbar, off the A1087 from the A1. There are barbecue stoves at Linkfield carpark for those with meat at hand. For help, contact the ranger service. Tel: 01368 863886

Just a few miles south of Dunbar is *Thorntonloch*, where you'll find a sandy beach with dunes behind it. Good for walking and birdwatching, although swimming isn't advised, as there is a strong undertow.

More facts about Dunbar can be had from the Tourist Information Centre at 143 High Street. Tel: 01368 863353

East Linton. One mile to the east, off the A1, is *Knowes Farm Shop*, where you can wander in their herb garden and generally take in the smells and realities of organic farming on a small scale. You won't leave empty-handed either! Open daily.

Also look out for the *Fenton Barns Farm Shop*, off the B1345 between Dirleton and Drem, via the B1377. Tel: 01620 860010

The local Tourist Information Centre is at Pencraig, one mile west of East Linton, on the A1. Open all year. Tel: 01620 860063

Gullane is a wild beach. So clean it wins awards, it is sandy, backed by a series of sand-dunes that provide protection from the wind, and it is great for paddling or swimming. It's also popular with windsurfers.

Haddington is a town jam-packed with history (see Historical Sites). For a gentle wander, try the *St Mary's Pleasance Garden*, within the walls of the grounds of a seventeenth-century town house. The garden has been developed by the Haddington Garden Trust, to the appropriate level of splendour. Open all year, daily from dawn to dusk. Tel: 01620 822838

Inveresk Lodge Garden on the A6124 south of Musselburgh, is a small, attractive garden, cared for by the National Trust for Scotland.

Longniddry might be a place with a strange name, but *Gosford House* is a treasure. Owned by the Earl of Wemyss, you will be stung a quid to go into the house. Instead, take a leisurely stroll for free round the gardens, which are extensive and in parts gently returning to nature.
Longniddry beach is another windsurf spot.

Musselburgh is the place to go for the races, although we all know that isn't free! Neither is the ice-cream at Luca's, which I recommend highly.

North Berwick has two great beaches and a severe parking problem. Climb the 'Law' – a weird geological protuberance – or just stare at the guano-encrusted Bass Rock, the largest single stack of rock in the world. The rock is home to 100,000 gannets – so how do they know which spot is theirs?
For a park, try the *Lodge Grounds*, which has wonderful summertime fun like crazy golf and table-tennis, at a small charge. There is even an aviary.
North Berwick Law is a 200-metre high volcanic plug (or similar!), like Traprain Law, only a little less intimidating. See the whale's jawbone at the summit (infinitely more entertaining than a Napoleonic watch-tower). Just the kind of place to film a pop video.
Tourist information is available all year at 1 Quality Street. Tel: 01620 892197

Prestonpans, also known as 'the Pans', is the site of *Preston Tower Gardens*. These gardens, which surround a fifteenth-century tower house, have been restored to perfection. Stroll under the laburnum arch and smell the scented delights of the herb garden. Open all year, daily from dawn to dusk (so that's for about three hours in December!). Tel: 01875 810232

Traprain Law is off the A1, five miles west of Dunbar. Get up to the summit to see the iron-age fort, but it'll take a bit of climbing! Stout shoes and a bit of resolution.

Yellowcraig has a beach and a nature trail through the dunes, as well as barbie pits for roasting plastic dolls from China. Take the access road from the B1345 about two miles west of North Berwick. Beware parking charges, though . . . and the unpredictable east coast haar – sea fog, to the unknowing.

If you do get to Yellowcraig, look for Fidra, the island upon which Robert Louis Stevenson based *Treasure Island*.

City of Edinburgh

Airport – yes, I know it sounds bizarre, but as long as you don't mind the smell from Marshalls down the road, there is plenty of entertainment to be had from watching the planes just come and go . . . (My God, I am a sad soul.) Tel: 0131 333 1000

There is a Tourist Information Desk on the main concourse. Open all year. Tel: 0131 333 2167

Balerno is a small village to the south-east of the city, just a bus ride away. Look for *Malleny Garden*, a National Trust for Scotland property off the A70. Good for big yews and glorious for bonsai – it houses the national collection for Scotland. (A secret until now.) Pop a coin in the honesty box to show your appreciation. Tel: 0131 449 2283

Whilst in Balerno, take the kids to *Dean Park*, which has play areas for toddlers and juniors.

Blackford Hill and Pond are to the south-east of the city. The quiet pond is good for feeding ducks, whilst the steep slopes up to Blackford Hill, home of the Royal Observatory, will give any hardy walker a refreshing view and the chance to get his/her breath back.

Bonaly Country Park is on Bonaly Road, to the south of the city. This is the ideal place from which to walk into the Pentlands, with wonderful views. Stroll round Bonaly Reservoir or take a picnic. There is also fishing in the reservoir. Tel: 0131 445 3383

Braidburn Valley Park is on Comiston Road to the south of the city, on the way out past Morningside. Steep hillsides have made a natural amphitheatre, which is used for puppet shows in July and August twice a week.

The Braid Hills are across Comiston Road from the Braidburn Valley Park. The view north across the city from this 600-foot vantage point is superb.

The Brass Rubbing Centre could be the place for you if it rains and you need a pew. The centre has a variety of replica brasses, so get rubbing! All you pay for are the materials – and how much does a crayon cost? Open Monday to Saturday from 10 a.m. to 5 p.m. (till 6 p.m. in summer); also Sunday at Festival-time from 12 noon to 5 p.m. Find the centre at Trinity Apse, Chalmers Close, off the High Street. Tel: 0131 556 4364

Calton Hill is at the east end of the city centre, easily reached from Waterloo Place or Regent Terrace. A good grassy hill with assorted strange-looking monuments and a wonderful panorama of the city and Leith, away to the Forth bridges and Fife.

Cammo Estate is off Cammo Road, Barnton, to the west of the town. This was once a formal garden, which has reverted to a natural state and now has rangers to foster understanding of the current environment. Open April to September, Monday to Friday from 1 p.m. to 5 p.m.; October to March, Monday to Friday from 10 a.m. to 1 p.m. Tel: 0131 317 8797 (or 447 7145)

The **Clan Tartan Centre** could be the place to get to know your forebears. This exhibition is in the James Pringle Weavers shop, and features a video presentation to show it how it was. They also have a computer to trace your own clan. Open Monday to Saturday from 9 a.m. to 5.30 p.m. Find the Clan Tartan Centre at 70 Bangor Road, Leith. Tel: 0131 553 5100

Colinton Dell is a beautiful place for a riverside walk through the steep valley of the Water of Leith. You can follow the riverside walk to Juniper Green and *Spylaw Park*, for some wider, open spaces. Spylaw Park has adventure play areas for older children. There is a park at Colinton Mains with children's play areas for the youngsters.

Cramond is the home of the Cramond Association, which organises the annual Maltings Exhibition, which runs from June to mid-September. If you are interested in tracing the history of Cramond from prehistoric times, the best way to get involved is to take the hour-long tour on a Sunday at 3 p.m. Plenty of historical sites along the way. The exhibition is at the Maltings, Cramond Riverside, and is open Saturday and Sunday from 2 p.m. to 5 p.m. Further information can be obtained from Mrs Kathleen Dodds, 10 Cramond Gardens, Edinburgh EH4 6PU.

Cramond Island. Yes, you can walk across at low tide, but be very careful: your rescuers won't be pleased when they come to pick you up after getting marooned in the middle of the Firth of Forth!

The **Dean Village** is a historical, artisans' village close to the city centre, near the west end. In the valley of the Water of Leith, follow the path along the river, under bridges and past St Bernard's Well. The peace of the walk is amazing when you remember the bustle that is going on only a quarter of a mile away. You can follow the walk easily to Stockbridge and go on to cut across to the Royal Botanical Garden.

The **Forth Bridge** and **Forth Road Bridge** are sights to behold, especially as the rail bridge is now lit up at night. I love this kind of bridge, mostly because I get so scared. The Tourist Information Centre at the Forth Road Bridge, by North Queensferry, is open from Easter to October. Tel: 01383 417759

Gorgie City Farm is a really child-friendly place, with ponies and pigs, turkeys and tortoises. In a small area close to central Edinburgh, the farm is a wonderfully compact place; it is actually located on the derelict site of the original City of Edinburgh refuse collection yard. Don't be put off, they even sell their own organic produce and compost! Tel: 0131 337 4202

Greyfriars Kirk, home of the famous Greyfriars Bobby, is a must for any serious grave-looker. There are lots of wonderful structures here, complete with skulls and sorrowful carved elegies. Find Greyfriars on Candlemaker Row, near the city centre. Tel: 0131 225 1900

The **Hermitage of Braid**, on the edge of Morningside, lies below Blackford Hill with its famous observatory. The Hermitage is a beautiful woody valley, with good paths. There is even a visitor centre and ranger service. Tel: 0131 447 7145

Hillend Country Park or **Pentland Hills Country Park** takes you right into the Pentlands, and has chairlift access to the ski slopes. Tel: 0131 445 4433

Holyrood Park is an easy walk from the foot of the Royal Mile, past Holyrood Palace. This is a huge open space, with the scenic geological wonder of Arthur's Seat and the Salisbury Crags occupying the whole skyline. Probably the best place to fly a kite in Edinburgh, it is also a haven for serious runners and sporty folk. There are two lochs here too, Dunsapie Loch and St Margaret's Loch. The ducks, geese and swans are very well fed indeed.

It is a short walk through the park to Duddingston Loch – this is a quality loch, not a mere pond. Remember the famous old master (a Raeburn, I think) of the Reverend skating upon it?

The Meadows is a vast area of green space, great for sporty types. There are several play areas around the Meadows, suitable for wee ones and slightly larger wee ones. There is actually an enclosed toddlers' play area at the east end, with a paddling pool. Watch out in summer for the Meadows Festival and the 'shows' (that's the fair, if you're confused). Wander further along the Meadows to Bruntsfield Links for the pitch and putt. Find the Meadows off Melville Drive, to the south of the city centre, near the University.

Portobello is a real seaside resort, with shows and even donkey rides in the summer. A healthy walk along the promenade is advised. The promenade is good for rollerblading, and the beach attracts a lot of beachcombers, with those embarrassing-looking metal detectors. (Not recommended in the height of summer, though!) The park at Mount Lodge has play areas for toddlers and slightly older kids too.

Princes Street Gardens are in the heart of the city. With the castle on one side, the shops on the other, it is amazingly tranquil and green. Look out for daffodils galore, the floral clock, and nippy squirrels, depending upon the time of year you visit. Enter Princes Street Gardens from Princes Street or Castle Terrace.

The **Royal Botanic Garden** at Inverleith Row is worth a visit any time of the year, with enormous glasshouses that include Britain's tallest palm house. For the initiated, find the fish tanks beneath the ponds, and try to hypnotise the albino carp. Is it illegal to attempt to feed the pitcher plants with dead flies? A word of warning: the squirrels may be tame, but their teeth, honed on the bones of small children, are remarkably sharp. Tel: 0131 552 7171

Inverleith Park is adjacent to the 'Botanics' and will keep the wee ones happy with play areas for the very smallest, as well as open spaces for kicking a ball (if you so desired).

Saughton Park Winter Gardens at Balgreen Road is a well-kept secret. With a small-scale hothouse and a little café, this is a quiet refuge on the south-west side of the city. In the park nearby the sunken Italian garden is actually less than cosmopolitan, but the children's adventure playground, widely agreed to be the best in the city, 'Fort Saughton', will tire them out.

Swanston Village is a little known seventeenth-century whitewashed hamlet, nestling at the feet of the Pentlands. Walk through the village up to the ski slope at Hillend, or simply wander to the nearest attractive viewpoint for a rest, picnic and a super view back to Edinburgh. Get to Swanston from the city bypass to the south of the city, taking the Oxgangs turn-off and following the signs going right to Hunter's Tryst, then right again to Swanston.

The Tourist Information Centre for the city (and the rest of Scotland) at 3 Princes Street is open all year. Tel: 0131 557 1700

Water of Leith Heritage Centre is at 24 Lanark Road, Slateford, and has displays and information on this often-overlooked city river, the 'Water of Leith'. Open Monday to Friday from 9.30 a.m. to 3.30 p.m. Tel: 0131 445 7367

Midlothian

Flotterstone Visitor Centre is at Easter Howgate, off the A702 in the Pentland Hills. Displays are of natural history and conservation. A good place to walk from for a bit of peace.

Newtongrange has the Scottish Mining Museum, which I am sorry to say isn't free. There is a Tourist Information Centre here though, at the Lady Victoria Colliery. Open April to October. Tel: 0131 663 4262

Old Craighall Tourist Information Centre, off the A1 at the Granada Service Station, is open all year. Tel: 0131 653 6172

Penicuik has a Tourist Information Centre, which is at the Edinburgh Crystal Visitor Centre in Eastfield! Open May to October. Tel: 01968 673846

Roslin Glen Country Park is by Roslin near Penicuik, off the A701. Get a great woodland walk by the river with the added attraction of caves, weirs and waterfalls. Rosslyn Castle and Chapel are also worth a look (see Historical Sites).

Vogrie Country Park by Gorebridge is off the B6372. Take time to enjoy this excellent park, with its walled gardens, nature trail and woodland walks. There is even a small golf course and, of course, plenty of rangers to go round. Get all the information at the visitor centre. Tel: 01875 821990

West Lothian

Almondell and Calderwood Country Park is near East Calder. Turn off the B7015 (from the A71) at East Calder. Lots of wildlife, woods, rangers and a brilliant visitor centre with a freshwater aquarium and local natural history displays. The visitor centre is open from April to September, Monday to Saturday from 9 a.m. to 5 p.m., Sunday from 10.30 a.m. to 6 p.m.; October to March, Monday to Thursday from 9 a.m. to 5 p.m., Sunday from 10.30 a.m. to 4.30 p.m. Tel: 01506 882254

Beecraigs Country Park is just two miles south of Linlithgow. Take the Preston Road and it is signposted on your left. Excellent for kids: there is a decent playpark and the usual walks around the park are gentle and easy. Try feeding the fish at the fish farm. Get into some real added value with a peek at the deer park. For more adventurous sportspeople, there is archery and rock climbing and more sedate angling. Of course, there are charges for some of the facilities. Tel: 01506 844516

Linlithgow. The palace itself can be seen for miles, situated by Linlithgow Loch and right in the heart of the prosperous village. Pop into the Tourist Information Centre for a booklet on The Linlithgow Trail, which will guide you past everything you would want to see of historical interest in the town. The palace sadly isn't free; but don't be deterred. You can walk right round the loch in under one hour, get a feeling for the Mary Queen of Scots story, and see the palace from all angles. There is a variety of wildlife on and around the loch, as well as sailing, canoeing and windsurfing. A good bit of trout fishing too. The park is known as *The Peel*, and has a large kids' play area.

The Tourist Information Centre (open all year) is at Burgh Halls, The Cross, Linlithgow. Tel: 01506 844600

For an unusual trip, with but a small price to pay, try a short canal ride, on *Victoria*. The *Linlithgow Union Canal Society* (LUCS), a charity manned by volunteers, runs two canal trips on Saturday and Sunday afternoons from 2 p.m. *Victoria* is a diesel-powered replica of a Victorian steam-packet – unlikely on the Union Canal, but true. Ticket prices for a 20-minute trip are £1.50 for adults and 75 pence for children and concessions. *St Magdalene* chugs over the dizzy heights of the Avon Aqueduct. This trip takes two and a half hours and is much dearer, at £5 and £3. All boat trips depart from the Canal Basin, Manse Road, Linlithgow. Tel: 01506 671215

LUCS also runs the Canal Museum which you might stumble into once your land legs have returned (see Museums).

Polkemmet Country Park is near Whitburn. Take the B7066 going west from Whitburn for two miles, and it is signposted on your right. The park was once an estate, and today elements of the estate are part of the facilities open to the public – like the golf course and putting green (there is a charge for these). Go for a woody walk or have a ranger-chat. Tel: 01501 743905

THE BORDERS

Dumfries and Galloway

Castle Douglas. Here in Kirkcudbright (a challenge to pronunciation – wait until a local says it for you) you will find *Threave Garden and Estate* a mile to the west of town. There is a visitor centre, as well as a wildfowl reserve, with five observation hides open in winter. In spring there are apparently 200 varieties of daffodils here. (I don't believe a word of it!) There are charges for the 66-acre gardens although the four and a half miles of paths through the wildfowl reserve are free. Tel: 01556 502575

In Castle Douglas itself look out for *Lochside Park*, with bowling, putting, boating and sailing, and even play areas for kids. Call in at the Tourist Information Centre (open Easter to October) at Markethill. Tel: 01556 502611

For a glorious walk to the Solway coast through a majestic Douglas Fir forest, head for *Doach Wood*, two and a half miles to the south on the B736. This Forest Enterprise wood is well signposted, with a convenient carpark. Tel: 01556 503626

Dalbeattie can offer *Colliston Park*, for watery fun in the boating and sailing area; kids' playground, trampolines and putting, too.

Dalbeattie Forest is just to the south of town on the A710. This forest is run by Forest Enterprise; it has picnic places and miles of waymarked woody and hilly walks. There are also mountain-bike trails.

Screel Hill is another Forest Enterprise area near Dalbeattie. This walk will take you to a rocky hillview of the hills and the coast. Find Screel Hill on the A711, five miles south-west of Dalbeattie. Mountain-bike routes here are more rigorous. Tel: 01556 503626 (Castle Douglas district office)

If the worst comes to the worst, there is a Tourist Information Centre (open Easter to October) at the Town Hall. Tel: 01556 610117

Dumfries is one of many places in this part of Scotland with a strong Robert Burns link. Apparently, everything there is to know (unlikely!) about the bard can be learnt at the *Robert Burns Centre*. This is an award-winning visitor centre, with exhibitions, an audio-visual show and, naturally, a bookshop, so you can get a rucksackful of poetry to make your road a lyrical one. The audio-visual show costs 80 pence for adults and 40 pence for children. Open April to September, Monday to Saturday from 10 a.m. to 8 p.m., Sunday from 2 p.m. to 5 p.m.; October to March, Tuesday to Saturday from 10 a.m. to 1 p.m. Tel: 01387 264808

Dock Park has a good children's play area and paddling pool, and lots to keep the pounds off the adults too – putting, crazy golf, trampolines and tennis. Other Dumfries parks include *Castledykes Park* at the site of a former castle, which also has a children's play area, as does *Mill Green*. Mill Green has the added bonus of a deer enclosure, as well as a woody walk and a picnic area. There is also a specially designed *Cresswell Play Area*.

Barony College Countryside Walks. The college is situated just off the A701, about eight miles from Dumfries towards Moffat. Get some really fresh air and good walking here, in farmland and woods. Open all year from 9 a.m. to 4 p.m. Tel: 01387 286251

An unusual and fun place to visit is the *Camera Obscura*. Panoramic views of Dumfries with a real difference. There is a charge of 80 pence for adults and 40 pence for children and concessions. Open April to September, Monday to Saturday from 10 a.m. to 1 p.m., Sunday from 2 p.m. to 5 p.m. Tel: 01387 253374

Ae Forest is the strangest-named wood in the book. This is a Forest Enterprise wood, with characteristic waymarked walks. For the truly athletic there are some tricky mountain-bike routes. For the more rural tastes, have a wander round the display of ploughs, which is out in the open air beside the picnic area. Turn off the A701 about seven and a half miles north of Dumfries. Tel: 01387 860247

Mabie Forest has a children's play area and graded walks to get you going gently. This is the Dumfries forest most likely to leave an impression on you. There is a 50 pence parking charge.

For something a little different, pay a visit to the *Netherfield Heather Nursery* on Dalbeattie Road. You can get heather cuttings for next to nothing, and take a seat on one of the benches outside the idyllic white farmhouse to enjoy the home-cooked food. Why not take home some free-range eggs? Tel: 01387 730217

Dumfries has a Tourist Information Centre (open all year) at Whitesands. Tel: 01387 253862. There are good markets on Saturday and Sunday at Whitesands, just opposite the Tourist Information Centre.

Eskdalemuir, 15 miles from Langholm on the B709, is the home of the *Samye Ling Tibetan Centre*. There is a magnificent temple and tranquil riverside grounds open all year daily. This is a special place, and you will want to rest and meditate quietly over a cup of something herbal in the café, and perhaps even buy something exotic in their little shop. They have a series of courses, and even accommodation. You might like it so much that you stay! Tel: 013873 73232

Garlieston, Wigtownshire, is the home of *Galloway House Gardens*. Wonderful at azalea and rhododendron time, the gardens extend down to a sandy bay. Show your appreciation of the growers' skill by putting a pound in the box as you go. Open March to end October, daily from 9 a.m. to 5 p.m. Find Garlieston south of Newton Stewart, taking the A746 then B7004. Tel: 01988 600680

Gatehouse of Fleet has one of those shops with a difference – *Galloway Country Style* in the High Street. Here you can see how a kilt is made, and then buy one too! Open all year, daily from 10 a.m. Tel: 01557 814001

Cream o' Galloway is a milk bar with a difference. Here your kids (and you) can romp over nature trails and snack at picnic sites, before trying some delectable farm-made ice-cream. Open April to end September, daily from 11 a.m. to 6 p.m. Find it on the Sandgreen Road, off the A75. Tel: 01557 814040

Fleet Forest just east of Gatehouse of Fleet has an 'Oaklands Interpretive Trail', which is really an all-weather two-mile trail through broad-leaved woods. Plenty of birds and such like.

Cally Gardens are at Gatehouse of Fleet, off the A75 to the A727. This eighteenth-century walled gardens has an amazing collection of plants, shrubs and climbers. Open mid-April to October, Saturday and Sunday from 10 a.m. to 5.30 p.m. Donations are welcome.

If you get stuck for ideas in Gatehouse of Fleet, try the Tourist Information Centre (open Easter to October). Tel: 01557 814212

Glen Trool is a stunning area, with a Forest Enterprise visitor centre and walks and views to die for. Take the A714 going north from Newton Stewart for about 12 miles, then an unclassified road at Bargrennan, to reach the visitor centre, which is open from April to October, daily from 10.30 a.m. to 5 p.m. Serious walkers and climbers can get off to Merrick, the highest peak in southern Scotland (843 metres). There is also a campsite, a mere four and a half miles round the loch (see Accommodation). Tel: 01671 402420

Gretna Green is the first stop for many on their journey into Scotland. It is a touristy place, with plenty of cafés and shops battling for your custom. There are two places where you will hear all you ever wanted to know about the blacksmith and his wretched anvil. Both charge, but not a lot.

The *Famous Old Blacksmith's Shop Centre* features an Anvil and Coach Museum. (Hold me back!) As well as the 'interactive-type' displays there is a gallery, café and, naturally, a shop. Open all year, daily from 9 a.m. to 5 p.m. (later in summer), this experience costs £1 for adults. Tel: 01461 338441/338224

Gretna Hall Blacksmith's Shop will tell the same story. Here an experienced guide will give you all the gen on Gretna Hall, for 80 pence (60 pence for OAPs). Open April to October, daily from 9 a.m. to 5 p.m.; November to March, daily from 10.30 a.m. to 4 p.m. Tel: 01461 337635

Gretna has its own Tourist Information Centre (open all year) at the M74 Service Station. Tel: 01461 338500. There is a centre in the town too, at the Old Blacksmith's Shop, open from Easter to October. Tel: 01461 337834. If you arrive on a Sunday, there is a great Sunday Market.

Kirkcudbright – to be fair, there are several towns in this area that only a local can pronounce. This is an example, but once you have it, you'll be in an élite group (*Ker-coo-brie*). Just to the north on the A711 look out for *Tongland Power Station*. There are tours of the station, to illustrate how the place fits in with the environment. Be impressed by the size of the turbine hall, and the dam and fish ladder. Open May to September, there is a small charge. Tel: 01557 330114.

From Easter to October pop into the local Tourist Information Centre at Harbour Square. Tel: 01557 330494

Langholm was the home of poet Hugh MacDiarmid, and you can visit his incredible memorial on the hillside above the town. In the form of a gigantic metallic book, open on the hillside, this will make for unusual holiday snaps.

Get tourist information here from Easter to October at Kilngreen. Tel: 013873 80976

Lockerbie has an excellent children's play area. Look for *McJerrow Park*. You will also find public tennis courts here.

Moffat has parks with plenty to do. *Station Park* has boating, sailing and putting, whilst *Beechgrove Park* has bowling and tennis on offer. At Beechgrove you can try putting too at the sports centre. There is a Tourist Information Centre (open Easter to October) at Churchgate. Tel: 01683 220620

Grey Mare's Tail is the spectacular 60-metre waterfall, off the A708 about ten miles north-east of Moffat. Take care, because this is a serious walk – a two-hour round trip – with plenty of wild goats on the way. There are guided walks too in summer. Tel: 0141 616 2266

New Galloway. Six miles to the west on the A712 is *Clatteringshaws Forest Wildlife Centre.* This is a Forest Enterprise centre, with displays about forest ecology and a brilliant reconstruction of an ancient Romano-British homestead. *Bruce's Stone* is nearby. Look out for wild goats, and talk to the rangers about the red deer here. Open April to October, daily from 10 a.m. to 5 p.m. The red deer and wild goats can be seen on a guided tour; these run from 27 June to 10 September, on Tuesday and Thursday at 11 a.m. and 2 p.m. and Sunday at 2 p.m.

Stay on the A712, along the Queen's Way Tourist Route between New Galloway and Newton Stewart, to find *Talnotry.* More Forest Enterprise at work here, with forest trails, a waterfall, wild goat park – even a campsite (see Accommodation). Tel: 01556 503626

Newton Stewart. The *Kirroughtree Visitor Centre* is three miles south-east of Newton Stewart, off the A75 at Palnure. This Forest Enterprise display and audio-visual exhibit gives detailed information on forest management. There is also an adventure playground and a bird trail forest garden. The centre is open from April to September, daily from 10.30 a.m. to 5 p.m. Tel: 01671 402420

Barwinnock Herbs offers the opportunity to learn about the ancient, as well as the more modern, uses of herbs. This is an organic herb garden and nursery with a great assortment of plants. Open April to end October, daily from 9 a.m. to 7 p.m. You will find it off the B7027, north-west of Newton Stewart. Tel: 01465 821338

Also north of Newton Stewart, about four miles north via Minnigaff, you can take a walk through the *Wood of Cree.* This is an RSPB Nature Reserve, with impressive waterfalls.

For additional local information from Easter to October, try the Tourist Information Centre at Dashwood Square in Newton Stewart. Tel: 01671 402431

Port Logan is a small village in the Rinns of Galloway area, where you will find the *Logan Fish Pond.* This is actually a 200-year-old tidal pond containing up to 150 species of saltwater fish (impossible, surely, I hear you cry!). Take the A716 from Stranraer and then the B7065. Tel: 01776 860300

Rockcliffe is an area of unusual beauty, often overlooked and consequently nice and quiet. Head for the romance of Castlehill Point, where there is a compass point aid to identify the places in the view, from Workington and Whitehaven right across the Solway. Off the A710, about seven miles south of Dalbeattie, you will find Muckle Lands and the Jubilee Path. This is a rough coastline area with tiring but rewarding walks. Rough Island bird sanctuary and the oak woodland nature reserve at Southwick are also nearby.

Sanquhar is a place with a name that you would be well advised *not* to say, until a local has pronounced it correctly for you. The best park is *Lorimer Park*, which has a bowling green (for woody types), kids' play area (for younger types) and putting (for another type altogether). Have a chat from Easter to October with the Tourist Information Centre at the Tolbooth, High Street. Tel: 01659 50185.

Stranraer. The *Meadowsweet Herb Garden* is off the A75 near Dunragit. This garden is on the lochside site of a twelfth-century abbey, and has a collection of over 150 herbs! Ratatouille will never taste the same again. Open April to end August, daily except Wednesday, from 12 noon to 5 p.m. There is a £1 charge for adults, but children are free. Well worth it. Tel: 01581 400222

Parks in Stranraer include the excellent *Agnew Park*, which has crazy golf, putting, boating and sailing, even canoeing and windsurfing on Marine Lake for the waterproof amongst you (there is a charge for these adventures). If in doubt try the local Tourist Information Centre (open Easter to October) in Bridge Street. Tel: 01776 702595

Wigtown is the home of the *Bladnoch Visitor Centre*. For the uninitiated, this is the site of a former malt whisky distillery, with the whole sorry tale told in audio-visual splendour. Open Easter to end October, Monday to Friday from 10 a.m. to 4.30 p.m., Saturday from 12 noon to 4 p.m. Tel: 01988 402605. To get there, follow the A746 going south out of Wigtown for half a mile.

Scottish Borders

Berwick-upon-Tweed. Purists might suggest it shouldn't be in this guide, but let's stretch the rules shall we? Find the *Chain Bridge Honey Farm* at Horncliffe, on the River Tweed just to the south-west of Berwick. The visitor centre at this working honey farm has all kinds of information on bees, as well as observation hives. There is a shop too, where you can buy the products, including beeswax and propolis. The visitor centre is open only from Easter to October; not surprising, really, as it would be pretty dull looking at a hive full of dead bees. Tel: 01289 386362

It is a quick walk to the *Union Chain Bridge*, which was the first suspension bridge ever to carry commercial traffic. And you can cross back over to Scotland here too!

Cockburnspath is the place to head for *Pease Sands,* a mile of sandy beach backed by red cliffs. Take the turning off the A1 eight miles south of Dunbar or off the A1107 just south of the junction with the A1, about 20 miles north of Berwick.

Coldstream. Just to the west of town on the A697 is *Hirsel House* and *Hirsel Country Park*. The park is part of a vast estate, with a couthy 'homestead museum' and an arts and crafts centre (see Museums). You could even get stung in the tea-room. Tel: 01890 882834. Alternatively, stick to our usual plan, and have a free wander up Hirsel Law. This hill was once the site of a prehistoric ring enclosure. Say no more.

In the town, walk along the riverside to *Henderson Park* and gaze into England. That bridge is pretty damn famous! Get some facts from the Tourist Information Centre (open April to October), at the Town Hall in the High Street. Tel: 01890 882607

Duns Park has a trim track if you feel the need and you are in the area.

Eckford, south of Kelso, is the home of the *Teviot Water Gardens*, where you can see bog plants you didn't know existed, beside the River Teviot. Look for *Kirkbank House* at Kelso. Open April to September, Monday to Saturday from 10 a.m. to 4.30 p.m., Sunday from 11 a.m. to 4 p.m. Tel: 01835 850734

Eyemouth is a pretty harbour town. You can go sea fishing from here if you have the stomach for it. During the summer there are attractions like giant chess and even a bouncy castle down at the seafront. Look into the Tourist Information Centre (open April to October) at the Auld Kirk in Market Place. Tel: 01890 750678

Galashiels is still pretty close to Edinburgh. (I once had a 'landlady from hell' who lived here, so it has never held much appeal for me personally!)

Scott Park has putting if you're keen. If you need something more adventurous, ask at the Tourist Information Centre (open April to October) at St John's Street. Tel: 01896 755551

Hawick has a lovely park in *Wilton Lodge Park* on Wilton Park Road, just off the A7 near the town centre. Riverside walks, crazy golf – they've got the lot. Look out for the tropical glasshouse and the aviary. Tel: 01450 378023

The Tourist Information Centre (open all year) is at Drumlanrig's Tower in the High Street. Tel: 01450 372547

Innerleithen has the *Caerlee Hill*, or 'Curly' as it is known. Climb up for good views of the Tweed Valley. The hill also forms the 'high point' at the end of 'Games Week' in July, when a torchlight procession ends in a bonfire on top of the hill.

Traquair House, just south of Innerleithen, has lovely grounds, and entry to them is free. You can wander in and then have a look at the craft workshops, which include leatherworking, pottery, woodpainting and candle-making. Open April to end September from 12.30 p.m. to 5.30 p.m.; in July and August from 10.30 a.m. to 5.30 p.m.; the craft workshops are open on Wednesday and Thursday only.

Jedburgh can't be seen from the A68; come off the road and see the market square and all manner of historical joys.

About three miles to the north on the A68 look out for *Harestanes Countryside Visitor Centre*. It has walks, either alone or in the company of a ranger, a discovery room, play area and even an indoor games area and exhibitions, particularly useful if the weather turns rough. They run workshops throughout the season. Open April to end October, from 10 a.m. to 5 p.m. Tel: 01835 830306

Speak to the Tourist Information Centre in Jedburgh, which is open all year at Murray's Green. Tel: 01835 863435/863688

Kelso is the place for the races, which will, of course, cost you an arm and a leg! No room for that in this book. Try the Tourist Information Centre instead, at the Town House in The Square. Open April to end October. Tel: 01573 223464

For parks, try *Sheddon Park* with lots of stuff to keep you active – tennis, putting, swingball and even table-tennis. *Croft Park* has a trim track to keep you really in the pink.

Melrose isn't just the burial place of Robert the Bruce's heart, you know. A different kind of NTS garden exists here: at *Priorwood Garden and Dried Flower Shop* the majority of plants are grown with a view to drying (and giving to your granny). Talking about grannies, keep an eye out for the historic apple varieties . . . If you can't resist a visit, head off the A6091 by the Abbey. Open Monday to Saturday, from 10 a.m. to 5.30 p.m. Tel: 01896 822493

Gibson Park has pitch and putt to keep your handicap down.

Look for more ideas in the Tourist Information Centre (open April to end October), at Abbey House, Abbey Street. Tel: 01896 822555

Peebles is only 20 miles from Edinburgh, but a real Borders town on the River Tweed. Enjoy a riverside stroll – head upstream towards Neidpath Castle and watch the serious anglers at play. On the other side of the river, off Kingsmeadows Road, is an adventure playgound. Call in at the Tourist Information Centre in the High Street. Tel: 01721 720138.

Selkirk is about three miles east of *Bowhill House and Country Park*, the home of the Duke of Buccleuch and Queensberry, KT. (Pardon?) Access to the park is free from the end of April to the late summer bank holiday, from 12 noon to 5 p.m. The adventure playground includes giant slides and aerial ropeways! Hold me back! Tel: 01750 22204. A standard park in the town is *Pringle Park*.

Selkirk Glass Visitor Centre is right on the A7, and doesn't look too salubrious. However, if you want to see some crafty business, this is the spot. You might be tempted to veer off to the factory shop or the tea-room, but stay resolute and don't go home with a rucksackful of glass paperweights. Tel: 01750 20954

Lindean Reservoir has a round-the-reservoir walk, with rangers for those who need to be led. Find Lindean Reservoir three miles east of Selkirk, on a minor road linking the A7 and A699. It is open all year. Tel: 01835 823301

There is tourist information here too; the centre is at Halliwell's House and is open from April to end October. Tel: 01750 20054

St Abb's Head is a good place to watch seabirds, with puffins, kittiwakes and fulmars. The headland is a nature reserve, with a lighthouse keeping watch over the rocky shore – and a ranger. Tel: 018907 71443

Torness Visitor Centre offers tours with a difference. This nuclear power station is in a beautiful coastal situation, easy to find off the A1 six miles south-east of Dunbar. You can tour the station, view the reactor hall and see that legendary refuelling machine. I know I'm a product of the '70s, but I still find it all a bit SCARY! Tours are daily from 9.45 a.m. to 11.15 a.m. and 1.30 p.m. to 3 p.m. The visitor centre is open daily from 9.30 a.m. to 4.30 p.m. Tel: 0800 250255, or 01345 251251

CENTRAL, TAYSIDE AND FIFE

Clackmannanshire

Alloa is a metropolis to the folk of the 'wee county', as Clackmannanshire is known. Just two miles to the north-east is Sauchie, where you will see the *Gartmorn Dam Country Park and Nature Reserve*. There are plenty of picnic places; birds mooching about; fishing for those of that persuasion (not free, sadly); and a visitor centre – in and around this reservoir. Tel: 01259 214319

Alva is home to the *Mill Trail Visitor Centre*, which you will find at Glentana Mills, West Stirling Street. A visit to this centre is a good, quick way to get to grips with the heritage of the area, and see the wool industry at work. It is also probably the best first port of call on the established 'Mill Trail'; there are other sites in the 'Hillfoots' (the villages at the foot of the Ochils) to call in at. There is even a shop and a café. Open October to May, daily from 10 a.m. to 5 p.m.; June to September, daily from 9 a.m. to 6 p.m. Tel: 01259 769696 (also the local Tourist Information Centre)
    Silver Glen is a beautiful place to go walking. The glen once supported a silver mine, so watch for nuggets. The walk starts at the *Ochil Hills Woodland Park*.

Dollar Glen. It is a wonderful walk up this green ferny gorge to Castle Campbell. The atmosphere is all a bit swampy, with moss and dripping rock. Wear sensible shoes, and for mercy's sake don't take anything in a pushchair. Having said that, you do get an amazing view from the top, even though your legs are wobbly. Turn off the A91 just north of Dollar.

Muckhart. *Muckhart Mill* is near the exciting *Cauldron Linn*, a double waterfall that is easy to walk to from the village.

Rumbling Bridge is four miles east of Dollar. You can take a footpath on the north side of the gorge, to see these falls at their best. Turn off the A823 at the tiny village of Rumbling Bridge.

Tillicoultry is at the foot of *Mill Glen*, which leads away up into the foot of

41

the Ochils where you can see eight waterfalls close together. Turn off the A91 at Tillicoultry.

Dundee City

Balgay Hill is the home of the city's *Mills Observatory*; it also boasts two parks, Lochee Park and Victoria Park, and a spectacular view over the city. Victoria Park is rose gardens and beds of flowers – plus play equipment, whilst Lochee is an open-space, good-for-sport type of park.

Baxter Park, a classic Victorian park, with boating on Stobsmuir Ponds, is ideal for meandering walks. Shelter at the central sandstone pavilion. Tennis and bowling are available, and there is a playpark.

Caird Park is at the junction of Forfar Road and Kingsway. A gift to the city from past industrialists, the park includes Mains Castle, which is now a restaurant (see Historical Sites). This is a sporty park, with golf and athletics well catered for, as well as winter pitches. The conservation area of *Trottick Ponds*, with resident swans, is just to the north of the park.
   Further information about any of Dundee's parks can be obtained by ringing 01382 434000 ext. 4296

Camperdown Wildlife Centre is a great experience. The variety of birds and animals is impressive, with grey wolves, Arctic foxes and brown bears amongst the attractions. Here you can see those mammals you might spend a lifetime waiting to see wild in the Highlands, such as pine marten and polecats. The kind folk who run Camperdown even lend brollies for free on rainy days! The country park and Templeton Woods around the wildlife centre is wonderful for outdoor activities, from pitch and putt to play areas. For water-lovers there is a boating pond and model boats to play with. For those with an architectural leaning, the neo-classical Camperdown House is a glorious sight. Find Camperdown Country Park off the A923 Coupar Angus road. The Wildlife Centre is open March to September, daily from 10 a.m. to 4.30 p.m. (till 3.30 p.m. from October to February). There is a charge for the Wildlife Centre, adults £1.50, children over four and concessions £1.05. Tel: 01382 432689

Clatto Country Park is on Dalmahoy Drive, and is signposted off Kingsway. The park has a reservoir that is very popular with watersports enthusiasts, and a ranger service. Open all year, daily from 10 a.m. to dusk. Tel: 01382 436505 or 01382 435911

Dundee Law is an extinct volcano. I can barely believe this, volcanic eruptions and twentieth-century Dundee seem so distant! However, Law Hill offers brilliant views and wildlife-type walks. Get to the Law along Lochee Road heading towards Coupar Angus and Camperdown. The steep slopes of Dudhope Park, with Dudhope Castle, are nearby.

Mills Observatory has displays to take you to the moon. The best time to view the stars through the Observatory's ten-inch telescope is on a clear winter's evening. Regular planetarium shows. Open April to September, Monday from 11 a.m. to 5 p.m., Tuesday to Friday from 10 a.m. to 5 p.m., Saturday from 2 p.m. to 5 p.m.; October to March, Monday to Friday from 3 p.m. to 10 p.m., Saturday from 2 p.m. to 5 p.m. Tel: 01382 667138

Shaws Sweet Factory is difficult to find, being well out of the city centre, but it is well worth the effort. The place is a dream for anyone with a sweet tooth, and although they do charge (50 pence for four years and over), you can buy cut-price sweeties in their factory shop. They are open all year, except for two weeks at Christmas. The place has a 1950s feel to it; the machinery reminded me of those films 'through the round window' on *Playschool* many years ago. Part of the excitement is that they could be making *anything* when you arrive. Look out for Scottish favourites like Soor Plooms and Pandrops. Shaws Dundee Sweet Factory Ltd, Keillers Building, 34 Mains Loan, Dundee. Tel: 01382 461435

Tourist information on Dundee is available all year from the centre at 4 City Square. Tel: 01382 434664

Falkirk

Airth has a small claim to fame: it houses the Tourist Information Centre for the Kincardine Bridge, at Pine 'n' Oak, Kincardine Bridge Road. Open from Easter to September. Tel: 01324 831422

Another delight at Airth, *The Pineapple,* has to be seen to be believed. A 45-foot carved structure that resembles – yes, a pineapple. Take a stroll around the gardens of this bizarre building, you might even want to get a sample from the crab-apple orchard. To find this hidden gem, turn off the A905 seven miles east of Stirling, then off the B9124.

Bo'ness has *Kinneil Park,* off Provost Road. Here you will find some nice woody walks, pitch and putt, putting green and even a lump of the Antonine Wall left by the Romans.

You can get tourist information from April to September from the centre at Union Street. Tel: 01506 826626

Falkirk has some parks to try out. The most obvious is *Dollar Park,* just half a mile from the town centre, on Kilns Road. In the summer you'll find giant chess and draughts, putting, tennis, a paddling pool and even a pets' corner. *Callendar Park*, on Callendar Road, is a little further out. Open daily from dawn to dusk. During the summer there are attractions like crazy golf and a bouncy castle. Remember, though: there are small charges for the best extras!

Bantaskine Park is a spacious park. There is a trim track for the keenest amongst you. Get to the park from Gartcows Road.

For tourist information head for 2 Glebe Street. Open all year. Tel: 01324 620244

Grangemouth has *Zetland Park* on Abbots Road. Try out the boating pond, tennis courts, bouncy castle, crazy golf and even the mini-cars; all of these are available in summer, but may have a small charge.

Muiravonside Country Park is near Linlithgow, but falls into the Falkirk area. Find it on the B825 west of Whitecross, three miles west of Linlithgow. If you're looking for animals go no further. A little farm area has all the domesticated wildlife your heart could desire, and once that gets boring, trek off along the river walk or wander round the visitor centre in search of rangers. Tel: 01506 845311

Fife

Aberdour. If you're looking to bask, this is the beach for you. A clean, traditional beach that deserves the accolades it has received as one of Britain's best.

Balmerino Abbey Gardens is owned by the National Trust for Scotland, so pop something appreciative in the honesty box. Suitably decrepit ruins of a thirteenth-century Cistercian monastery are out of bounds. However, on a wander round the gardens you might glimpse possibly the oldest chestnut tree in the country! Turn off the A914, about five miles south-west of Newport-on-Tay.

Burntisland has a Tourist Information Centre at 4 Kirkgate. Open all year. Tel: 01592 872667

Crail also has a Tourist Information Centre, at Crail Museum and Heritage Centre in Marketgate. Open Easter to September. Tel: 01333 450869

Cupar possesses a garden to make the back of your neck go goose-pimply. (At least, that's how I felt when I first saw the film.) The *Douglas Bader Gardens* (now am I making sense?) were designed primarily for use by disabled people. Situated in Duffus Park, Cupar, they even have an aviary for guaranteed birdsong.
    There is a Tourist Information Centre (open Easter to September) at The Granary, Coal Road. Tel: 01334 652874

Dunfermline. Situated right in the town centre near the railway station, *Dunfermline Park* has pleasant walks and children's play areas. Crazy golf, tennis, table-tennis and even trampolines in the summer. Open all year. There is good disabled access, too.
    Pittencrieff Park is known locally as 'The Glen'. A tiny zoo, formal gardens, a mini street area for kid cyclists to practise. Thank heavens for Andrew Carnegie's generosity! There is also a museum in the park (see Museums).
    Townhill Country Park (on Townhill Road) is a large park with wooded areas, a loch and plenty of space for kite-flying or wild ball-games. There is also a ranger service in this park, which to the uninitiated means guided walks and advice on such arcane matters as what to do with a wounded newt. The visitor centre is open Monday to Friday, from 9 a.m. to 5 p.m. Tel: 01383 725596
    Saint Margaret's Cave can be reached from Glen Bridge carpark. It is open Easter to September, daily from 11 a.m. to 4 p.m. St Margaret used to pray in this cave, which was her own special shrine. Take the 84 steps down to it and

you'll understand how it came to be buried by a carpark. Tel: 01383 721814

Get tourist information at 13 Maygate all year round. Tel: 01383 720999

East Wemyss has an *Environmental Education Centre* which is particularly good if you have kids. The visitor centre has natural history displays and local fossils. You can walk to nearby caves from here. Open all year, Monday to Friday from 9.30 a.m. to 12.30 p.m. and 1.30 p.m. to 4 p.m. Tel: 01592 414479

Elie is one of the picturesque villages of 'East Neuk' fame; consequently it is chock-a-block with Edinburgh lawyers and senior managers from commerce justifying the expense of their second homes. The exclusive golf attracts them. My advice is to avert your gaze from the excesses of the executive régime and repair to the delightful beach. (Don't get run over by a sporty little number on the way.)

Visit *Macduff's Cave* at the far end of West Bay, or take the chain walk along the rocks between Shell Bay and Elie. Taste that sea spray – it'll take for ever to wash out of your hair.

Glenrothes. *Riverside Park* is beside the River Leven, and sports the usual paddling pool and formal gardens.

There is a Tourist Information Centre (open all year) at Rothes Square, Kingdom Centre. Tel: 01592 754954/610784

Kingsbarns. If you can find this beach, then you deserve to have it to yourself. Expect solitude.

Kirkcaldy has good open-space parks, such as *Beveridge Park* on Abbotshall Road. There is a boating pond and a small aviary. Get into some crazy golf or table-tennis in the summer. The mini railway is ace too! Open all year, although the facilities are available in summer only, from 12 noon to 8 p.m.

Dunnikier Park is on the A910. This is another spacious place with putting, paddling, playing and picnicking. Even a skateboard rink for the criminally insane.

Ravenscraig Park is on the A955, just before Dysart. Go for the pitch and putt or tennis if you're sporty, or head for the seashore rockpools if you fancy a crabby paddle. *Ravenscraig Castle* is here too (see Historical Sites).

Go for tourist information to 19 Whytescauseway. Open all year. Tel: 01592 267775

Leven. The *Silverburn Estate* gardens are open all year, from dawn to dusk. Plenty of walks, plus some small farm animals (you don't get much smaller than pygmy goats) to enjoy. Find the estate half a mile east of Leven, off the A915. Tel: 01333 427568

Letham Glen, in Leven itself, is a little park but it has a lot packed in, including a pets' corner, putting and a deer enclosure.

Especially exciting for children, the *Praytis Farm Park* offers hands-on experience of your common-or-garden farm animals. Whilst admission is free, there are a number of attractions that you *can* pay for (if you so desire), such as go-karts and a floodlit golf range. The park is on the A916 between Kennoway and Cupar. Tel: 01333 350209

Tourist information here is at The Beehive, Durie Street. Open all year. Tel: 01333 429464

Lochgelly is near Dunfermline, and you will find *Lochore Meadows Country Park* between Lochgelly and Ballingry on the B920. The park covers a former coal-mining area, so don't expect it to be packed with full-grown trees. There is a visitor centre too, which is open April to September, daily from 9 a.m. to 8 p.m.; October to March, daily from 9 a.m. to 5 p.m. Tel: 01592 860086

Lower Largo, on the A915 a few miles north of Leven, has a monument to Alexander Selkirk, the real Robinson Crusoe, who was born here in 1676. There is a lovely wood and beach walk – the Serpentine Walk – between Upper and Lower Largo. Start at the Upper Largo Hotel.

Markinch has a beautiful park. *Balbirnie Park* is vast – 415 acres – and even houses an 18-hole golf course. This is an excellent all-round attraction, with a crafts centre also *in situ*. Furniture-making, glass-blowing, jewellery and leatherwork; you won't get much craftier than that. Tel: 01592 645661

St Andrews. *Kilburn Park* has a scented garden guaranteed to revive those noses other parks don't reach. Here you will also find the St Andrews Museum (see Museums). There are tennis courts, a bowling green and putting, which all carry a charge. (Why bother when you can get a noseful in the scented garden?) Tel: 01334 477706

If you want to take off your clothes (or most of them) try *West Sands Beach* for size. (Not that size matters of course.)

For a really natural time, try the *Eden Estuary Local Nature Reserve,* which is mudflats to you and me. Good for sea walks and birds from hides. Open all year, although rangers during working hours only! Tel: 01334 472151

Another reserve is close by, the *Tentsmuir Point National Nature Reserve.* You could take a proper nature trail from here. Open all year. Tel: 01334 654038

Tourist information is available all year at 70 Market Street. Tel: 01334 472021

Valleyfield Wood. There are some beautiful woodland walks in these old mansion-house gardens.

Perth and Kinross

Aberfeldy is a pretty town on the River Tay. Only two miles to the east on the Weem–Aberfeldy road you'll find the *Tombuie Smokehouse.* Here they have a farm walk, a cheese-press collection (fascinating!) and plenty of deer and sheep. Open April to end October, daily from 11 a.m. to 6 p.m. Tel: 01887 820127

There is pleasant walking country at *Birks O'Feldy,* which you can reach from the A826 Crieff road. Woodlands and the Moness Falls.

If you are looking for more in Aberfeldy, there is a Tourist Information Centre (open all year) in The Square. Tel: 01887 820276

Auchterarder has a Tourist Information Centre (open all year) at 90 High Street. Tel: 01764 663450

Birnam is just over the River Tay from Dunkeld, the place of *Macbeth* fame. I bet you don't know about the village's other literary claim to fame – Beatrix Potter! You can visit for free the garden where the writer spent her childhood summers; it is, of course, the home of Mrs Tiggywinkly et al. Sick yet? The gardens are open all year. Birnam is just off the A9.

Take a stroll along the River Walk, and take in the delights of the Tay, which include the legendary Birnam Oak.

Blair Atholl. The beautiful *Falls of Bruar* are just three miles west of town, off the A9. The walk along the gorge to the falls is well marked.

Blairgowrie is *the* place for berries. To shake off any excess weight, try a good walk along the bank of the River Ericht, through *Wellmeadow* up to where the river gets quite white and exciting.

There is a Tourist Information Centre (open all year) at 26 Wellmeadow. Tel: 01250 872960/873701

Coupar Angus has a great park – *Larghan Park*. There is a paddling pool, play area, putting, pitch and putt and even a bouncy castle in summer (some of which you will pay for). Great place for picnics, too.

Crieff is popular with tourists – and quite deservedly so. There are plenty of things to do here for nothing!

Try *Strathearn Pottery* on West High Street, where you can watch a potter at work (Tel: 01764 656100), or pop along to the *Stuart Crystal* Factory on Muthill Road to watch a craftsman engraving crystal (Tel: 01764 654004). In *Woolieminded* – part of the complex on Muthill Road – there are kilt-making demonstrations to watch (Tel: 01764 653478). These places make their money from the shops on site, so if you are on a budget, stick to the cheaper souvenirs!

Glenturret Distillery is a hop, skip and jump from Crieff, and you can wander in and look about for absolutely nowt; you only pay if you want a 'guided' tour. Open March to December, Monday to Saturday from 9.30 a.m. to 6 p.m., Sunday from 12 noon to 6 p.m.; January, Monday to Friday from 11.30 a.m. to 4 p.m.; February, Monday to Saturday from 11.30 a.m. to 4 p.m., Sunday from 12 noon to 4 p.m. Find Glenturret on the A85 Crieff to Comrie road. Tel: 01764 656565

For the sweet-toothed, visit *Gordon and Durward* on West High Street. There you can see traditional sweetie-making (viewed from the shop). Open all year, Monday to Saturday from 9 a.m. to 5.30 p.m.; also Sunday afternoons in summer. Tel: 01764 653800

If you need a rest or a place to let the kids run wild, try *MacRosty Park*. There's a paddling pool and attractions such as trampolining, putting and giant draughts (all of which are under £1). If you feel more energetic, you could attempt the four-mile Glen Lednock Circular Walk to the Deil's Cauldron – get a leaflet from the Tourist Information Centre! Or, you could walk up Knock Hill, near the Hydro Hotel, for a glorious view of the area.

If after all this mind-and-body-improving activity you fancy a greasy bite, try Mac's Café beside the main post office: old-world charm with calories for value.

Get all the gen, all year, from the helpful folk at the Tourist Information Centre at the Town Hall. Tel: 01764 652578

Dunkeld is a charming place. The National Trust for Scotland owns 20 houses in the village, so beware tweeds and other worthy visitors. Take a gentle walk along the River Tay, past the ancient Birnam Oak (see Birnam).

Dunkeld Cathedral is atmospheric, if ruined. There are lovely walks here too, beside this wide river.

The Hermitage, off the A9, is a beautiful area to walk through, with woody trails leading to a picturesque folly overlooking the gorge of the River Braan. *Ossian's Cave*, apparently once the home of some poor hermit soul, is here, as is the tallest tree in Britain (allegedly), a Douglas fir that stands near the River Braan, easily seen from the Hermitage folly. You might need ranger help. If so, call 01350 728641.

Just two miles north-east of Dunkeld, off the A923, is *Loch of the Lowes*. Here you can watch an osprey's nest and waterfowl from a hide. There is also a wildlife exhibition and displays in the visitor centre.

If you need tourist information in Dunkeld, try the centre at The Cross from March to October. Tel: 01350 727688

Killiecrankie is off the A9, just three miles north of Pitlochry. Learn about the history of the area at the visitor centre – there is a £1 charge for adults; children and National Trust for Scotland members are free. Here a government soldier fighting the Jacobite army in 1689 leapt over the gorge – the Soldier's Leap. Impossible! Open Easter to end October, daily from 10 a.m. to 5.30 p.m. Tel: 01796 473233 (visitor centre)

Kinloch Rannoch is exciting countryside. The walk along the River Tummel up on to the hillside starts at Allt Mor Crescent and is about three miles in all. Take stout shoes and a good camera.

Kinross has a super park right by Loch Leven. *Kirkgate Park* offers putting, a children's play area, trampolines, bouncy castle, crazy golf and draughts! All available from April to September, though you will pay a small charge for the activities. Tel: 01577 863161 (You could also take a boat to Loch Leven Castle from here, which you would also pay for, I'm afraid!)

The Tourist Information Centre here is at the Kinross service area, off Junction 6 of the M90. Tel: 01577 863680

Linn of Tummel. Forty-seven acres of woodland walks beside the foaming wrath of the Rivers Tummel and Garry in their Highland setting. Turn off the B8019 two and a half miles north-west of Pitlochry. You should have provisions, a camera, stout shoes, and a sense of purpose. Tel: 01796 473233 (Killiecrankie Visitor Centre)

Loch Tummel. The finest views are from Queen's View, don't forget your camera. An exhibition and audio-visual show will make the whole thing easier to digest. (And less embarrassing than standing awestruck in the carpark for ten minutes or so.) There is a parking charge, so perhaps you would be permitted to do that kind of thing in the carpark anyway. Open April to October, daily from 10 a.m. to 6 p.m. Get to the Queen's View six miles west of Pitlochry. Tel: 01350 727284

Meikleour Beech Hedge is amazing, particularly in autumn and spring. This hedge is now 600 yards long and 110 feet high – the biggest hedge in the world! It is five miles south of Blairgowrie on the A93. The hedge was first planted in 1746.

Perth is the place for glass-making. The famous *Caithness Glass* have visitor centres at their 'factories' in Perth, Wick and Oban. Here in Perth you can watch the gorgeous paperweights being made, and see the engraver etching glass. Fall in love with any of these beauties and you'll find the factory shop irresistible. To tire out the kids before they go wild and break a wallet's worth of paperweights in the gallery, take them to the play area cunningly provided! Caithness Glass are at the northern edge of Perth on the A9, at the Inveralmond roundabout/industrial estate. The visitor centre is open all year, Monday to Saturday from 9 a.m. to 5 p.m., Sunday from 12 noon to 5 p.m. (from 10 a.m. Easter to September); glass-making Monday to Friday from 9 a.m. to 4.30 p.m. Tel: 01738 637373

If you want to lose your hat, look out for the date of the next meeting at Perth racecourse (which is definitely not free, or even cheap!).

Perth has a *North Inch* and *South Inch* – it sounds peculiar, but these are two parks beside the river. You can wander and watch the sporty types at the North Inch, or play a quiet game of pétanque. The South Inch has boating, trampolines, putting and crazy golf, all for a small charge. For less strenuous parks, try the Norrie Miller Walk and Bellwood Park, which borders the River Tay, or *Quarrymill Woodland Park* on Isla Road, just half a mile north of Perth on the A93. The latter has walks (open all year), as well as a visitor centre and tea-room (open May to September). Tel: 01738 633890

If you fancy an altogether different day out, you could go along to the livestock market at the Agricultural Centre, which has sales on Mondays and Fridays from 11 a.m.

Get tourist information from the centre (open all year) on the High Street, Tel: 01738 638353. If you are on the outskirts of town, try at Inveralmond, on the A9 city bypass, from April to October. Tel: 01738 638481

Pitlochry. The town is full of tourists, so give all the wool shops a body swerve and take a walk down to the dam. There you will find a visitor centre (to tell you everything your heart desires about dams and such). The salmon ladder is a brave and laudable concept, although I have yet to see a fish in it. The Festival Theatre here is renowned.

Edradour is Scotland's smallest distillery (not including my mother-in-law's kitchen), and is only a few miles north-east of Pitlochry, off the A924. Their free tours include a taste of the malt! Open April to October, Monday to Saturday from 9.30 a.m. to 5 p.m., Sunday from 12 noon to 5 p.m. Only the shop is open in winter. Tel: 01796 472095

Pitlochry has a Tourist Information Centre (open all year) at 22 Atholl Road. Tel: 01796 472215/472751

Rannoch Forest is looked after by the Forestry Commission. Thank goodness. And thank goodness they put up all these nice signposts so you don't get lost. Just keep going along the B8019 to Kinloch Rannoch, then take the B846 and look out for the Forestry signs.

Scone, near Perth, has a lovely walk – the *Coronation Walk* — up to the Murrayshall Monument where you can see right over the Tay Valley. The starting-point is behind the Murrayshall Hotel.

Tummel Forest is getting into really wild country. Take the B8019 from Pitlochry to Kinloch Rannoch and then look out for the Forestry Commission signs and walks that are either lochside, or right up the hillside, depending on your state of fitness!

Stirling

Aberfoyle. At the *Queen Elizabeth Forest Park* the walking is tranquil and easy. If you have a bike, there are cycle trails to follow, too. Turn off the A821 a mile north of Aberfoyle. The visitor centre with its audio-visual delights is open from March to October, daily from 10 a.m. to 6 p.m. Tel: 01877 382258

Tourist information here in Aberfoyle is available at the Main Street from April to October. Tel: 01877 382352

Callander is a busy tourist town in summer, with plenty of souvenir shops and small hotels and B&Bs. The spectacular *Bracklinn Falls* can be reached on foot from the Stirling end of the town. Follow the path on for a wilder walk. Alternatively, you can see the *Falls of Leny* if you continue through Callander on the A84 for about two miles. There is a much shorter path to these rushing falls: keep on along the A84 to Loch Lubnaig for a lochside picnic or wander.

Tourist information is available at the Rob Roy and Trossachs Visitor Centre (worth a look in itself). Find it in Ancaster Square. Tel: 01877 330342

Doune is my current home. It is a small village, with a few shops and pubs, but boasts an outstanding castle and river walk. The castle was in *Monty Python and the Holy Grail*, and recently, *Ivanhoe* (sadly my family didn't get a walk-on part even after standing looking hopeful for half an hour). Don't pay to go into the castle on a sunny day, walk round it and wander along the River Teith. The views are quiet and rural, and the whole place exudes tranquillity. You could walk to Doune Ponds to feed the ducks if you preferred. (Tel: 01786 432365). If you need more action, try *Moray Park* for kite-flying and the kids' playground.

For a junk shop that is full of delights at reasonable prices, try *Jimmuck's* at the Cross. If you need a few provisions pop into *Sam's* (also the post office). Sam is chatty and kind, and he sells 'the cheapest fish food in Scotland' (a great boon to the weary traveller). If night falls and you need to drink copiously and possibly even fall asleep at the bar, try the *Highland Hotel* in Main Street.

Drymen has a Tourist Information Centre at the library in The Square. Open May to September. Tel: 01360 660068

Dunblane has a couple of good parks, which could be tricky to find without asking a few directions! Try *Laighhills Park*, for example; it is great for small kids, with a brilliant sand play 'ship'. *Ochlochy Park* is in a different part of the village, up towards the golf course on the Sherrifmuir Road. This is more of a wandering-through-woodland type of park.

You could take a wander by the Allan Water beside the cathedral and the older part of town; there is another, smaller kids' playpark here.

Get your tourist information from April to October from the centre on Stirling Road, near the station. Tel: 01786 824428

Fallin, near Stirling, has *Polmaise Park* on Polmaise Road. This park caters for kids of all abilities, with a giant sandpit and even a spectacular aerial runway.

Inversnaid has an *RSPB Reserve* with a nature trail and views overlooking Loch Lomond. Take the B829 and head a mile north of Inversnaid itself. There is a warden at Garrison Cottage if you get lost! Tel: 01877 386244

Killearn is near the *'Pots' of Gartness*, an exciting waterfall on the Endrick Water. If you come here at the right time you might see some salmon leaping.

Killin doesn't just have a beautiful waterfall. There is a Tourist Information Centre too, in Main Street, which is open from March to December. Tel: 01567 820254

Loch Katrine is a glorious ten-mile-long loch in the heart of the Trossachs. Sir Walter Scott drew much of his inspiration from the scenery around here, so don't be alarmed if you take a poetic turn. Access is from the pier at the end of the loch (follow the Trossachs Trail from either Callander or Aberfoyle). The glamorous way to see the loch is from the SS *Sir Walter Scott*, which takes groups of tourists up and down the water in summer, for a price which includes queueing for quite some time! A really fun way to see the flora and fauna, *and* take in the view, is to walk as far as your feet will carry you, along the lochside paved footpath. The loch is Glasgow's water supply, so it is impeccably well kept. You can also hire bicycles at the pier, and cycle the length of the loch. For the weary, there is a shop, tea-room and visitor centre at the pier, too.

Plean Country Park is just south of Bannockburn, on the A9. Lots of waymarked walks so no need to take that ball of string (but you can take the compass if it makes you feel more comfortable). Open all year during daylight hours. Tel: 01786 432364

Stirling has plenty to keep the whole family amused. *Parks* include *Causewayhead Park*, which has a great kids' playground, and *Beechwood Park*, off St Ninian's Road, which has putting, bike tracks and a peculiar mini road system with bikes for hire. Tel: 01786 479000. A large municipal park with space to fly kites for miles is *King's Park* (where the circus pitches its tents in the summer). There is also an area of 'facilities' like giant draughts, crazy golf and putting for the summer. Special areas for bikes and for really small kids make this a superb all-round park, although it isn't truly in the centre of town.

Tourist information at Stirling is a many-splendoured thing. Look either at Dumbarton Road (open all year), Tel: 01786 475019; or at the excellent Royal Burgh of Stirling Visitor Centre at the Castle, Tel: 01786 479901. You can also get information at the Pirnhall motorway service area from March to November (off the M9). Tel: 01786 814111

Stirling University has *Airthrey Castle* hidden in its midst. There are some nice places to walk round here. Take it from me, you'll be surprised.

Stirling Visitor Centre is up on the Castle Esplanade. (You get an incredible view from here, too.) This is an excellent audio-visual, hands-on centre, where you come out knowing more about the place than most of the locals. Open all year daily from 9.30 a.m. to 5 p.m. (from 9 a.m. to 6 p.m. in July and August). Tel: 01786 479901

The Wallace Monument is the strange, slightly sexual thing that overlooks the Stirling area, from a high point over by the University towards Bridge of Allan. The monument itself isn't free; it is also a frightening round-and-round-up-interminable-tiny-stairs-enough-to-induce-evil-dreams-for-months kind of experience (similar to the Scott Monument in Edinburgh). Ascend if you dare; but otherwise, simply make your way up to the carpark, and then walk up to the monument, to enjoy a brilliant view.

Tyndrum has a Tourist Information Centre in the Main Street. Open April to October. Tel: 01838 400246

GRAMPIAN

Aberdeen City

Beaches. Aberdeen Beach is a two-mile stretch of sand, with the strange sight of oil platforms adorning the sea horizon. There are plenty of things to see here, the usual arcades and some healthy, sporty stuff too including crazy golf, putting and tennis at the *Queen's Links Park* at the Esplanade. *Balmedie Beach* to the north of town, off the A90, is excellent too, with over ten miles of sands and a visitor centre.

Countesswells Forest is on Countesswells Road, and has lots of good tracks for horses and brave hikers with boots.

Den of Maidencraig Local Nature Reserve is near Hazlehead Park (see below). This is an area of woodland thought to be at least 200 years old.

Donmouth Local Nature Reserve is on Donmouth Road at Bridge of Don, to the north of Aberdeen. This is a coastal reserve, sand-dunes and the like. Bats at night too. Eerie!

Doonies Farm, on the coast road between Nigg Bay and the village of Cove, is a working farm of rare breeds. They have sheep, goats, pigs, cows, horses and a variety of feathered things. Try a visit in spring to see the lambs. The farm (open all year) has space for picnics and has a kids' playground area. It's not a zoo, it's much too real for that. Tel: 01224 523400

Dyce isn't just where the airport is, you know! Look for *Tyrebagger Wood* and go on a trail to the Robber's Cave. Lots of other interesting things too, like a walk through sculptures. Tel: 01224 790432

Fish. Another place to have a laugh is the *Fishmarket*, off Market Street. Get there in the early morning to see the tons of fish being unloaded and sold.

Hazlehead Park, on Groats Road, is at least an afternoon out. The park is at its floral best in spring and summer, with an azalea garden and rose gardens to relax in. More entertaining might be the maze, or the pets' corner for the kids. The park is home to an impressive range of sculpture, including the poignant Piper Alpha Memorial and a classic Ian Hamilton Findlay sundial. If you felt the urge, you could pay for the pitch and putt. This park has everything, from azaleas to adventure playground. There is even a small zoo. Sports include table-tennis, trampolines and swingball in summer. It is open all year from 8 a.m., with sports activities available from 10 a.m. Tel: 01224 276276

Parks in Aberdeen range in size from the small ones, such as *Johnston Gardens*, on Viewfield Road, right up the scale to the wonderful *Hazlehead Park* (see above). *Duthie Park and Winter Gardens* are excellent too. They have plenty of activities available, like tennis and putting. The glass-roofed Winter Gardens are glorious – especially if it rains – with terrapins and fish in the ponds and a very zen Japanese garden. Open all year, from 10 a.m. to dusk. Get to Duthie Park either from Polmuir Road, or from Riverside Drive. Tel: 01224 583155

A couple of other small fun parks are: *Seaton Park* on Don Street, beside the River Don, which is quite a formal park, with great daffys in the spring, Tel: 01224 276276; and *Westburn Park* on Westburn Road which has a mini roadway system for child cyclists, Tel: 01224 276276. If this is all too much, you could explore the maze at *Victoria Park* on Westburn Road. There is a conservatory here, for a restful time, and giant chess for the thinkers amongst you.

Scotstoun Moor Local Nature Reserve is on Scotstoun Road, near Bridge of Don. There is an amazing variety of wildlife living here, surprisingly close to the city.

Tourist information in Aberdeen is available all year at St Nicholas House, Broad Street. Tel: 01224 632727

Aberdeenshire

Aboyne. At Dess nearby you will find *Bellwade Farm,* a centre that belongs to the International League for the Protection of Horses. Try to avoid leaving with a pony. Spend **one** if you must. Open Wednesday, Saturday and Sunday from 2 p.m. to 4 p.m. Tel: 01339 887186

Also nearby is *Braeloine Visitor Centre*, at Glen Tanar. It has displays on local natural history and all the kinds of things that good rangers can offer. Find Braeloine off the B976. Open April to September, daily from 10 a.m. to 5 p.m. Tel: 01339 886072

Tourist information is available at the Ballater Road carpark from Easter to October. Tel: 01339 886060

Aden Country Park, at Mintlaw near Peterhead, is another remarkable centre which features everything from an adventure playground to a working farm and 'heritage centre'. Tread gently over the nature trails and you might get as far as the kitchen of the horseman's house and see oatcakes in the making. There is a caravan/camp site too. Find Aden on the A950, between Old Deer and Mintlaw. Tel: 01771 622857

There is tourist information here from April to October. Tel: 01771 623037

Alford. Six miles south of town, off the A980, is *Craigievar Castle*, a fairy-tale postcard site and property of the National Trust for Scotland. There is a charge to go into the house, but an honesty box for the grounds. Go low-season for the best result. Tel: 01330 844651 (ranger at Crathes)

Haughton Country Park is just north of Alford, and you can pack in a woodland walk, a bit of putting and a play for the kids quite easily. There is a visitor centre open from Easter to September at weekends from 8.30 a.m. to 4.30 p.m.; the park is open all year. Tel: 019755 62453

Tourist information can be obtained from April to October, at the Railway Museum, Station Yard. Tel: 019755 62052

Ballater has the *Loch Muick and Lochnagar Wildlife Reserve*. This is glorious walking country. Watch out for the wild red deer. You can also wander through the Forestry Commission's *Cambus o'May Forest Walks*. I would be far too nervous to go across the shaky bridge over the Dee, mind you!

For a really sweet treat, go to *Dee Valley Manufacturing Confectioners* at Station Square. Here you can see those boilings being boiled, if you know what I mean . . . Open for viewing all year, Monday to Thursday from 9 a.m. to 5 p.m., Friday from 9 a.m. to 12.30 p.m. Tel: 01339 755499

The local Tourist Information Centre, at Station Square, is open Easter to end October. Tel: 013397 55306

Balmedie Country Park, eight miles north of Aberdeen, is a coastal park with a sandy beach. You can romp in the dunes or have a picnic. The park is open all year; the visitor centre is open from October to March, Monday to Saturday from 9 a.m. to 5 p.m.; also Sunday in summer. Tel: 01358 742396

Banchory is near to *Mulloch Forest* (off the A957), which is a superb area for walking with views of the Feugh Valley and Deeside. Look out for the stone circles.

Shooting Greens is another walking place, in Blackhall Forest.

Banchory has a Tourist Information Centre (open all year) at Bridge Street. Tel: 01330 822000

Banff is home to the *Colleonard Sculpture Garden and Gallery*, on Sandyhill Road. Unusual sculptures varying in height from 25 feet to ten inches – figurative, but weird. Open March to September from 9 a.m. to 7 p.m. Tel: 01261 818284.

Banff also has a Tourist Information Centre, which you will find at Collie Lodge. Open April to October. Tel: 01261 812419

Bennachie Hill Walks and the West Gordon Way are a series of long and short forest hilltop walks with excellent views. You can get up there from the respective carparks at Donview, Esson's and Back o' Bennachie. Tel: 01467 794161

Braemar Highland Heritage Centre is located in Braemar village centre. It features the award-winning film and exhibition of the colourful history of the Royal Highland Games, and Queen Victoria's arrival in Deeside, as well as material about the building of Balmoral and the local wildlife. Open daily from 10 a.m. to 6 p.m. (longer in summer). Tel: 013397 41944

At Braemar there is the most beautiful birch woodland for walking in. Go to Chapel Brae to find *Morrone Birchwood*.

Tourist information is available all year from The Mews, Mar Road. Tel: 013397 41600

Brimmond and Elrick Country Park is near Aberdeen, off the A96/A944. Plenty of rangers, and the Robber's Cave to look forward to as well. Open all year.

Buchan Ness is at Boddam, by Peterhead. The headland and lighthouse here mark the most easterly point on the Scottish mainland.

Collieston, off the A90/A975 north of Aberdeen, has the *Forvie National Nature Reserve* which is founded on dunes. Good for walking and birdwatching. The visitor centre is open in summer, daily from 10 a.m. to 5 p.m.; in winter at weekends only. Tel: 01358 751330

Crathie has a Tourist Information Centre, romantically positioned in the carpark at Balmoral Castle. Open Easter to October. Tel: 013397 42414

Crimond, three miles south of Fraserburgh, is where you will find the RSPB's *Loch of Strathbeg Reserve*, signposted from the A90. This is an excellent place for keen birdwatchers, with hides and binoculars supplied. Open daily from dawn to dusk. Tel: 01346 532017/513017

Cruden Bay Beach is a lovely place for a sandy stroll of an afternoon. It is about eight miles south of Peterhead.

North of Cruden Bay, on the A975, is the *Bullers of Buchan*, a breathtaking sea chasm and stunning cliff scenery.

Ellon has a useful Tourist Information Centre at the Market Street carpark. Open April to October. Tel: 01358 720730

Fetterangus is west of Peterhead and near *Drinnie's Wood and Viewpoint*, a restored nineteenth-century vantage-point, with lovely walks. Open mid-May to September, daily from 10 a.m. to 5 p.m.

Fettercairn, near Laurencekirk, has the *Fettercairn Distillery*, one of the oldest licensed distilleries in Scotland. You can have a free guided tour and a dram. Open May to September, Monday to Saturday from 10 a.m. to 4.30 p.m. Tel: 01561 340205

Finzean is near Banchory. Here you might come across the *Finzean Bucket Mill*. It is a nineteenth-century water-powered mill producing steel buckets and tubs! Outlandish. Open Tuesday to Friday from 10 a.m. to 5 p.m., weekends from 2 p.m. to 5 p.m. Tel: 01330 850633

Fraserburgh has a pleasant beach with a three-mile stretch of sand. It also has a great *Fishmarket* if you want a smelly start to your day.
For tourist information try at Saltoun Square from April to October. Tel: 01346 518315

Fyvie, eight miles south of Turriff, has one of Aberdeenshire's baronial castles. The grounds and Fyvie Loch were designed and landscaped in the eighteenth century, so be sure to put your contribution in the National Trust for Scotland honesty box, to show how much you enjoyed yourself. You would pay to go into the castle. Tel: 01330 844651 (ranger at Crathes)
About six miles north-west of Fyvie is Kirkton, Millbrex, where you will find the *Fluffsfield Donkey Sanctuary*. Admission is free, but you try coming away without a donkey, or at least a pledge to supply one with carrots for the rest of its life! Open daily except Tuesday, from 10 a.m. to 5 p.m. (till 2 p.m. in winter). Tel: 01771 644770

Haddo House is one of the poshest houses in the country. Wander in the gardens (pop a donation in the box) and feel the quality, but go off-season to avoid the crowds. Aberdeenshire Council now run the adjacent *Country Park*, which is a better bet for a freebie, but not as up-market. Take in Haddo off the B999, ten miles north-west of Ellon. Haddo Country Park is at Tarves, and it is open all year, from 9.30 a.m. to dusk. Tel: 01651 851440

Huntly has *Cooper Park* with table-tennis, tennis and trampolines in summer, even cross-country skiing! (And associated charges too.) Get down on the ski trail.
Bin Forest is just out of town, with a series of waymarked walks through a varied woodland scene. Tel: 01466 794161
For more ideas try the Tourist Information Centre, at 7 The Square, from April to October. Tel: 01466 792255

Inverey, west of Braemar, is where you will find the *Linn of Dee*, which is a narrow chasm of the River Dee, and quite a local beauty spot.

Inverurie has a Tourist Information Centre at the Town Hall. Open April to October. Tel: 01467 620600

Macduff is a few miles along the B9031 from *Crovie Viewpoint*, which is a clifftop vantage-point from where you can see the little fishing village. There is a picnic area here too.

Maud is 12 miles west of Peterhead. Here they have a big livestock market every Tuesday and Wednesday at 10 a.m.

Mar Lodge Estate, five miles west of Braemar, can be your route and introduction to the Cairngorms, the most important nature conservation landscape in Britain. This has the three 'Ms' – Majestic Mountainous Moorland. Serious walks, wildlife and even patches of Caledonian forest. The rangers here are more like the SAS. No joking. Tel: 01339 741433

Monymusk. The *Monymusk Walled Garden* at Home Farm is an eighteenth-century nursery garden full of hardy perennials (they would need to be hardy). Open March to November, Monday to Saturday from 10 a.m. to 5 p.m., Sunday from 2 p.m. to 5 p.m.; in winter, Tuesday to Saturday from 10 a.m. to 2 p.m. Tel: 01467 651543

Muir of Dinnet Nature Reserve is halfway between Ballater and Aboyne, off the A97. You can walk along to the exciting watery *Burn o' Vat* from here, or call in at the visitor centre. Open mid-May to September, Thursday to Monday from 10 a.m. to 6 p.m. Tel: 01339 811667

Pennan, an old smugglers' village which was the location for the film *Local Hero*, is on the B9031 coast road from Fraserburgh. Nearby is *Cullykhan Bay*. A lovely sandy beach isn't all you'll find here: there is a bronze-age fort and even a sea tunnel – Hell's Lum!

Peterhead has a beach that is popular with watersports enthusiasts. It is quite sheltered, too. The harbour and the fishmarket are worth a visit, particularly in the early morning to see the boats coming in.

Look out for the Tourist Information Centre at 54 Broad Street. Open April to October. Tel: 01779 471904

Portsoy has a park at *Loch Soy* where you can hire a paddle boat in summer. There is also putting for you clubbers. Find the park at Seafield Street.

You could look in at the *Marble Workshop and Pottery* where they make items on the premises. Tel: 01261 842404

Sandhaven is near Fraserburgh, and is the home of the *Sandhaven Meal Mill*. This place has been lovingly restored to full working glory, and also features a visitor centre so you can sort the wheat from the chaff. Open May to September, Saturday and Sunday from 2 p.m. to 4.30 p.m.; also weekdays in July and August.

Stonehaven. About three miles to the south, off the A92 near Crawton, is

Fowlsheugh Nature Reserve, an RSPB-run reserve. This has one of the biggest seabird colonies in Scotland. The best time to go is spring or summer. There is also an exhibition centre. Tel: 01224 624824

There is tourist information here too, at 66 Allardice Street, from Easter to end October. Tel: 01569 762806

Strathdon is on the A944 north of Ballater. Here you will find the *Candacraig Walled Garden* with the kind of flora your mum hoped you'd like. Open May, June and September from 2 p.m. to 5 p.m.; July and August from 10 a.m. to 6 p.m. Tel: 01975 651226

Look for another super garden, the *Old Semeil Herb Garden,* which has 200 varieties of herb! Open April at weekends; May to September, daily from 10 a.m. to 5 p.m.; closed Thursdays in September. Tel: 019756 51343

Turriff has tourist information to impart, at the centre in the High Street. Open April to October. Tel: 01888 563001

Angus

Arbroath seafront is the home of the *West Links,* near the well-used caravan parks to the south of town. Come here for some gentle activity, pitch and putt, tennis and even trampolines. More recent additions include mini racing cars. An engaging place to see the sea from April to October. Tel: 01241 431060

For a brilliant beach, head for *Lunan Bay* which is four miles north of Arbroath, and is a sandy unspoilt beach. Good for swimming except at the river mouth.

The thing that is a *must* whilst you are in Arbroath, is, of course, the smokie!

Try the Tourist Information Centre at Market Place (open all year). Tel: 01241 872609

Brechin has a Tourist Information Centre (open April to September) at St Ninian's Place. Tel: 01356 623050

Carnoustie has a Tourist Information Centre in the High Street, which is open from April to September. Tel: 01241 852258

Crombie Country Park. The pond (formerly a quarry) that sits in the centre is one of Dundee's old reservoirs. Have a go at their orienteering course! I dare you! (For young kids there is even Animalteering, an easier form of orienteering.) Find Crombie off the B961 about 12 miles north-east of Dundee. Tel: 01241 860360

Forfar. *Forfar Loch Country Park* is close to the junction of the A94, A932 and B9128, north of Dundee. Watch for rangers and the special events throughout the year, especially the hands-on for kids variety. The visitor centre is open all year, Monday to Friday from 2 p.m. to 4 p.m.; also Sunday in summer, from 12 noon to 4 p.m. Note that you will pay for activities like pitch and putt. Tel: 01307 461118

Forfar has a Tourist Information Centre (open April to September) at 40 East High Street. Tel: 01307 467876

Kirriemuir. The RSPB runs the *Loch of Kinnordy Reserve*, which is a freshwater marsh full of birds. Find it on the B951, a mile west of Kirriemuir. It is open daily.

Monikie Country Park is on the B962 near Monifieth just outside Dundee. In 1845 reservoirs were created to provide a water supply for the people of Dundee; now, made redundant by the larger reservoirs of the 1970s, Monikie is a great place for wildlife and sport. A children's adventure playground and superlative watersports are key parts of the park. Rangers too, if you feel the need. Tel: 01382 370202

Montrose. Off the A92 north of Montrose, just a mile before St Cyrus, is the *St Cyrus Nature Reserve*. There is a visitor centre with local natural history on display and even a salt-water aquarium. Open May to September, Wednesday to Sunday from 9.30 a.m. to 5.30 p.m. Tel: 01674 830736

The beach at Montrose stretches for four miles, between the two rivers, the North Esk and South Esk. Don't swim near them as the currents are treacherous.

Get tourist information at Bridge Street from June to September. Tel: 01674 672000

THE HIGHLANDS

Moray

Aberlour is a village in the middle reaches of the Spey, where you will find *The Village Store* in the Square. No ordinary store though, as it preserves items sold from the 1920s to the late 1970s, in a real 'glimpse into the past'. A modern craft shop, too. Tel: 01340 871243

Brodie Castle Gardens are another triumph for the National Trust for Scotland. As usual, a small contribution to the honesty box is well worth while. Plan your visit for the off-season for purest peace and quiet. Woodland walks and fine views of the castle. Brodie is about five miles west of Forres. The grounds are open all year, daily from 9.30 a.m. to sunset.

Brodie also has *Barleymill Dried Flower Centre*. Say no more. Tel: 01309 673847

Buckie has a Tourist Information Centre at Cluny Square. Open May to September. Tel: 01542 834853

Craigellachie. Here, by Aberlour, the Speyside Way Visitor Centre and Ranger Service Headquarters can give you all the facts you will need. At Boat of Fiddich. Tel: 01340 881266

Look out for *Craigellachie Bridge* too, a single, cast-iron span bridge designed by Thomas Telford and put up in 1814.

Cullen. Between here and Sandend to the east is *Sunnyside Bay*, with Charlie the Hermit's cave at the Cullen end. Sometimes I know just how Charlie felt. There is a Tourist Information Centre at 20 Seafield Street. Open from May to September. Tel: 01542 840757

Dolphins are often seen off the coast of Moray, and there are plenty of good places to go spotting. Try by the Culbin Sands (see Highland Heartlands: Nairn), but take binoculars. A couple of miles north of Inverness on the A9 there is a *Dolphin and Seal Centre* at the Tourist Information Centre carpark.

Dufftown is the home of the *Glenfiddich Distillery*, Wm Grant and Sons Ltd. They are open all year except two weeks at New Year, Monday to Saturday from 9.30 a.m. to 4.30 p.m. There is plenty to see, bottling and the like! Tel: 01340 820373

There is also a Tourist Information Centre (open April to November) in the Clock Tower at the Square. Tel: 01340 820501

Elgin is where you will come across the *Old Mills* working watermill. This unique attraction stands by the banks of the River Lossie, to the west of the town. The miller himself will explain the workings. As if that wasn't enough, after looking at the exhibitions, you can even get close to a working beehive. Open May to September from 10 a.m. to 5 p.m. (closed Wednesday and Thursday). There is a small charge: £1 for adults and 50 pence for children and concessions. Tel: 01343 540698

Johnston's Cashmere Visitor Centre at Newmill has an audio-visual programme, and will fill you in with everything you ever wanted to know about cashmere. Open all year, Monday to Saturday from 9 a.m. to 5.30 p.m.; also Sunday from June to September, from 11 a.m. to 5 p.m. Mill tours are available on weekdays. Tel: 01343 554099

Cooper Park is great to let off steam, with a range of recreational activities. For more countryside, opt for *Millbuies Country Park*, five miles south of town, off the A941 to Rothes. Wayfaring and nature trails, even fishing. Open all year, from 8 a.m. to dusk. Tel: 01343 860234

Roseisle Forest can be reached from the B901 Elgin road. There are walks from here to lovely secluded beaches.

Blackhills House is three miles east of Elgin via the A96, then B9103. You need to phone in advance to see round this 70-acre wild garden, packed with rhododendrons. Donations to charity. Tel: 01343 842223

There is a Tourist Information Centre at 17 High Street, Elgin. Open all year. Tel: 01343 542666

The Findhorn Foundation is an international spiritual community, founded in the 1960s by Peter and Eileen Caddy and Dorothy MacLean. The place is well worth a visit, as it is genuinely serene (perhaps that is the inhabitants). The community is highly organised, with ecological buildings (some made of old whisky barrels), celebrated organic gardening and even a publishing business. The bookshop is excellent, with all kinds of new-age titles, as well as unusual gifts. (Look out for 'angel cards' and the 'transformation game'.) In the summer, tours of the Foundation run daily at 2 p.m. from the Phoenix Bookshop. There is also a caravan park here (see Accommodation). Tel: 01309 690311

For walks alongside the *River Findhorn*, head for the *Dunearn Burn Walk*, which starts about five miles south-west of Forres. Great views guaranteed. You can see the gorge at its best (I struggled there with 'gorgeous'!) at *Randolph's Leap* at Logie, which is seven miles south of Forres. Take the A940 then the B9007 towards Carrbridge.

Fochabers – another tricky name; try saying it *Fokabers*, with equal stress throughout. This is the home of *Baxters*, the famous manufacturers of fine foods (particularly delicious soups). Visit Mrs Baxter's Victorian kitchen and have a good gawk in the factory itself. This is a day out in itself, with an audio-visual display, a great shop and, of course, a restaurant. Open all year, Monday to Friday from 9.30 a.m. to 5 p.m., weekends from 10 a.m. to 5 p.m. Factory tours are available only on weekdays. Tel: 01343 820393

The *Tugnet Ice House* is an unusual attraction if ever there was one! It is the largest ice house in Scotland, and was built in 1830 to store ice from the River Spey for use to pack salmon. Now the ice house has been restored, and an exhibition and an audio-visual show added. Open May to October, daily from 11 a.m. to 5 p.m. Tel: 01309 673701

Another weird attraction just outside Fochabers are the *Earth Pillars*, which have been formed by erosion. They are a mile south of town, off the Ordiquish to Boat o' Brig road at Aultdearg. Spooky.

Forres has an unusual park feature: incredible floral sculptures can be seen in summer in *Grant Park* on Victoria Road. In the past these have included the Teddy Bears' Picnic, Owl and the Pussycat and the Buckie Drifter. There is a children's playground, as well as walks up Cluny Hill for views of Forres and Findhorn Bay.

Tourist information is available at the centre at 116 High Street. Open April to November. Tel: 01309 672938

Garmouth, near Elgin, has a footpath extending across a viaduct to the bay of the Spey. Good sharp intakes of breath now please.

Keith. The *Drummuir Castle Walled Garden* is just off the B9014 Dufftown road, six miles from town. This is a traditional walled garden, using organic methods. Fruit, flowers and vegetables. Make a donation. Open May to September, Monday to Friday from 9 a.m. to 4 p.m. Tel: 01542 810300

You could pop into the Tourist Information Centre, in Church Road, which is open from May to September. Tel: 01542 882634

The Lein Nature Reserve can be found at the mouth of the Spey, at Kingston on Spey. The area beside the shingle beaches is now a Scottish Wildlife Trust reserve. The shingle ridges themselves are quite awe-inspiring when you consider they were formed by the river over thousands of years.

Lossiemouth. Three miles to the west of town is *Covesea Caves*, a series of sea-cliff caves. Rumour has it that one of them has a link, in the form of a passage to Gordonstoun House.

At Lossiemouth the sand and shingle beaches stretch for miles. *Silversands* is to the west, and has the nicest bathing beach. Visit the harbour and see the fishmarket before breakfast.

At the park in Lossiemouth, *Burghead Fun Track*, you'll find go-karts nestling beside sporty attractions like putting and pitch and putt. *Marine Park*, on Stotfield Road, has a bit more to add, in the form of croquet and trampolines in the summer.

Tomintoul – or rather, the wilderness ten miles north of Tomintoul – is the home of *The Glenlivet*. You can visit this distillery for free, and hear all about the secrets of the famous 12-year-old malt whisky. Open mid-March to end October, Monday to Saturday from 10 a.m. to 4 p.m., Sunday from 12.30 p.m. to 4 p.m. (In the height of the summer they stay open till 6 p.m.) Give a call before you go, as they are due to be refurbishing in 1997. Find The Glenlivet on the B9008, north of Tomintoul. Tel: 0154 278 3220

You can visit the *Tomintoul Peat Moss* just north of town to see the peats being dug. Far more inspiring when you recall that this place supplies peats for barley malting, the first stage of whisky production!

The *Glenlivet Estate* offers miles of wild, spectacular waymarked walks (thank God they are waymarked!), well watched by rangers and with wonderful wildlife. Visit the Glenlivet Estate Information Centre on Main Street, Tomintoul. Tel: 01807 580283

There is also a Tourist Information Centre at Tomintoul, in the Square. Open Easter to October. Tel: 01807 580285

Tomnavoulin has *The Old Mill Visitor Centre*, which is an old carding mill. The visitor centre has an audio-visual presentation about the making of whisky, even a dram. Open April to October. Tel: 01807 590442/590432

Highland Heartlands

Aviemore will be a familiar name to anyone with a skiing bent. If you take the B951 road from Aviemore to Glenmore Forest Park, you will cut right across *Rothiemurchus Highland Estate*. Pop into the visitor centre to see their touch-table and get a feel for the area! Other activities here have a cost involved, but you might want to pick up some information to mull over. You might like the idea of pathfinding – a gentler version of orienteering with a certificate on completion. Tel: 01479 810858

Tourist information is available all year from the centre on Grampian Road. Tel: 01479 810363

Ballachulish Bridge, near Glencoe, is a scenic delight. By the bridge on the north side of Loch Linnhe, off the A82, you will find the *Confectionery Factory*. You can watch tablet and truffles being made, and even taste the wares. It is a small-scale home-baking kind of operation, so they benefit from a speciality Scottish food shop next door. There is also a mail order service, so that you can send some tablet to your relatives at home without the possibly irresistible temptation of carrying it with you. They are open Monday to Saturday from 9.15 a.m. to 5.15 p.m. (10.15 a.m. to 4.15 p.m. from mid-November to March). Note that the factory isn't normally in production at the weekends. Find it all at Great Glen Fine Foods, Old Ferry Road, North Ballachulish, near Fort William. Tel: 01855 821277.

Ballachulish has a Tourist Information Centre, open April to October. Tel: 01855 811296

Beauly is an attractive village with a glorious salmon river. You can wander in the grounds of the ruined abbey, or head off up to Glen Affric, one of the most outstanding scenic glens in the whole of Scotland. Near Beauly, on the River Glass, is the Aigas Dam where fish are brought up into viewing chambers as they move up stream. Go from mid-June to mid-October, between 10 a.m. and 3 p.m. At *Aigas House and Field Centre* you can get a bit more of an insight into local natural history – particularly if you ask a ranger. Open May to October, 10.30 a.m. to 5.30 p.m.

Carrbridge has a Tourist Information Centre in the Main Street. It is open May to September. Tel: 01479 841630

Daviot Wood. The local Tourist Information Centre (open April to October) is right beside the A9. Tel: 01463 772203

Fort Augustus. You can while away a good hour or two just watching inexperienced boat-folk trying to get through the most fearsome series of lochs. There are also the monks at the Abbey to ponder. You can stay there, too (see Accommodation). For a quiet walk wander off along *Leiterfearn* beside Loch Oich. Other Forestry Commission walks from here are available at *Inchnacardoch Forest*.

If in doubt, try the Tourist Information Centre at the carpark. Open April to October. Tel: 01320 366367

Fort William. Take your taste buds to visit the *Ben Nevis Distillery and Visitor Centre*, which is at Lochy Bridge on the A82 near the turn-off for Mallaig. Here you can witness the miracle of whisky-making and hear about the legendary Hector MacDram and his role in the creation of John MacDonald's Dew of Ben Nevis. The centre is open all year, Monday to Friday from 9 a.m. to 5 p.m., Saturday from 10 a.m. to 4 p.m. Guided tours are available, which cost £2 for adults, £1 for concessions (including a dram). Tel: 01397 700200

The Tourist Information Centre (open all year) is at Cameron Square. Tel: 01397 703781

Foyers. Now I hope you didn't come here just to get a glimpse of Boleskine House, the old haunt of Aleister Crowley and then other madcap folk like Jimmy Page of Led Zep. They won't let you in, anyway. Instead, take a trip to the falls just off the B852. And keep a sharp eye out for the Loch Ness monster the whole time. Locals here really do believe you know!

Glencoe is just off the A82, 17 miles south of Fort William. You would be hard-pressed to find a more beautiful glen in the whole of Scotland. Towering mountains closing in on all sides, with water rushing through the glen, carving its way through the rock, this is wild Scotland in an accessible place. The wilderness itself is home to wildlife from red deer to golden eagles. If you visit the *Glencoe Visitor Centre* you will be able to piece together the tragic tale of the massacre of 1692, when the MacDonalds were slaughtered by King William's men.

Glenmore Forest Park can be reached from Aviemore. It is about seven miles east of the town, off the B9152. Expect solitude, because this is wilderness country. There is a visitor centre with an excellent audio-visual presentation, and guided walks are as full of fresh air as any walk could ever be. There is also camping and caravanning (see Accommodation). Tel: 01479 861220

Glen Nevis is surely one of the wildest parts of Scotland. Here you will find *Ionad Nibheis*, which houses an exhibition and video show about Ben Nevis and the history and wildlife of the Glen. Open April to October, daily from 9 a.m. to 5 p.m. Tel: 01397 700774/705922

Grantown-on-Spey has a Tourist Information Centre in the High Street. Open April to October. Tel: 01479 872773

Inverness is the capital of the Highlands. Try the *Bught Floral Hall and Visitor Centre* at Bught Lane. This is a great wet-weather venue for wandering through a sub-tropical landscape, complete with a waterfall, fountain and tropical fishpond. There is even a cactus house. Open April to end September, daily from 10 a.m. to 8 p.m. (till 6 p.m. at weekends); October to end March it closes at dusk daily. Tel: 01463 222755

Less exotic parks in Inverness can be found, too. *Bellfield Park* is an ideal area for picnics in landscaped gardens, with children's playground, paddling pool and tennis. *Ness Islands* is a pleasant riverside walk close to the centre of town, which leads to the centre of the Bught leisure complex. *Whin Park* is a great park, with a miniature railway, boating pond and children's play area. Why not try your hand at *Bught Mini Golf* (June to September – a small charge)? Tel: 01463 724224 (Highland Council Leisure Services)

There is a large Tourist Information Centre in Inverness, at Castle Wynd, which is open all year. Tel: 01463 234353

Kilchoan, Ardnamurchan, has a Tourist Information Centre to see you through. Open from April to October. Tel: 01972 510222

Kingussie. The RSPB's *Insch Marsh Reserve* is nearby. Great habitat if you are a waterfowl: pleasant walks if you are human. Open all year. Find it on the B970 a mile and a half from Kingussie. Donations are encouraged. Tel: 01540 661518

There is a Tourist Information Centre here too. Open May to September. Tel: 01540 661297

Kinlochleven has a very unusual visitor centre. In this mountain site, close to Fort William, you will find the *Aluminium Story*, the tale of a community that worked with hydro-electric power to produce aluminium from the mountains.

Open mid-April to mid-October, daily; only Tuesday and Saturday in winter (and who can blame them). Tel: 01855 831663

Kintail and Morvich is an enormous Highland crofting estate looked after by the National Trust for Scotland. This kind of scenery and wild grandeur are the real Scotland. This estate includes the Falls of Glomach and the Five Sisters of Kintail. It will take you five to seven hours to traipse to the falls, so get serious if you decide it is for you. Try the *Countryside Centre* at Morvich Farm, off the A87 about 16 miles east of Kyle of Lochalsh, which has the best access to the mountains. More than serious shoes are required in this region. Take flares (not the leg-wear variety) if possible. Tel: 01599 511231 (resident manager and ranger)

Mallaig is the place for ferries. To Skye, for example, or the Outer Hebrides. Pop into the transcendent Ceilidh Place Bookshop to kill some time (why not eat here, and stay here?), or trot to the Tourist Information Centre, which is open April to October. Tel: 01687 462170

Nairn is a charming seaside town, with a beautiful beach, seaside links and occasional sitings of dolphins and porpoises. The super *Nairn Leisure Park* offers the lot. For kids there's the woodland fort and adventure trails as well as a toddlers' playground. An outdoor games complex gives sporty types their just deserts, whilst the more sedate can laze by the beach or take in the swimming pool and steam room (a charge for these). Open daily from Easter to September. Tel: 01667 453061

Close to Nairn (go out of town towards Forres and turn left down Lochloy Road, past the golf course on your left, now follow the signs), you will come across the *Culbin Sands and Culbin Forest*. This area of moving sand-dunes on the Moray coast has already swallowed up a whole village (back in 1694). Hence, Forestry Enterprise back the dunes with plantations in an attempt to stabilise them. The effect is pleasing, with wildlife and plants now flourishing. Make your way over the dunes for the views and walk along the sandflats. Exhilarating! Tel: 01343 820223 (Forestry Enterprise at Fochabers)

There is a Tourist Information Centre at Nairn too, head for 62 King Street. Open April to October. Tel: 01667 452753

Newtonmore. The *Ralia Highland Gateway Centre* is nearby. This visitor centre has touch-screen computers to help you discover all manner of secrets about the Highlands! Open June to September, from 10 a.m. to 5 p.m. Tel: 01540 673650

Shiel Bridge has a Tourist Information Centre you can call into from April to October. Tel: 01599 511264

Spean Bridge is where you should go if you want to watch Angus Macleod weaving tartan and tweeds. Angus won a prestigious competition for his Skye tartan design, and now he can be found demonstrating his art at the Woollen Mill. Tel: 01397 712260

The Tourist Information Centre here is open from April to October. Tel: 01397 712576

Strontian is beginning to get wild. The delights of Ardnamurchan await you. Golden eagles and singing sands. Single-track roads for miles and miles. Sigh. There is a Tourist Information Centre here, which is open from April to October. Tel: 01967 402131

Tomich is close to the beautiful *Plodda Falls*. You can take the track from the village quite far, so it isn't a long walk to the falls. There is an old Victorian bridge right over the falls, which makes it all the better for trembling knees.

The Northern Highlands

Balmacara. Take a wander round *Balmacara Estate and Lochalsh Woodland Garden,* on the A87 about two miles east of Kyle of Lochalsh. This is a vast crofting estate with amazing views and access to treasure spots like Applecross and Knoydart. Plockton will be familiar to fans of *Hamish Macbeth.* There is no formal admission charge, just an honesty box, for the stunning Lochalsh Woodland Garden. The estate and the garden are owned by the National Trust for Scotland, so expect the usual high standard of facilities and rangers with an air of superiority. Tel: 01599 566325 (Balmacara Administrator); 01599 511231 (Ranger/naturalist for Kintail)

Beaches. For unspoilt beaches, the strands along the coast of Caithness and Sutherland (where there aren't cliffs plunging vertically into the sea, of course) take some beating. Dornoch beach is particularly good, as are the beaches at Talmine near Tongue, Achmelvich to the north-west of Lochinver, and Duncansby Head near John o' Groats.

Bettyhill has a Tourist Information Centre at Clachan, which is open from March to September. Tel: 01641 521342

Black Isle Country Park is first right after the Tourist Information Centre at North Kessock. This is a park jam-packed with birds and small friendly animals just ready for some heavy petting. Open all year, from 10 a.m. to dusk. Tel: 01463 731656

Bonar Bridge. Five miles to the north, on the A836, you will come across the *Falls of Shin* and the accompanying visitor centre. If you are really lucky you may get to see a salmon leaping up the falls. Spectacular. There are forest walks and even a kids' play area and café here. Open April to October, daily from 10 a.m. to 5.30 p.m. Tel: 01549 402231

Braemore. Here the gorge at *Corrieshalloch* is 200 feet deep and about a mile long, with a beautiful waterfall and a suspension bridge a little way down from the falls. Refreshing and unusual, the gorge is owned by the National Trust for Scotland, so watch out for rangers and put some pennies in any honesty boxes you pass. On the A835, 12 miles south-east of Ullapool. Tel: 01445 781200 (Administrator)

Dingwall. To the south-west of town is Marybank, where you will find the

Torrachilty Dam. There is a fish lift here which you can see in operation; it works naturally.

Dornoch has an unusual claim to fame. Here you'll see the *Witch's Stone*, which marks the place where the last witch was burned in Scotland, in 1722. Not so long ago really . . .

You could visit the *Old Post Office Visitor Centre*, which has displays on south-east Sutherland. Get your tourist information at the centre in the Square. Open all year. Tel: 01862 810400

Duncansby Head and Stacks are just west of John o' Groats. Walk from the carpark near the lighthouse on Duncansby Head along the cliffs to see the stacks.

Dunnet Bay has incredible views and an awesome sea and stretch of strand. Go into the *Pavilion* for a look at the natural history exhibition. Open April to September, Tuesday to Friday from 2 p.m. to 5 p.m., weekends from 2 p.m. to 6 p.m. Tel: 01847 821531

Durness Visitor Centre is at the northernmost point of mainland Scotland. They have good displays relating to the landscape and the wildlife; and heaven knows, you might also want to get in there to shelter from the wind. Open Easter to October. Tel: 01971 511259

Durness is also close to *Smoo Cave*, a huge limestone cavern with three compartments. There is a walkway and you can take a boat trip.

For more ideas try the Durness Tourist Information Centre, which is at Durine. Open late March to October. Tel: 01971 511259

Forsinard Nature Reserve and the Flow Country Visitor Centre are at Forsinard on the A897. The centre is an excellent guide to this boggy experience. There are guided walks for the more serious, which may incur a charge. The visitor centre is open April to October, daily from 9 a.m. to 6 p.m. Tel: 01641 571225

Gairloch has a Tourist Information Centre at Auchtercairn, which is open all year. Tel: 01445 712130

Golspie. A mile south of the town, off the A9, you will come across *West Drummie Garden*. Woody gardens. Open April to October, Wednesday only from 10.30 a.m. to 12.30 p.m. and 2 p.m. to 4.30 p.m. Tel: 01408 633493

Helmsdale is ten miles from the *Wolf Stone*, the place where the last wolf in Scotland is said to have been shot, in 1700.

At nearby Loth you will come across *Crakaig Gardens*. There are plenty of interesting plants, even palms! Peacocks wander round the shrubbery, too. There is a charity box for donations. Open April to October, Thursday and Sunday afternoons. Tel: 01408 621260

There is a Tourist Information Centre at Coupar Park, which is open late March to September. Tel: 01431 821640

John o' Groats has a Tourist Information Centre, on County Road. Open April to October. Tel: 01955 611373

There are also great views here and wonderful walks!

Kinlochbervie Harbour is another place to see fish being landed in the early hours of the morning. An important west coast port.

Knockan Cliff Visitor Centre is in the Inverpolly National Nature Reserve, near Ullapool. This is a thorough centre with displays on geology together with nature trails, and great views. You will never see scenery like this anywhere else in the world. Open all year; visitor centre open May to early September.

Kyle of Lochalsh is the place you will find the Skye road bridge. There is a Tourist Information Centre here too, which is open April to October. Tel: 01599 534276

Lairg. The *Ferrycroft Countryside Centre* is across the River Shin from the centre of the town. At Ferrycroft you can get tourist information and take a spooky audio-visual journey through time and space. It is the archaeological centre for the north; mind you, even the kids will be amused in the indoor puzzle area or the outdoor play area. Open April to October, Monday to Saturday from 9.30 a.m. to 5.30 p.m., also Sunday in the height of the summer from 10 a.m. to 3 p.m. Tel: 01549 402160 (also the Tourist Information Centre)

Take a walk from here up Ord Hill (which is covered in prehistoric sites) to get a great view, or take the forest walk through Ferry Wood. Tel: 01549 402160

Only ten miles to the west, off the A839 are the *Cassley Falls*, which have a walkway that runs alongside them. In the season you might glimpse the silver of a leaping salmon.

Lochcarron has a Tourist Information Centre in the Main Street, which is open Easter to October. Tel: 01520 722357

Lochinver Visitor Centre in Assynt is open Easter to October. They have good displays on the local wildlife, the lives of the people and the land they inhabit; and ranger information. Tel: 01571 844330

Lochinver harbour is a good place to be early in the morning to see the large fishing boats landing their catches.

While you're here, pop into the Tourist Information Centre in the Main Street, which is open late March to October. Tel: 01571 844330

Lybster has a little factory worth visiting. At *Kyle Burn Confectionery* you can even see them putting the writing in the rock. I haven't seen that since they used to take us 'through the round window' on *Playschool*! Tel: 01593 721353

Munlochy has the *Clootie Well*, a bizarre wishing well. To get your wish, you must spill some water and tie a piece of cloth to a nearby tree. The well has been so surrounded by legend that there are rags all round the place. Take a rag with you, so you don't have to rip your shirt off.

North Kessock has a Tourist Information Centre; it is just over the bridge to the Black Isle. Open all year. Tel: 01463 731505

The Old Man of Stoer is an incredible sea stack, which the most adventurous, and fit dare I suggest, could walk carefully to from Stoer Lighthouse. It is a two-mile walk. Head for Culkein, north of Lochinver.

Rosemarkie has a couple of strange attractions. There are weird fossils to be found at *Eathieburn* near Eathie Mains Farm. You can imagine what properties these peculiar-shaped stones are thought to have. If they aren't strange enough for you, why not have a jolly through the *Fairy Glen*, which is actually a glorious scenic walking area with waterfalls and wild cherry trees.

Sandwood Bay is an isolated beach – the kind you may only see once in a lifetime! It is almost a five-mile walk and wild as hell. Look on the map, just down from Cape Wrath and up from Kinlochbervie. Whew!

Strathpeffer. Two miles to the west are the *Falls of Rogie*. This is yet another scary place where you get to view the water from a suspension bridge. Nature at its most raw and real.
There is a Tourist Information Centre in The Square, which is open April to November. Tel: 01997 421415

Strathy Point is for the twitchers. This northern point is a good place to see unusual birds flying by on their migration routes!

Stromeferry is the perhaps unlikely home of the *West Highland Dairy*. You can call in and watch yoghurt, cheese and even ice-cream being made from different kinds of milk (including sheep's milk!). Give them a call; they are at Dailfern, Achmore. Tel: 01599 577203

Syre in Strathnaver is the site of the *Rosal Clearance Trail*. There is a pre-Clearance village here which is of particular interest. Take a walk to it from the forest carpark, it is only a mile.

Tain has the wonderful *Highland Fine Cheeses Factory*, where you can watch cheeses being made – even go on a guided tour. This is my kind of visit! Open Monday to Friday from 9 a.m. to 5 p.m. Tel: 01862 892034

Thurso has a Tourist Information Centre on Riverside, which is open April to October. Tel: 01847 892371

Tongue, or rather Kyle of Tongue Causeway, is the place to go for great views of Ben Loyal to the south and the Rabbit Islands and open sea to the north. There are lay-bys.

Torridon Countryside Centre is nine miles south-west of Kinlochewe on the

A896. Walks from here are strictly for the well equipped, but there are plenty of rangers for the keen. Open May to September, Monday to Saturday from 10 a.m. to 5 p.m., Sunday from 2 p.m. to 5 p.m. Tel: 01445 791221

Ullapool has a Tourist Information Centre at Argyle Street that is open April to November. Tel: 01854 612135

Whaligoe Steps are a flight of scary steps down the cliffs to a tiny harbour at an old herring station, off the A9 between Lybster and Wick. An exhilarating place to visit, but not for the feeble, and not in bad weather at all.

Wick has a *Caithness Glass* factory, complete with visitor centre and the chance to see glass-makers, cutters and engravers at work. Here, as at the Caithness Glass centre at Perth, you will find excellent facilities, including a glorious factory shop and a restaurant. The factory is on the north side of Wick, beside the A9 to John o' Groats. Open all year, Monday to Saturday from 9 a.m. to 5 p.m.; glass-making Monday to Friday from 9 a.m. to 4.45 p.m. Tel: 01955 602286

Try to find the *Brig o' Trams*, which is a natural rock arch formed by erosion over hundreds of years.

Tourist information can be obtained from the centre at Whitechapel Road. Open all year. Tel: 01955 602596

ISLANDS

The Inner Hebrides

SKYE

Beaches include the beautiful white coral shell beaches near Dunvegan. Take the tiny road to the coast about three miles north of the village.

Braes is south of Portree by the A850 and B883. You will find *Glamaig Garden*, at nearby Peinchorran. This informal garden, with waterfalls, is open Easter to mid-September, daily during daylight hours. Donations please. Tel: 01478 650226

Broadford is to the south of the island. Here you'll find a Tourist Information Centre at the carpark. Open April to October. Tel: 01471 822361

Kilt Rock is off the A855 about 17 miles north of Portree. Take a walk to the waterfall, and see strange tartan rock formations on your way.

Kylerhea Otter Haven is just brilliant. There is a flourishing community of otters here, and hides from which to view them. A nice place for a picnic, too! On the road from Kyleakin to Broadford, then follow the signs through Glen Arroch.

Portree is a lovely little harbour town, and is where it all happens as far as Skye is concerned! You will find the Tourist Information Centre at Meall House. Open all year. Tel: 01478 612137

The **Talisker Distillery** has a visitor centre and offers tours. See the amber nectar in the raw! The visitor centre is open weekdays from 9 a.m. to 4 p.m., November to March from 2 p.m. to 4 p.m. Also watch out in the winter, the distillery may not always be in full production. The Distillery is at Carbost. Tel: 01478 640314

Uig is the place for the ferry for Lewis; it also has a Tourist Information Centre at the Ferry Terminal. Open April to October. Tel: 01470 542404

MULL
Craignure is one of the island's ferry ports. The Tourist Information Centre at Pierhead is open April to October only. Tel: 01680 812377

Tobermory is as pretty a town as you'll find anywhere in the world, and it comes complete with a different pace of life. Relax and enjoy!
Just a quarter of a mile from town is *Mull Cheesemakers*, a working farm that you can visit. See the cheese store and have a wander round the farm, perhaps watch the milking. They also have a tea-room, the Garden Barn. The Cheesemakers is open Easter to end September at all reasonable times; closed on Saturday. Find the farm at Sgriob-ruadh; the tea-room is signposted. Tel: 01688 302235
Tourist information is in the Main Street and is open all year. Tel: 01688 302182

IONA
You have to pay the ferry to get here, but you'll never regret it. What a timeless place it is. Every time I've been here the sun has shone, even in October. Look out for seals around the ferry. Walk right across the island for the beaches and the peace. Visit the Abbey and just drink in the peace. The *Iona Heritage Centre* is at the Manse, and here you can learn all you need to know about island life over the past two centuries. Tel: 01681 700364

ISLAY
Bowmore has a Tourist Information Centre (open all year). Tel: 01496 810254
Look for the Kirk, you won't miss it. It is the circular building – the Devil can't hide if there aren't any corners!

Carraig Fhada Open Farm is by Port Ellen Lighthouse, so it is part of a potentially good afternoon's mooching about. There are enough friendly animals here to keep any kids amused, and a small donation is all that is required. The farm is open May to September, daily from 10 a.m. to 5.30 p.m. Tel: 01496 302114
You could also walk down to the singing sands whilst you are here.

JURA

The **Corryvreckan Whirlpool** is between Jura and Scarba; it makes a terrific noise at low tide, when you can see the whirlpool itself from a vantage-point at the north end of the island.

GIGHA

Gigha is an enchanting wee island, reached by ferry from Tayinloan, on the west coast of Kintyre. (Gigha actually means 'God's island' in Gaelic.) As the whole island is only six miles long, most people hire bikes from the island post office and cycle along the only road on the island. Be brave and remember: nowhere on Gigha is more than three miles from the pier. The gardens at Achamore House are owned by the National Trust for Scotland. There is a charge, but there are few ways to spend your money on Gigha, anyway! One way of course, is to head for the Gigha Hotel, near the pier. Tel: 01583 505254

COLONSAY

Kiloran Gardens, Colonsay House, feature natural woodland, rare plants and rhododendrons. Open daily from dawn to dusk. Tel: 01951 200312

The Western Isles

BARRA

Airport. It might not sound exciting, but this is an airport with a difference. At Barra the plane lands on the beach, at *Traigh Mhor*. Only when the tide is out of course!

Castlebay is home to the Tourist Information Centre, which you will find on Main Street. Open Easter to October. Tel: 01871 810336

HARRIS

Beaches. The glorious beach at *Hushinish* has views of the uninhabited Isle of Scarp. Take the B887.

Three of the best beaches in the isles can be found at *Traigh Sgarasta, Losgaintir* and *Taobh Tuath*. Take a spade and a sense of awe.

The Clisham is the highest point in the Western Isles, at 799 metres high. Get up there and get the view. Off the A859.

Harris has a Tourist Information Centre in Tarbert on Pier Road. Open Easter to October. Tel: 01859 502011

LEWIS

Beaches. There are brilliant beaches here, as there are on many of the islands. Try *Traigh Mor* and *Port Geiraha*, which are at the end of the B895.

Bridge to Nowhere was built by Lord Leverhulme for a road to Ness that he never got round to building. (It sounds like my ironing pile, which is sure to still be lying there, useless, many years after *my* death.)

Butt of Lewis isn't just a name from the solemn Radio 4 weather forecast. Here you can see it in the flesh, so to speak, and it isn't a surprise at all that there is so much weather round here. There is a working lighthouse perched on the cliffs here at Ness.

Stornoway has a fishmarket at North Beach Quay, where early risers can see fish being landed. If you are on the look-out for a place to saunter, try *Lady Lever Park* in the town centre.

For more help, try the Tourist Information Centre at 26 Cromwell Street. Open all year. Tel: 01851 703088

Tiumpain Head Lighthouse is a good vantage-point, with views across the Minch to the mainland. You might even glimpse a whale or a basking shark!

Tolsta to Ness Waymarked Walk is a good ten miles, so take stout shoes and a sandwich. Allow four hours at least for this coastal stroll.

Whalebone Arch is something to see at Bragar on the west coast of the island. The blue whale that owned the jaws which make up this gruesome arch must have been massive!

NORTH UIST
Balranald/Baile Raghaill is an RSPB reserve, and there is a resident warden to fill you in. This is twitcher country, low lochans and shelter at a premium. The reserve is off the A865, three miles north of Bayhead.

Clachan Sands is a large beach near the village of Clachan, which is on the B893.

Langass Walk is a circular walk round the island, details can be obtained from the Tourist Information Centre in Lochmaddy. The centre is at Pier Road and is open Easter to October. Tel: 01876 500321

SOUTH UIST
Lochboisdale is the place to go for tourist information; the centre on Pier Road is open Easter to October. Tel: 01878 700286

Loch Druidibeg Nature Reserve covers a wide area either side of the A865 at Loch Druidibeg. Plenty of geese and listen out for those distinctive corncrakes! (No, I said *corncrakes*, not cornflakes!)

Orkney

MAINLAND
Deerness on Mainland is the village from where you can find your way to the 'Gloup' – a spectacular natural arch – and Mull Head. The local reserve of Mull Head covers 300 acres of maritime grassland and heath, home to thousands of seabirds. You can also see the ruins of a Norse chapel and village as you wander the paths.

Kirkwall is one of the best preserved examples of an ancient Norse town, with sites galore to prove it. Tankerness House, as well as containing an excellent museum, is surrounded by gardens, which are free and open all year.

The park to try out is *Brandyquoy Park*, which also has a putting green (there is a charge for this). Find the park on Palace Road.

For tourist information try the centre at 6 Broad Street. Open all year. Tel: 01856 872856

Stromness is Orkney's main port after Kirkwall. Just north of town, off the B9056, you will find *Marwick Head Reserve*, which is an RSPB reserve. Wild, cliff scenery with puffins and other seabirds – and a dreadful smell! Tel: 01856 850176

If you are in need of a park in Stromness then *Marwick Park* has a radio-controlled model car track, with a modest charge. Who needs parks in Orkney anyway?

There is a Tourist Information Centre here at the Ferry Terminal Building at the Pier Head. Open all year. Tel: 01856 850716

Shetland

MAINLAND
Lerwick houses the Tourist Information Centre for the islands, at Market Cross. Open all year. Tel: 01595 693434

Sandwick is on the east coast of Mainland, halfway between Sumburgh and Lerwick. Go into *Hoswick* to spend a bit of time in the *Warp and Weft Visitor Centre*. Browse through their displays on the history of weaving (or simply head for the tea-room). Open Monday to Saturday from 10 a.m. to 5 p.m., Sunday from 12 noon to 5 p.m.

Scalloway. The *Crofting and Wildlife Trail* set up at Burland, Tondra, is between here and Burra. Unusual farm animals in a different kind of setting. There isn't any charge, but donations are welcome. Tel: 01595 880430

UNST
Unst is home to the *Hermeness National Nature Reserve*. An excellent visitor centre helps to make the whole bird thing a bit easier to handle. (Thousands of birds on cliffs to me and you.) Find it at the shore station, Burrafirth. It is signposted from Haroldswick. The visitor centre is open May to mid-September, daily from 9 a.m. to 5 p.m. Tel: 01595 693345

HISTORICAL SITES

If you like your days out to feature something just that little bit more mature, then this is the section for you.

As far as this book goes, historical sites refers to absolutely anything that is a tangible, visitable 'something' with a historical interest. This means that many castles and ancient monuments are included, whilst the majority of battle sites aren't. The most important battle sites are marked on every map, and many have visitor centres. Ones that are of particular interest, of course, are Killiecrankie, Glencoe and Culloden. Do not be perturbed, gentle reader, those stars of the warring firmament all feature here in some way or other!

Standing stones and prehistoric places are a bit of a problem. There is such a wealth of these kind of sites that to catalogue them all would take the best part of the rest of my lifetime. Again, lots are marked on good maps, and certainly the most interesting and accessible are here. With regards to any piles of stones that 'seem remarkably like a broch' that you might find on your travels, don't tell me about them unless you are utterly convinced that someone else after you would actually want to visit them.

Castles are endless fun; from the still-working to the completely flattened, they retain a real attitude from the day they were built. My favourite is just outside Wick. Check it out. Onwards and upwards. Another day, another ruin.

THE WEST

Argyll and Bute

Carrick Castle is a ruined fourteenth-century castle on the western edge of Loch Goil. Very romantic once you get there, but not easy to get to.

Dunoon has the *Castle House*, which was built by Lord Provost James Ewing of Glasgow in 1822 (see Museums).

Why not also try the *Ardnadam Heritage Trail*? This walk links a number of sites through which you can get an idea of the history of the Cowal peninsula. The trail takes about an hour and a half, and covers two miles, passing amongst other things an early field system and a 'flag' or 'clapper' stone bridge. The starting-point is the Ardnadam carpark, just off the A885 about two miles north-east of Dunoon.

Glendaruel, on the A886 south of Strachur, is the village to visit to see the *Clachan of Glendaruel*, which incorporates Kilmodan Church, dating from 1610. St Modan once established a monastery in the glen.

Innellan Church is in the pretty village of Innellan, overlooking the Firth of Clyde towards Wemyss Bay. So inspirational it even prompted the blind preacher, George Mathieson, to write 'O love that will not let me go'.

To the south of Innellan the wittily named *Toward Castle* sits in ruins looking over towards Bute. It was once a Clan Lamont stronghold, but was destroyed by the Campbells in 1646.

Inveraray is a lovely town. *All Saints' Episcopal Church* has a great Bell Tower which contains Scotland's finest bells! The campanologists amongst you will know about 'the heaviest ten in the world', of which this is number two. Open mid-May to end September, daily from 10 a.m. to 1 p.m. and 2 p.m. to 5 p.m. There is a free exhibition. If, however, you want to ascend the tower and see the bells and the views, there is a small charge. If the bells aren't chiming when you are there, you can listen to recordings!

Inverchaolain Church is in a village looking over Loch Striven. Ancient gravestones lie around this pretty church. Graves particularly interesting to Lamonts I suggest . . .

Kilfinan Parish Church is believed to have been built upon an earlier Celtic site.

Kilmun Church is close by the original cell of St Munn. It also has the burial ground of the Dukes of Argyll. Kilmun is across the Holy Loch from Dunoon.

Knockamillie Castle is on the A815 between Dunoon and Innellan. This was once one of the most important castles in the area; now it lies another ruin . . .

Strachur Church was built in 1787, with interesting sculptured stones.

Strathlachlan Parish Church was built in 1792, with a good belfry – if that's your scene!
   Have a look at *Castle Lachlan* on the banks of Loch Fyne. Parts of this ruin date from the twelfth century.

BUTE
Kilmichael, in the west of Bute, is the site of an old ruined chapel dedicated to a saint with a strange name – St Macaille.

St Blane's Chapel is in the south of Bute. These are the remains of an early twelfth-century chapel, with a fine example of a Norman arch.

St Mary's Chapel is near Rothesay. A superb medieval chapel. Look out for two wonderful tombs in recesses, with effigies of Walter the Steward and his wife Alice.

St Ninian's Chapel, or rather the remains of it, is in the west of Bute, looking over towards Gigha. Although there are many churches dedicated to St Ninian in Scotland, this one was actually founded by the saint, together with his disciples, in the sixth or early seventh century.

East Ayrshire
The **Ballochmyle Cup and Ring Markings.** This is one of the best sites in Britain for this type of early bronze-age marking, possibly 5,000 years old. There are over 200 separate markings here in the heart of the River Ayr valley. For further details, contact Mauchline Tourist Information Centre Tel: 01290 551916

Dalmellington is the site of *The Motte.* This is an ancient monument in a good state of preservation. As you'd expect, it is a flat-topped mound surrounded by a circular ditch!
   Dalmellington Parish Church is up from the town centre on Knowehead, and was built in 1846 by Patrick Wilson. Great windows and an impressive tower – neo-Norman, I think they say.
   Cathcartston Visitor Centre is just off the square, and is made up of restored weavers' cottages of 1774 (see Museums).

Fenwick Church was built in 1643 and has Covenanter tombstones, and other reminders of those times, including the Bible used on the scaffold by martyr John Parton in 1684. Find it just off the main road through High Fenwick.
   North of Fenwick, off the B764 to Eaglesham, you will find *Lochgoin.* This is a moorland farm which has a museum with relics of the Covenanters.

Galston has *Loudoun Castle*. The ruins of the castle are surrounded by a great park, with children's rides, pets corner – everything to distract you from the castle ruins themselves. (You have to pay to park, but all else is free.)

Galston Church has Covenanter tombstones and a couple of martyrs' monuments. Also look out for *St Sophia's RC Church*, which was built in the Byzantine style in the form of a Greek cross.

Kilmarnock is the site of the *Laigh Kirk* (right in the centre of town). The stone clock tower dates from the fourteenth century, and, you guessed it, there are more Covenanters buried in the churchyard.

Holy Trinity Scottish Episcopal Church stands opposite the Sheriff Court at the corner of Dundonald Road and Portland Road. This church was built in 1857 by James Wallace, with later additions in 1876 by George Gilbert Scott.

Kilmaurs has the *St Maurs-Glencairn Parish Church*. This is on the south-east side of town beside the A735 from Kilmarnock. It is a restored kirk built in 1888 with lovely stained glass including three rose windows.

Beside the church is the *Glencairn Aisle*, a vaulted burial aisle with an amazing wall sculpture.

Loch Doon Castle is two miles south of Dalmellington, off the A713. It was originally on an island, but the Hydro Electricity people, in their wisdom, re-sited it here. Plenty of walks nearby in Carrick Forest. There is an information desk here, which is open from April to September. Tel 01292 550165. Alternatively try Historic Scotland on 0131 668 8600.

Newmilns Keep was originally built in the fourteenth century, and was later used to imprison Covenanters. Quite right too.

Sorn Castle, also built in the fourteenth century, overlooks the River Ayr. Open mid-July to mid-August, daily from 2 p.m. to 5 p.m. The grounds are open from April to October. Tel: 01505 612124

Stewarton has *St Columba's Church* off Lainshaw Street. It dates from the seventeenth century.

East Renfrewshire

Eaglesham Village, on the B767 south-west of Newton Mearns, is a conservation area, and is actually one of the best examples of an eighteenth-century planned village built on an A plan by the tenth Earl of Eglinton.

City of Glasgow

Cathedral Church of St Mary is at 300 Great Western Road. One of Glasgow's Gothic revival edifices, it was designed by Sir George Gilbert Scott. Great modern murals inside. Open daily from 9.30 a.m. to 5.30 p.m. Tel: 0141 339 6691

The City Chambers are in George Square, and an imposing civic building they are too. Guided tours are a great way to see it all, and ask some pertinent questions. Tours are available Monday to Friday at 10.30 a.m. and 2.30 p.m. (depending on whether or not there is council business at the time). Tel: 0141 221 9600

Crookston Castle is off Brockburn Road, in Pollok. This tower house with Mary Queen of Scots connections dates from the fifteenth century, although a ruin on the site takes it back to the twelfth. Open April to September at all reasonable times. Tel: 0141 668 8600

Glasgow Cathedral is on Castle Street. This is a great Gothic building dating in part from the twelfth century, founded by St Mungo, the city's patron saint. Look out for his crypt! Open October to March, Monday to Saturday from 9.30 a.m. to 1 p.m. and 2 p.m. to 4 p.m., Sunday from 2 p.m. to 4 p.m.; in summer, Monday to Saturday from 9.30 a.m. to 6 p.m., Sunday from 2 p.m. to 5 p.m. Tel: 0141 552 6891

Govan Old Parish Church is at the Pearce Institute at 840 Govan Road. Some great early Christian sculpted stones inside this nineteenth-century building. Admission by arrangement really, so ring before you go. Tel: 0141 445 1941

Hutcheson's Hall is at 158 Ingram Street in the city centre – actually in the newly trendy 'Merchant's City'. The hall was built in 1802, to a design by David Hamilton. It is open all year, Monday to Friday from 10 a.m. to 5 p.m. Tel: 0141 552 8391

The Mackintosh House is at the Hunterian Museum and Art Gallery at the University of Glasgow on Hillhead Street (see Museums). Beautiful reconstructions of rooms from Mackintosh's Glasgow home. Open Monday to Saturday from 9.30 a.m. to 12.30 p.m. and 1.30 p.m. to 5 p.m. Tel: 0141 330 5431 or 330 4221 (Hunterian Museum)

The Necropolis is a graveyard with attitude; it is on Castle Street, and gives a great view (see Days Out).

Pollok House is in Pollok Country Park at 2060 Pollokshaws Road. Built around 1750, this ancestral home is now part-gallery, housing works by Goya and El Greco. Open Monday to Saturday from 10 a.m. to 5 p.m., Sunday from 11 a.m. to 5 p.m. Tel: 0141 632 0274

Provand's Lordship is an off-putting title for a place. It is actually the oldest building in Glasgow, built in 1471! It even has a medieval garden. Open Monday to Friday from 10 a.m. to 5 p.m., Saturday from 10 a.m. to 5 p.m., Sunday from 11 a.m. to 5 p.m. Tel: 0141 552 8819

Queen's Cross Church is the headquarters of the Charles Rennie Mackintosh Society – not surprising really, as they have renovated this, the only church he designed, to a state of splendour. There is an information centre with displays, as well as a shop. Open Tuesday, Thursday and Friday from 12 noon to 5 p.m.,

Sunday from 2.30 p.m. to 5 p.m. Find the church at 870 Garscube Road. Tel: 0141 946 6600

Queens Park Synagogue is on Falloch Road, off Ledard Road. Beautiful stained-glass windows depict the festivals of the Jewish calendar. Ring to find out times to go along. Tel: 0141 632 1743

Royal Highland Fusiliers Museum at 518 Sauchiehall Street is a building that features the work of Mackintosh, together with Honeyman and Keppie. Open weekdays from 8.30 a.m. to 4.30 p.m. (till 4 p.m. on Friday). Tel: 0141 332 0961

Ruchill Church Hall is a Mackintosh building on Shakespeare Street. Built in 1898, it is now a tea-room, but you can view if you ask at the church house in the courtyard. Open Monday to Friday from 10.30 a.m. to 2.30 p.m. Tel: 0141 946 1430

St Andrew's RC Cathedral is at 172 Clyde Street. This is a Gothic revival building, from 1816, designed by James Gillespie Graham. Tel: 0141 221 3096

St George's Tron Church is right in the city centre, on Buchanan Street. It was built by William Stark in 1807, and the steeple shows up well on the skyline. Tel: 0141 221 2141

Scotland Street School is the *Museum of Education*, at 225 Scotland Street. There is a permanent exhibition detailing the history of education since 1872, in this famous Mackintosh building. Open Monday to Saturday from 10 a.m. to 5 p.m., Sunday from 2 p.m. to 5 p.m. Tel: 0141 429 1202

Templeton's Carpet Factory can't be viewed from the inside; it is now a business centre. What a glorious building this is though, on Glasgow Green near the People's Palace. Colourful brickwork with panache, designed by William Lepier and built in 1889.

Trades Hall of Glasgow is a William Adam building at Glassford Street. Opened in 1794, the building still serves as a home to the trades houses of the city. Open Monday to Friday from 10 a.m. to 5 p.m. Tel: 0141 552 2418

University of Glasgow even has its own visitor centre, in tune with the times. The Uni was established in 1451 in the East End and moved to the Kelvingrove area much later, where now many of the buildings overlook Kelvingrove Park. The visitor centre is excellent, with good video displays and the answers to all your queries. Open May to September, Monday to Saturday from 9.30 a.m. to 5 p.m., Sunday from 2 p.m. to 5 p.m. You can even take a guided tour. Tel: 0141 330 5511

The Willow Tea Rooms on Sauchiehall Street are well worth a stare. Designed by Mackintosh for Miss Cranston, they were opened in 1903. Still a tea-room! Why not have tea here, and sit on one of those incredible chairs . . .

Open Monday to Saturday from 9 a.m. to 4.30 p.m. Tel: 0141 332 0521

Inverclyde

Gourock has *Granny Kempock's Stone*, which is a six-foot monolith that looks like a cloaked figure. Apparently it brings luck to sailors and newly-weds. To be found off Bath Street.

Greenock has much of interest, such as the *Cornalees Bridge Centre* (see Days Out) and some fine buildings too. Look particularly for the Municipal Buildings in Clyde Square and Greenock Custom House at Custom House Quay (see Museums).

Port Glasgow has a great big boat. Yes, it's the *Comet Replica*. The ship was launched at Port Glasgow in 1812, and was actually the first sea-going paddle-steamer to run commercially in Europe, taking passengers and freight between Greenock, Helensburgh and Glasgow.

North Ayrshire

Ardrossan Castle is a twelfth-century one, once sacked by Oliver Cromwell. Only part of it remains. Open all year.

Beith has a dominating Gothic T-plan church, *Beith High Church*, that was built in 1807–09.

Dalry has a great Victorian Gothic church in *St Margaret's Parish Church*, which is in the town centre.

Eglinton Castle. The ruins of this eighteenth-century castle is a splendid country park (see Days Out). Look out for the beautiful *Belvedere* – a classical temple of columns built on top of Belvedere Hill. If you like history, the story of the 'Landscape of the Knights' will interest you. Well worth a visit, for all the extras, like the playpark, the walks and even the tea-room. Other parts of historical interest include a raquet hall, ice house and even the remains of a mine. The visitor centre is open April to October, daily. Tel: 01294 551776

Irvine has a couple of castles: *Seagate Castle*, once visited by Mary Queen of Scots; and *Stanecastle*, only the remains of the square tower are left. Look for the graveyard at the *Parish Church*, as two of Burns' friends – David Sillar and Helen Miller – are buried here.
   If you catch a glimpse of a grey hump jutting out of the river, it could be the *Granny Stane*, thought to be the remains of a standing stone.
   Irvine Old Parish Church is in the Kirkgate, off Hill Street. The church is the design of David Muir, from the late eighteenth century.
   Glasgow Vennel Museum is an award-winning restored cobbled street and cottages (see Museums).

Kilbirnie has *Glengarnock Castle*, apparently the home of Hugh de Morville from the twelfth century.

Kilbirnie Place (*Palace*) is now a ruin. Legend tells of a secret tunnel that leads from the Castle to the Barony Church almost a mile away.

Kilbirnie Auld Kirk is at the junction of the B780 from Dalry and the B777 from Glengarnock. The church dates from 1470, and has magnificent woodwork.

While you're at it, look for the *Stables Museum* in Main Street under Walker Hall (see Museums). Access is through the gate beside Dr Walker's statue. This is actually part of the stable block of an old coaching inn.

Kilwinning has *Dalvargen Mill*, which is on the A737 a mile and a half north of town. This is a restored three-storey flour mill, which is now a museum of Ayrshire country life and costume. To get in for free, you'll need to wait until Doors Open Day in September!

While you are here, look for *Abbey Church* in Main Street, which was built by John Swan in 1774. There is even an *Abbey Church Tower Heritage Centre* in the centre of the town.

Largs. Look out for *Skelmorlie Aisle*, the remains of an old church (1636) in an Italianate design with a painted ceiling. Find it in the old burial ground, Manse Court, off the High Street. A newer church, *Clark Memorial Church*, is in Bath Street. This is an impressive early Gothic building from 1890 with a hammerbeam roof.

Pencil Monument – you can't miss it. Quite a good view from here too.

Haylie Chamber Tomb is in Douglas Park. This is a 5,000-year-old burial chamber, which contained flints and human remains. Also in the park, at the top of Castlehill, is an iron-age hill fort dating from 550 BC and AD 200.

Just out of town is Fairlie Glen and *Fairlie Castle*, a ruined tower dating from the fifteenth century.

Saltcoats. The *North Ayrshire Museum* is in Manse Street, in the former Ardrossan Parish Church, which was built in 1744 (see Museums).

Seamill, north of Ardrossan, has *Portencross Castle*, a ruined fifteenth-century keep used by early Stewart kings.

Stevenson has *Kerelaw Castle*, which was built in 1470 and burnt down soon after.

West Kilbride, north of Ardrossan, is where you will find *Law Castle*, a tower house dating from the fifteenth century.

ARRAN

Arran has plenty of places to visit if you are keen on the history of our forefathers/foremothers.

Auchagallon Stone Circle is the remains of a circle of 15 red sandstone blocks, possibly an encircled cairn.

Kildonan Castle is one of those romantic-looking ruins. Overlooking Brodick Bay, you can't miss it.

Kilmory Cairns are near the village of the same name, in the south of Arran.

Kilpatrick Dun is a bronze-age ring cairn, which you will find off the A841 at Kilpatrick, near Blackwaterfoot.

Lochranza Castle is about 400 years old, the remains of a hunting seat of Scottish kings. Lochranza is the port in the north of the island.

Machrie Moor Stone Circles are the impressive remains of a group of bronze-age stones. And what a view, too, from here on the moor near Ballymichael. Get to the stones along the footpath from Blackwaterfoot – beautiful views of the coast, mountains in the distance, and then the stones to round it up.

CUMBRAE

Millport has the *Cathedral of the Isles*, which is in fact the smallest cathedral in Europe. It is open daily.

North Lanarkshire

Airdrie is the home of the *Weavers' Cottages Museum* at Wellwynd. This is a reconstructed weaver's house dating from the nineteenth century (see Museums).

Shotts has the *Kirk o' Shotts Church*, which dates from 1821. A watch-house in the graveyard was for watchers to keep an eye out for bodysnatchers!

Renfrewshire

Castle Semple Collegiate Church was built in 1505. It is now a ruin, but contains a memorial to John, the first Lord Semple, who was killed at the Battle of Flodden. Find Castle Semple one and a half miles north of Lochwinnoch.

Paisley has many interesting buildings (see Days Out and Museums). *Paisley Abbey*, at Abbey Close, was founded in 1163, and has beautiful stained glass as well as the Barochan Cross. Tel: 0141 889 7654

Watch out, too, for the *Oakshaw Conservation Area*, which features churches, schools and homes of the eighteenth and nineteenth centuries. The Coats Observatory (Oakshaw Street), John Neilson Institution (Oakshaw Street), High Kirk and, of course, the *Sma' Shot Cottages* on Shuttle Street (see Museums) are of particular interest.

Thomas Coats Memorial Church in the High Street represents one of the finest Baptist churches in Europe. Open May to September, Monday, Wednesday and Friday from 2 p.m. to 8 p.m. You would do well to check the opening hours in advance. Tel: 0141 889 9980

South Ayrshire

Alloway. If you're here, you mustn't forget to visit the famous *Brig o' Doon* which is central to Burns' great poem 'Tam o' Shanter'.

Actually, if you are here, what else would you want to do but get knee-deep in Burns? There is a *Burns Monument and Gardens*, which actually gives you a good view of the Brig o' Doon.

The Auld Kirk, also in Alloway, is the setting for 'Tam o' Shanter'. It was here that Tam saw the witches, warlocks and Satan himself doing their diabolical dance! The kirkyard also contains the grave of William Burnes, Robert's father. Find it beside the B7024, south of Burns Cottage. Excellent stained glass in this Gothic-style 1857 building by Campbell Douglas.

Ayr is the home of *Greenan Castle*, a Kennedy stronghold built in the fifteenth century on an old site. Rumour has it that this may once have been Arthurian, perhaps even Camelot itself! Check it out with some divining rods and drop me a line.

Auld Kirk is where Burns was baptised. Lots of Covenanters' gravestones, too, beside the river. Find it off the High Street.

Another church to look for is *Holy Trinity Scottish Episcopal Church* at Fullarton Street by the bus station. This was built in the nineteenth century in a thirteenth-century Gothic style. Confused?

Take a stroll down to the harbour and check out the *Lighthouse*, which was built in 1841. Thank God for tradition.

Ballantrae, on the A77 south of Girvan, is the site of *Ardstinchar Castle*, which once gave shelter to Mary Queen of Scots. Sadly, it is now a ruin.

Colmonell on the B734 south of Girvan has a sixteenth-century Kennedy castle, *Kirkhill Castle*. It is now a ruin.

Look out too for *Knockdolian Castle*, a sixteenth-century tower house on the River Stinchar; it is inhabited by the Duchess of Wellington, so please don't try to get in.

Five miles east of Colmonell is *Pinwherry Castle*, another ruined sixteenth-century Kennedy stronghold, in the river valley.

Dailly has the two *Dalquharran Castles*. Both the fifteenth-century Kennedy mansion and the 'new' 1786 Robert Adam version are now ruins. Dailly is on the B741 from Girvan.

New Dailly Parish Church was mostly built in 1766, with a laird's loft.

Dundonald. On the A759 near Troon, the town has a great view of *Auchans Castle*, which was visited by Boswell. It is now a ruin, below *Dundonald Castle* (which isn't free).

Dunure Castle, on the A719 south of Ayr, is a picturesque ruin with a colourful past. Some poor soul was even roasted here! There is plenty of room here for a picnic though, if you can stomach it.

Girvan. *Carleton Castle* nearby is part of a chain of watch-towers along the coast. In a ballad this was sung of as the home of the baron who pushed seven wives over the cliff; he was disposed of in turn by his eighth wife, May Culean. Carleton Castle is off the A77 south of the town.

In Girvan itself, look for *St John's Episcopal Church* on Piedmont Road, off Dalrymple Street. It was built in 1859 by Alexander Thomson.

Another unusual one is the *Stumpy Tower* in the town centre, which is an eighteenth-century Tolbooth tower with clocks around it and an unusual design.

Kirkoswald is the home of *Souter Johnnie's Cottage*; it dates from 1786 and has a thatched roof. Find Kirkoswald on the A77 Maybole to Turnberry road.

Maybole has *Baltersan Castle*, a sixteenth-century laird's house, now in ruins. It is on the A77, near *Crossraguel Abbey* (which sadly isn't free). South of Maybole on the Girvan road you will see *Kilhenzie Castle*, yet another Kennedy stronghold. *Maybole Collegiate Church* is yet another roofless ruin you may pass.

Monkton Church, near Ayr, dates from the twelfth century, and was the scene of William Wallace's inspiring dream of Caledonia.

Old Dailly Church was built no later than the fourteenth century. You will find Old Dailly about three miles east of Girvan.

Prestwick is the site of *Old St Nicholas Church*, twelfth-century ruins. It was built by Walter, High Steward of Scotland. There are even some ancient Mort Safes (ugh!). Tel: 01292 282842
   If you get a bit thirsty in Prestwick, you could try *Bruce's Well*. Apparently, it cured Robert the Bruce of leprosy . . . think what it could do for you!

Symington, near Troon, has one of the oldest churches in Ayrshire. *Barnweil Church* was closed in 1673, but has a tower built in memory of William Wallace in 1855. You can view it by appointment. Tel: 01292 282842
   Symington Parish Church was built around 1150 in Romanesque style. The ancient roof is open timber, with fine stonework walls and round-topped Norman windows. It is open on request – look for the notice on the door. Find it in the centre of the village, off the A77.

Troon has *St Ninian's Scottish Episcopal Church* in Bentinck Drive. Built by James Morris in 1912–13, it features beautiful carved oak doors and furniture with the carved 'mouse' mark of Robert Thompson of Kilburn.

South Lanarkshire

Biggar has the only remaining gasworks in Scotland, now a musuem (see Museums).
   Biggar Kirk was the last pre-Reformation church to be built in the whole of Scotland. Some stonework and relics inside date from the previous twelfth-century church. Open daily.
   Coulter Motte, an early medieval castle mound which was originally moated, is about two miles from Biggar. There should always be access to Coulter Motte.
   If you have two or three hours to spare, and plenty of energy, then a climb to the top of *Tinto Hill*, five miles west of the town, will show you one of the country's largest bronze-age cairns. (Sensible shoes, now, everyone!)

Blackhill offers another viewpoint, this time topped with the largest iron-age fort in Lanarkshire, and a bronze-age cairn too. Access available at all times, this hill reaches 951 feet, and the view really is great. Turn off the B7018 Kirkfield to Lesmahagow road.

Candymill is where you can visit *Hugh MacDiarmid's Brownsbank Cottage*. This is the house where the Scots poet lived in 1952–78, now restored to what it was during his lifetime. There is even a writer-in-residence thrown in free. Although admission is free, donations are welcome. Admission is by arrangement, so ring before you descend. Tel: 01899 221050

Crawford is a village in the Lowther Hills, a pretty area for walking and days out. *Crawford Castle* is a ruin, dating from around 1600 and situated on the banks of Camps Water.

Douglas is another village in the Lowther Hills. Head for the viewpoint at the north of the village, for the view and a look at the Cameronians Regimental Memorial.

Douglas Heritage Museum is in the former dower-house of the old castle (see Museums).

Old St Brides is a fourteenth-century church. In the chancel are tombs of the Douglas family. The church tower has the oldest working town clock in Scotland. (Although our one in Doune acts as though it came out of the Ark.) The clock was a gift from Mary Queen of Scots, famous horologist(!) Look at the board by the gate to check times for access.

Douglas Castle was once the home of the powerful Douglas family. Only the tower now remains, along with some pleasant walks in the 'policies'.

Hamilton is the site of *Chatelherault*, a fabulous William Adam designed building, now beautifully restored (see Days Out).

Hamilton Old Parish Church dates from 1734, and is the only church designed by William Adam. Plenty of interesting things to see inside. Open Saturday at 11 a.m. (guided tour and coffee), Sunday at 12 noon (guided tour), and from Monday to Friday phone to find out if it is possible to see inside. Tel: 01698 420002

Leadhills and Wanlockhead has the oldest subscription library in Britain, the *Alan Ramsay Leadhills Miners' Library*. Established in 1741, the library has a collection of rare books, old mining records and maps. Open the first Saturday in May to the last Saturday in September, Wednesday, Saturday and Sunday from 2 p.m. to 4 p.m. Tel: 01659 74326

Lesmahagow Priory is the excavated remains of a twelfth-century priory dedicated to St Machatus. Is that more than you needed to know? The only bits that remain today are the foundations of the cloister and refectory.

Strathaven Castle dates from the fifteenth century, and was once home to the Earls of Douglas and later the Dukes of Hamilton. Open all year.

THE EAST

East Lothian

Bolton, on the B6368 south of Haddington, is where you will find the *Burns Family Grave*. In the churchyard here is a gravestone marking the graves of Robert Burns' mother, Agnes Brown, sister Annabella and brother Gilbert.

Dunbar. The castle is a ruin, and you will probably see it at its best from the harbour.

John Muir House is the birthplace of John Muir, the founder of America's national parks. Open June to September, Monday to Saturday from 11 a.m. to 5.30 p.m.; closed Wednesday, except in August. Find the house at 126–128 High Street, Dunbar. Tel: 01368 863353

Dunbar Parish Church has evolved from seventh-century beginnings. It was destroyed by fire in 1987, but has been restored. Open June to September, Monday to Saturday from 10.30 a.m. to 4 p.m., Sunday from 2 p.m. to 4 p.m. Tel: 01368 863316

Haddington is the nearest town to *Hailes Castle*. This is an impressive ruin from the thirteenth to fifteenth centuries, with Mary Queen of Scots associations.

In town, look in at *St Martin's Kirk* which is the ruined nave of a Romanesque church, altered in the thirteenth century. Open all year, at reasonable times.

Another very special Haddington church to see is *St Mary's Collegiate Church* at Sidegate. There has been a church on this site since the twelfth century. It lies in a peaceful spot by the River Tyne. Open April to end September, Monday to Saturday from 10 a.m. to 4 p.m., Sunday from 1 p.m. to 4 p.m. To get full fun value, go on Saturday afternoon (April to June) or Monday, Thursday, Friday and Saturday afternoon (July to September) and you will get a chance to do some great brass rubbing! Tel: 01620 825111

On top of Byres Hill, to the north of town, is the *Hopetoun Monument*. Not terribly exciting in itself, but you'll get a great view!

Traprain Law is an even more imposing hill, this time the site of an iron-age fort.

City of Edinburgh

Calton Hill has some unusual features: the *City Observatory* was built by W. Playfair in 1818, whilst the *Observatory House* is one of the few buildings by the planner of Edinburgh's New Town, James Craig, that survives. Look out for the unfinished replica of the Parthenon too.

Canongate Kirk has an interesting graveyard. The church was built in 1688, and can be found on the Canongate. This is one of the oldest parts of the city's Old Town.

Charlotte Square is a New Town square which illustrates the eighteenth-century architectural dream for the city. No. 5 Charlotte Square is a Robert Adam building and is now the headquarters of the National Trust for Scotland, and one of their most interesting properties.

George Square, in the city's southside, now forms part of an area dominated by the university. The square was the first major residential square built outside the Old Town. Nos. 23 and 25, built between 1770 and 1775, were the homes of Conan Doyle and Sir Walter Scott respectively.

Greyfriars Bobby might not seem like a truly serious 'historical site', but how much more serious can you be than a dog that pines away on the grave of his master? There is a charming little statue, but beware: if you stand too long to take a photo you may get run over by students. The graveyard at Greyfriars Kirk is full of over-the-top memorials and well worth a look.

Lauriston Castle is on Cramond Road South, in Cramond, on the west side of the city. Although it isn't free to get into the castle itself, the lovely grounds are free, and are open all year, from 9 a.m. to dusk. Tel: 0131 336 2060

The McEwan Hall is the University building where many graduations take place. A beautiful round building with a theatrical Greek interior, it was built by Sir Robert Rowand Anderson in 1874.

Parliament House is one of many interesting buildings on Parliament Square, off the Royal Mile. Parliament House was built in the 1630s.
The *Council Chambers* are on the west side of Parliament Square; they were built in the early years of this century.

The Royal Mile is one of the most famous streets in the city, and a walk from the Castle Esplanade right down to Holyrood Palace at the foot of the Royal Mile will really show you what the Old Town is all about. As you wander, look up into some of the vennels and closes, and imagine the overcrowding and squalor of medieval Edinburgh.

St Bernard's Well is one of those strange things you come across once in a while that make you smile. A little folly along the Water of Leith Walkway, this little Doric rotunda was designed by Alexander Nasmyth in 1789.

St Giles' Cathedral (on Parliament Square) dates from 1120, and is a truly historical building. The site of many royal and famous connections through the years, it also has wonderful stained glass, a glorious organ and the Thistle Chapel. Open all year, Monday to Saturday from 9 a.m. to 5 p.m., Sunday from 1 p.m. to 5 p.m. Tel: 0131 225 9442

Tron Kirk Information Centre (on the Royal Mile) is worth a visit, to get all the information about Edinburgh's Old Town. There you will also find the remains of a seventeenth-century street, houses and cellars. Open April to June, Thursday to Monday from 10 a.m. to 5 p.m., and in October. In summer they stay open till 7 p.m. and open Tuesday and Wednesday too. Tel: 0131 225 8818

Midlothian

Borthwick, off the A7 near Gorebridge, has both a castle which dates from the fifteenth century, and a church, which is a Gothic-revival type. The castle isn't free to get into, unless you wait for Doors Open Day in September!

Crichton Collegiate Church is in Crichton village, off the B6367 south-west of Pathhead. This is one of the few remaining pre-Reformation churches (1449) in Lothian.

Newbattle Abbey is on the site of a Cistercian abbey. This mansion house might need to wait until Doors Open Day for a proper viewing.

Rosslyn Chapel, by Roslin, dates from the fifteenth century and has the world famous Prentice Pillar with a spiral of beautiful leafy carvings. Some people talk about Rosslyn and the Holy Grail . . .

West Lothian

Mid Calder has the *Kirk of Calder*; it is over 450 years old, and was recently restored. Tread in the footsteps of John Knox and David Livingstone, they visited once. Well organised for modern-day visitors, with tea and biscuits, a guidebook, and even a quiz for your kids . . . Open May to September, Sunday from 2 p.m. to 4 p.m.; other times by arrangement. Tel: 01506 440449

Torphichen. Close to the village is *Cairnpapple Hill*, one of Scotland's most important archaeological sites. The hill is high in the Bathgate Hills with great views. It was actually a temple where prehistoric man buried his dead and worshipped over 3,000 years ago. A little tingle runs down your spine. The prehistoric burial chamber can still be visited. At the end of Torphichen village turn left, after a mile bear left and then turn right following the signposts. The hill is 200 yards further on, on the right. It isn't free to get right in there, but you can get a good look at it anyhow!

Torphichen Preceptory was established in 1153 by the Knights of St John of Jerusalem. It is a mysterious building rich in history. Unfortunately you will need to pay a little for admission.

THE BORDERS

Dumfries and Galloway

Canonbie. Two miles south of town is *Scot's Dyke*, a sixteenth-century trench and dyke, dug to mark the border between Scotland and England at times when feuds raged over this area of 'debatable lands'. Find Canonbie on the A7 south of Langholm.

Carsluith. *Cairnholy*, the impressive remains of two chambered cairns which date from around 2000 BC, are off the A75 Newton Stewart–Gatehouse of Fleet road, to the east of Carsluith.

Carsluith also has a four-storeyed tower house dating from the sixteenth century; it is beside the A75, one and a half miles south of Creetown.

Castle Douglas. On the outskirts of town is *Threave Castle*, a massive tower built on an island in the River Dee by Archibald the Grim in the late fourteenth century. Not a happy chappy clearly. Open Monday to Saturday from 9.30 a.m. to 6.30 p.m., Sunday from 2 p.m. to 6.30 p.m.; closed in winter. Find it three miles west of Castle Douglas on the A75. Tel: 0131 668 8600 (Historic Scotland). Free, but there is a charge for the ferry.

Dalbeattie is just two and a half miles away from the *Motte of Urr*. This motte and bailey earthwork castle is the most extensive in Scotland. Go off the B794 north of Dalbeattie and get to the castle via the riverbank and footbridge.

Close to Dalbeattie is the village of *Buittle*, where you can see *Old Buittle Tower*, a sixteenth-century L-shaped tower with the ruins of a thirteenth-century motte and bailey in the grounds.

Drumcoltran is a fortified sixteenth-century L-plan tower house, right next to a mid-eighteenth-century farmhouse. The two are a mile north of Kirkgunzeon, off the A711 seven miles north of Dalbeattie.

Dumfries has the *Lincluden Collegiate Church*, built in the early fifteenth century. The church was built by the Duke of Tourian to accommodate his canon. Now only remains remain. Open all year. Go off the A76 one mile north of Dumfries town centre. Tel: 0131 668 8600 (Historic Scotland)

Midsteeple dominates the high street of the town, and was built early in the eighteenth century. Also look in at the *Old Bridge House Museum*, which was built in 1660, into the fabric of Devorgilla Bridge. This is the oldest house in Dumfries (see Museums). Tel: 01387 256904

Don't forget to visit *Dumfries Museum and Observatory* either. The museum is a windmill remodelled in 1835 to form the observatory, and it now houses the world's oldest camera obscura – which isn't free, although the museum is (see Museums).

St Michael's Churchyard is the burial place of Robert Burns, and houses the *Burns Mausoleum*. *St Michael's Church* is the oldest in Dumfries, built in 1742 (find it in St Michael's Street!). *Ellisland Farm*, the farmhouse built by the poet, is just off the A76 six miles north-west of Dumfries. It has audio-visual shows for your edification, also for your payment. Tel: 01387 740426. For real Burnsaholics, pick up a copy of 'Dumfries – A Burns Trail' from the Tourist Information Centre, and you will be able to wander the town with impunity. (And all the locals will know *exactly* where you are going.)

Other churches in Dumfries worth a mention are *Crichton Royal Memorial Church* at The Crichton, Glencaple Road – this is a cathedral-style church from 1890 by Sydney Mitchell – and *St George's Church* in George Street which dates from 1843.

Ecclefechan. Three miles north of town is *Burnswark*, which is a native hilltop earthwork that dates from about the sixth century BC. Two Roman siege camps alongside these remains date from the second century AD. A nice walk to get there. The rest is history.

Gatehouse of Fleet. A mile to the north-east is *Cardoness Castle*. This is a well-preserved ruin of a tower house from the fifteenth century. The ancient home of the McCullochs. Open Monday to Saturday from 9.30 a.m. to 6.30 p.m., Sunday from 2 p.m. to 6.30 p.m.; in winter, Saturday from 9.30 a.m. to 4.30 p.m. and Sunday from 2 p.m. to 4.30 p.m. There is a charge, £1.50 for adults, 75 pence for children. Tel: 01557 814427. To book you can also contact Historic Scotland. Tel: 0131 668 8600

Glenluce Abbey is a twelfth-century Cistercian Abbey, founded in 1190. The remains include an attractive chapter-house. Open Monday to Saturday from 9.30 a.m. to 6.30 p.m., Sunday from 2 p.m. to 6.30 p.m.; in winter Saturday from 9.30 a.m. to 4.30 p.m. and Sunday from 2 p.m. to 4.30 p.m. The Abbey is two miles north of Glenluce. Another Historic Scotland property, there is a charge of £1.50 for adults, 75 pence for children. Tel: 01581 300541, or Historic Scotland, Tel: 0131 668 8600

Keir Mill, off the A76 Dumfries to Sanquhar road, is three miles south-west of Thornhill. In this village Kirkpatrick Macmillan built the world's first pedal cycle, around 1840. He is buried in Keir Mill Churchyard.

Kirkcudbright is the home of *MacLellan's Castle*. It was built in 1577 as a town house by the Provost, MacLellan, who pinched the stone from a ruined monastery nearby! Open Monday to Saturday from 9.30 a.m. to 6.30 p.m., Sunday from 2 p.m. to 6.30 p.m.; in winter Saturday from 9.30 a.m. to 4.30 p.m., Sunday from 2 p.m. to 4.30 p.m. Historic Scotland will charge you £1 for an adult, 50 pence for a child, for admission. Tel: 01557 331856. Historic Scotland, Tel: 0131 668 8600

Six and a half miles south-east of Kirkcudbright is the village of Dundrennan. It has a wonderful twelfth-century Cistercian Abbey – *Dundrennan Abbey* – where Mary Queen of Scots spent her last night in Scotland before departing for exile and prison in England. Open Monday to Saturday from 9.30 a.m. to 6.30 p.m., Sunday from 2 p.m. to 6.30 p.m.; in winter closed Thursday afternoon, Friday and other days at 4.30 p.m. Tel: 01557 500262

Kirkpatrick-Fleming, near Gretna, is the site of *King Robert the Bruce's Cave*. This is a pretty famous one. Turn off the A74 into Kirkpatrick-Fleming and follow the signs; it is in the grounds of the Cove Estate caravan and camping site. Open Easter to end October. There is a charge – 35 pence for adults and 25 pence for children. Tel: 01387 870249

Lochmaben Castle, near Lockerbie, is a thirteenth–fourteenth-century ruined castle on a promontory in Castle Loch, Lochmaben. It was once the seat of Robert the Bruce's family.

Palnackie, near Dalbeattie, is in a beautiful area. Even more lovely is *Orchardton*, a cylindrical tower house that dates from the fifteenth century. Find it one and a half miles south of Palnackie, off the A711.

Portpatrick, south of Stranraer, is near *Dunskey Castle*. Actually, these are the ruins of the castle, and are quite dramatic on the cliff top. Just five miles to the south-east of Portpatrick.

Port William has a tenth–eleventh-century chapel – *Chapel Finian* – named after the saint who studied at Whithorn. The low walls of it remain, on a long raised beach. Take the A747 and you will find it five miles north-west of Port William.

Rockcliffe has an imposing hill fort *Motte of Mark*, which is a fifth–sixth-century site that has a great view.

Ruthwell, near Annan, is close to *The Brow Well*, which is where Burns sought a cure for his final illness. There is a walk from the well to Clarencefield. By the B725, one mile east of Ruthwell.
   The Ruthwell Cross is a carved cross which is now known to be one of the first preserved pieces of Middle English text. You can make a donation if you are impressed.

Sandhead is the place to see the *Kirkmadrine Stones*. These date from the fifth century, and after Whithorn they are the earliest Christian memorials in Scotland. Turn off the A716 and it is two miles south-west of Sandhead.

Sanquhar has the world's oldest post office – at least the oldest still in use, since 1738. Post your cards off here!

Thornhill. Some six miles to the north is *Durisdeer Church*. The church includes the elaborate Queensberry Aisle which commemorates the second Duke. Built around 1699, the well path, which incorporates this church, was part of a medieval pilgrimage route to Whithorn.
   Only one mile off the A76, and three miles from Thornhill, is *Morton Castle*, the ruins of a Douglas castle from the fourteenth century.

Torthorwald is a village to the east of Dumfries, where you will find *Cruck Cottage*, one of the few surviving examples of a cruck framed cottage in the area.

Whithorn. The famous *St Ninian's Cave* lies about three miles south of Whithorn. Look out for the eighth-century carving. This cave is said to have been used as a retreat by the saint. It is a pretty walk from the farmhouse to get there.

Wigtown is close to the *Torhousekie Stone Circle*. This circle of granite boulders goes back to the second millennium BC, and surrounds three central eerie stones. This is one of the best of its kind in Britain. By the B733, four miles west of Wigtown.

Scottish Borders

Duns. One of the few iron-age brochs in Scotland, *Edin's Hall Broch*, which is unusually large too, can be found near Abbey St Bathans, about five miles north of Duns off the B6355.

Edrom Church has a richly carved Norman doorway. An even older church is in the Kirkyard. The village of Edrom is three and a half miles north-east of Duns off the A6105.

Foulden, on the A6105 between Berwick-upon-Tweed and Chirnside, is where you will see the *Foulden Tithe Barn*. It isn't open to the public, so you will need to gawp from the road.

Gordon. The *Greenknowe Tower*, an L-plan tower house built in 1581, is half a mile west of Gordon on the A6105, north-west of Kelso. It is open all year, daily.

Hume Castle, off the B6364 north of Kelso, has great views of the Merse of Berwickshire right across to Carter Bar. The castle is open from April to October during daylight hours; in winter it is kept locked, but you can get the key from the people at the house opposite.

Innerleithen has a few places of interest to take you off your beaten track. The *Cuddy Brig* is an old stone-built arch across the Leithen Water, built in 1701.
   St Ronan's Well takes its name from St Ronan, an early seventh-century monk who came to the area to banish evil! Taste the sulphurous water and reflect on Sir Walter Scott. The museum and interpretation centre is open from Easter to October from 2 p.m. to 5 p.m. (see Museums). You could even have a Victorian tea on the verandah!

Jedburgh has an ongoing archaeology project – Border Burghs Archaeology Project – which has uncovered the sixteenth-century Franciscan building of *Jedburgh Friary*. This is open to view Monday to Friday from 9 a.m. to 4 p.m. For further information about the project, or to organise a guided tour Tel: 01573 25211.

Kelso Abbey is one of four great Borders abbeys. It is in ruins now, but still elegant in its own way! Open all year. The Abbey is near the town-centre square.

Peebles. *Cross Kirk* is just a few minutes' walk from the High Street. This is actually the nave and tower of a Trinitarian Friary, founded in the late thirteenth century. Open all year.

CENTRAL, TAYSIDE AND FIFE

Dundee City

Broughty Castle is at Castle Green, Broughty Ferry. It is now a museum (see Museums). Look out too, for *Claypotts Castle* on Claypotts Road, West Ferry; it is a sixteenth-century Z-plan castle with two round towers.

Cathedral Church of St Paul is in the High Street. This beautiful neo-Gothic building was built in 1853, and is the work of Sir George Gilbert Scott. Tours and refreshments are available. There is also a gift shop. Open Monday to Friday from 10 a.m. to 4 p.m., Saturday from 11 a.m. to 3 p.m., Sunday from 12.15 p.m. to 12.45 p.m. Tel: 01382 224486

Churches to visit if you fancy, are as follows: *The Gilfillan Memorial Church* in Whitehall Crescent; *St Peter's McCheyne Church* in Perth Road, opposite Blackness Library; *St Salvador's Scottish Episcopal Church* in Church Street, off Carnegie Street in Hilltown; *The Steeple Church and Slessor Centre* in the High Street; *Meadowside St Paul's Church* in the Nethergate; *St Andrew's RC Cathedral* also in the Nethergate, opposite South Tay Street; and the *Scottish Episcopal Cathedral Church of St Paul* in Castlehill, High Street. Broughty Ferry has *St Luke's and Queen Street Church*, *St Stephen's and West Church*, *St Mary's Scottish Episcopal Church* and *St Aidan's Church*.

Dudhope Castle is on Barrack Road and was built in the thirteenth century. It is situated in Dudhope Park.

The Howff is at Meadowside, and for a graveyard, it is a nice one. Many graves show symbols of craft guilds, reminders that members of these guilds used to meet here. Peaceful.

Mains Castle is in Caird Park (left off the A929 at Claverhouse Road and then first left into Caird Park). Once known as Fintry Castle, it was built in the sixteenth century and later went to ruin. Now restored, it is a central feature of the park. Tel: 01382 456797

St Andrew's Kirk and the Glasite Church are in King Street (next to the Wellgate Centre). Great stained glass. The Kirk was designed by Samuel Bell in 1772. Open Tuesday and Thursday from 10 a.m. to 12 noon.

St Mary's Tower and City Churches are on the Nethergate. This is the most substantial medieval church tower in Scotland, dating from around 1460. Bear in mind the 232 steps to the view! The church itself has a hammerbeam roof and galleried aisles. Open mid-May to end August, weekdays except Wednesday, from 10 a.m. to 12 noon; Sunday from 10 a.m. to 1 p.m.

Tay Road Bridge. OK, I know it is the rail bridge that is famous, but you can't *walk* across that, can you! You *can*, however, walk right down the middle of this bridge, and at one and a half miles long, it is one of the longest in Europe. (The rail bridge, incidentally, is two miles and 73 yards long!)

The Wishart Arch is an old city gateway that has recently been restored. It is on the Cowgate. Dating from before 1548, the arch is named after the man who used it as a pulpit to preach to the faithful during the plague. Fascinating!

Falkirk

Callendar House is a great many things – museum, historical research centre, and the basis of an amazing culinary history tour. It is also an incredible building, as the house encapsulates 600 years of history, from medieval times to the twentieth century. It was even visited by Mary Queen of Scots, Oliver Cromwell and Bonnie Prince Charlie. Callendar House is just off the A803, easily reached from the town centre, or Falkirk Grahamston station. Open all year, Monday to Saturday from 10 a.m. to 5 p.m.; also Sunday from April to September from 2 p.m. to 5 p.m. Tel: 01324 503770

Rough Castle is on the B816, about six miles west of Falkirk. It is open at all reasonable times, and is worthy of a visit, for a picnic or a stroll. Tel: 0131 668 8600 (Historic Scotland)

Fife

Aberdour isn't just a great beach. Visit *St Fillan's Parish Church*, which dates from 1123.

Burntisland has the *Burgh Chambers*, built in 1843. Plenty of old paintings deck their walls. Tel: 01592 872667
You could try the *Parish Church*, the first post-Reformation church to be built in Scotland, in 1592. An unusual one. Tel: 01592 874303

Ceres is the site of *Scotstarvit Tower*. This is a sixteenth-century keep, owned now by the Wemyss family. Ask for the key at Hill of Tarvit Mansionhouse, which is in Cupar on the A916. Open May to October, daily from 1.30 p.m. to 5.30 p.m. Admission is free, but you will be asked for a deposit for the key.

Charlestown, on the north shore of the Firth of Forth, is the place for *limekilns*. I'm sure someone knows what a limekiln is, and perhaps has an interest in them. You can get a guided walk around them from May to September. (This is also a town built by the fifth Earl of Elgin in the shape of an E!) Tel: 01383 872006

Dunfermline Abbey and Palace Visitor Centre. Here you will find the burial place of Robert the Bruce. Open April to September, Monday to Saturday from 9.30 a.m. to 6.30 p.m., Sunday from 2 p.m. to 6.30 p.m.; October to March, Monday to Wednesday and Saturday from 9.30 a.m. to 4.30 p.m. Tel: 01383 739026
St Margaret's Cave was used by the saint for periods of contemplation. It is now a shrine. Open Easter to October, daily from 11 a.m. to 4 p.m. Tel: 01383 622290/721814
Abbot House, the remains of a sixteenth-century town house, is now a museum and visitor attraction.

Dysart has 'Pan Ha' – a group of seventeenth-century fisher houses now restored by the National Trust for Scotland. A nice wee harbour, too.
St Serf's Tower is a battlemented church tower. You can get a brilliant view of it from the harbour.

East Wemyss has the ruins of *Macduff's Castle*. (Yes, the one from *Macbeth*.) Spooky!

Inverkeithing Town House has a pepperpot belfry, quoins and a pedimented tower which dates from 1574. Lovely.

Kinghorn has the *Alexander III Monument*, which was erected in 1887 to commemorate the death of Scotland's last Celtic king, in 1286.
   Kinghorn also has an interesting town hall and parish church.

Kirkcaldy is the site of *Abbotshall Kirk*, an ancient kirk with a crypt dating from the eighth century. Also look to the coast for *Seafield Tower.*
   Kirk Wynd is the home of some of the oldest houses in Kirkcaldy, including more churches, such as *St Brycedale*, with a 200-foot spire. At *Sailor's Walk* is the oldest crow-stepped house in the town, dating from the time the castle was built, talking of which . . .
   Ravenscraig Castle dates from 1460, and was built by James II to protect the burgh from pirates, and the English! Open daily from dawn to dusk. You could even get a guided tour. (And you are guaranteed a view.) Tel: 01592 642090
   Town House is a building that began in 1939 – after an architectural competition. Open all year, Monday to Friday from 9 a.m. to 5 p.m. Tel: 01592 645000

Leven has an interesting *Mercat Cross*, built between 1623 and 1700, since when it has been moved around the town a few times! Why?

Markinch has *The Stobb Cross*, which once marked the boundary of an early sanctuary. (In other words, a gyrth cross.) Am I making any sense? Only those in the know will know!

Pittenweem has added value in *St Fillan's Cave*. It dates from the seventh century and was used by a missionary – St Fillan! Open all year, but collect the key from the Gingerbread Horse Craft Shop and Coffee Shop, 9 High Street, Pittenweem. I challenge you to take the key back afterwards, and *not* be drawn in by the idea of a quick cuppa and a cake! Tel: 01333 311495

St Monans Windmill dates from 1780, and was used to extract salt from the salt-pans. It has been restored, and has a viewing platform and a display about the excavation of the salt-pans. Unusual. Open June to September, daily from 11 a.m. to 4 p.m.

West Wemyss is the site of *St Adrian's Church*. St Adrian was a missionary to Fife in the ninth century.

Perth and Kinross

Aberfeldy is the place for *Wade's Bridge*, a famous bridge dating from 1733 and designed by William Adam. Part of the vital business of General Wade's road-building programme.

Abernethy Round Tower is eight miles south-east of Perth, and stands in a conservation village. This round tower is one of only two in Scotland. It does look strange – 74 feet high and barely a window. I guess they did that kind of thing in the eleventh century. Open April to September, at reasonable times.

Alyth Arches are at the north end of the village of Alyth and can be seen at all times. They are all that remains of a sixth-century church, St Moluag's.

Amulree Church is off the A822, about 14 miles north of Crieff. The scenery around here is unusual, almost lunar in places. Anyhow, this is a pretty eighteenth-century church. Open all year.

Ardoch Roman Camp is one of the largest Roman stations in Britain. The earthworks date from the second century. Open all reasonable times. Find the Roman Camp off the A822 at Braco, about ten miles south of Crieff.

Auchterarder. About ten miles to the south-east is *Tullibardine Chapel*. This fifteenth–sixteenth-century chapel is built in the shape of a cross. Open at reasonable times.

Bandirran Stone Circle is a few miles to the north-east of Balbeggie, along the B953. Look for a stile at the end of a strip of woodland to the left beside the road. If you cross the stile and take the faint path into the woods for 500 yards, you will see the stone circle right ahead.

Burleigh Castle is two miles north-east of Kinross. You can only view the outside of this tower house, which dates from 1500.

Colen Stone Circle isn't easy to find, but persevere. Take the A93 Blairgowrie road from Perth past the Scone Palace entrance, then go left to Waulkmill/Stormontfield. Just over three miles along is a sign for the circle. You need to traipse a bit across the field now. Bear in mind many of the stones are sunken, and they may be covered in crops!

Comrie is positioned on the Highland Fault, geologically speaking. This accounts for the position of the tiny *Earthquake House*. Here the world's first seismometers were set up in Victorian times.

Crieff has a number of little things of interest, and bear in mind everyone has been here – Romans, Picts, Vikings, Jacobites, you name them! The small square on the High Street in the centre of town has a Pictish cross (encased for protection) which once marked the centre of the *kirktoun*.
   The *Old Parish Church* is on Church Street, built on the site of an earlier church in 1786; the graveyard (if you're interested) is in Bank Street (plenty of Crieff 'worthies' in there, too!).
   A wander around the town will show you many architectural styles, in a quiet, market-town kind of way. You might want to try the *Crieff Heritage Trail*, a booklet showing the route is available from the Tourist Information Centre (see Days Out).

Dunfallandy Stone is slightly off the beaten track. It is on a minor road one and a half miles south-east of Pitlochry. Worth the trip, this is an eighth-century carved Pictish slab.

Dunkeld Cathedral is in a truly tranquil spot. The original structure was built in 1318, although it was largely ruined in the Reformation. The choir part is still a church. Look out for the tomb of the 'Wolf of Badenoch', the infamous son of Robert II.

Dunning has a twelfth-century church with an imposing tower, *St Serf's*. The village is laid out in a traditional pattern around the church. *Maggie Wall's Monument* commemorates a friendly local neighbourhood witch-burning in 1657.

Dunsinane Hill Vitrified Fort can be reached by a steep footpath on the north side of the hill, south-east of Collace. (Take the A94 Perth–Coupar Angus road.) There are wonderful views too from the summit.

Fortingall, near Aberfeldy, has two somewhat dubious claims to a place in history. Number one – the yew tree in the churchyard is said to be Europe's oldest living thing, at 3,000 years old. Number two – Pontius Pilate was allegedly born here (son of a soldier stationed here). If you do get to Fortingall, the thatched cottages are delightful.

Fowlis Wester has *St Bean's Church*, which dates from the thirteenth century. There you will find a leper's squint. (Don't tell me, I'd rather not know.)

Grandtully is two miles east of Aberfeldy. (Take the A827.) *St Mary's Church* is a sixteenth-century church with an amazing painted wooden ceiling. Get the key to let you in from Pitcairn Farm nearby.

Invergowrie is just outside Dundee, on the A90. Here you will see *St Peter's Church*, which was built in the sixteenth century on the site of the first Christian church on the banks of the Tay.

Loanhead Stone Circle is near the village of Guildtown. Take the A93 north out of Perth, and after Guildtown take the first right, towards Wolfhill/Burrelton. After 330 metres turn right up the road to Loanhead Farm. Go straight up the track for another 500 metres and look for the sign and two remaining uprights of the circle, beside the track to your left. The two stones are both over one and a half metres high.

Muthill is a conservation village near Crieff, dating from the eighteenth and nineteenth centuries. The *Parish Church* is an important fifteenth-century monument, with a tower that dates from Norman times.

Perth has some great civic buildings. Look too for *St John's Kirk*, which is a fine church dating from the fifteenth century, and was the scene of John Knox's momentous sermon in 1559. Open all year, Monday to Friday from 10 a.m. to 12 noon and 2 p.m. to 4 p.m.

Stirling

Stirling. There are many interesting sites in and around the town.

Cambuskenneth Abbey is near the Wallace Monument, a mile east of Stirling, off Causewayhead Road. The monastery where once Robert the Bruce held his parliament is just ruins today. Open April to September, Monday to Saturday from 9.30 a.m. to 6.30 p.m., Sunday from 2.30 p.m. to 6.30 p.m.

Stirling Castle sadly isn't free or cheap (wait for Doors Open Day in September). However, you can wander around beside it up at the highpoint of the town and pop into the good visitor centre whilst you are there (see Days Out).

The *Wallace Monument* stands tall on a rocky promontory overlooking Stirling and the whole valley. There's really no need to go up and into the monument, unless a bravery of 'I can go into very small places and survive endless stair torture' overcomes you. Walk up to the foot of the monument for the view, taking your time as it is a challenging climb (and the minibus is 50 pence). Take the Bridge of Allan road from the centre of town, and follow the signs straight ahead at the roundabout. You can't miss it!

GRAMPIAN

Aberdeen City

Balgownie is a 'bridge and cot-town' in Old Aberdeen. As you cross the fourteenth-century bridge over the River Don, the quaint cottages are revealed.

Bridge of Dee is a seven-arched sixteenth-century bridge on the outskirts of town. There are walks along the riverside beside it.

Castlegate on Union Street has been the centre of Aberdeen's happenings since the twelfth century. There are still market days here all year round.

Churches. There are many churches in Aberdeen. As well as the ones with their own towers, look out for: *St Peter's Roman Catholic Church* in Justice Street, *Salvation Army Citadel* on Castlegate, *St Mark's Church* on Rosemount Viaduct, *St James' Scottish Episcopal Church* at Holburn Junction, *Queen's Cross Church* at Carden Place and Albyn Place, *Melville Carden Place Church* at the end of Albert Street, *Beechgrove Church* on Mid Stocket Road and Beechgrove Avenue, *St Mary's Scottish Episcopal Church* at Carden Place and *Rubislaw Church*.

The Fire Station at King Street is an imposing building which opened in 1899. If you can persuade them to let you in, look out for their artefacts and hosepipe memorabilia.

The Langstane Church, Union Street, is a Gothic church with a vast galleried nave and a magnificent steeple.

Marischal College has a museum and interesting nineteenth-century architecture. It is the second-largest granite building in the world; the largest is the Escorial, Madrid. Find the college on Broad Street.

Provost Skene's House is one of the city's few remaining examples of early burgh architecture. Built in the sixteenth century, the house is now open as a museum of local history and an interesting period home in its own right. Rooms are wonderfully reconstructed, like the Georgian Dining Room and the yellow Regency Parlour. Open Monday to Saturday from 10 a.m. to 5 p.m. Find the Provost Skene's House in Guestrow, off Flourmill Lane. Tel: 01224 641086

The Rhynie Man is a Pictish stone-carved figure. You can see the stone in the foyer of Woodhill House, the headquarters of Aberdeenshire Council, and you can view it during normal working hours (8.30 a.m. to 5.30 p.m.).

Robert Gordon's College has an interesting oldest part; it was designed by William Adam and construction began in 1731. Get there via Schoolhill.

St Andrews Scottish Episcopal Cathedral in King Street was designed by Archibald Simpson in 1816. Gothic on the inside.

St Nicholas Kirk and Kirkyard are tucked away in the busiest part of the city, right beside Union Street, Schoolhill and the St Nicholas Centre. Although it was once the largest medieval burgh kirk in Scotland, the kirk is now mostly eighteenth-century, with a beautiful fifteenth-century *St Mary's Chapel*. The most-used area is *St John's Chapel*, which was refurbished by the oil industry in 1990. Take a wander round this churchyard and look out for some famous Aberdonians: Dr Robert Hamilton, William Penny and, most exciting, John Anderson – the Wizard of the North. The kirk is open May to September, Monday to Friday from 12 noon to 4 p.m., Saturday and Sunday from 1 p.m. to 3 p.m.; October to April, ring the bell at the office door between 10 a.m. and 1 p.m. to get in. The kirkyard is open May to September from 8.30 a.m. to 9 p.m. and October to April from 8.30 a.m. to 4.30 p.m. Tel: 01224 646333 ext 250 (Aberdeen Art Gallery)

The Town House is in Castle Street, and comprises the Tolbooth of 1618 and the Municipal Chambers in an unusual Flemish Gothic style. Also in Castle Street is the *Sheriff Court House*.

Aberdeenshire

Banchory. Cairn o' Mount has never been excavated, so you are standing on a mystery! The main cairn is 3.5 metres high, and about 15.5 metres across. The cairn, with the remains of another nearby, stands by the road at the top of the hill, on the B974 from Banchory to Fettercairn. Choose a clear day for a good view.

Banff is the place to find the beautiful *Duff House*. This magnificent Georgian mansion was designed by William Adam and is now open as a country house gallery, managed by the National Galleries of Scotland. Open in summer, daily except Tuesday, from 10 a.m. to 5 p.m.; in winter, Thursday to Sunday from 10 a.m. to 5 p.m. Tel: 01261 818181

Banff Castle was built back in 1750 to a John Adam design, and remains largely unaltered. You might have to look from the outside only.

Banff Parish Church in the High Street was built around 1790, and later altered. Other churches in Banff to look out for are the *St Andrews Scottish Episcopal Church* in the High Street, built by Archibald Simpson in 1833, and *Our Lady of Mount Carmel RC Church and Presbytery* in Sandyhill Road, which was built in 1870 and has a beautiful altar.

Bennachie is the site of *Mither Tap*, an ancient hill fort.

Braemar is where you will find *Kindrochit Castle*, on Balnellan Road. These ancient ruins are always open.

Clune Hill features an ancient recumbent stone circle, as well as a ring cairn inside the circle, which was built by the beaker people, or their bronze-age descendants. Recumbent stone circles are unique to Grampian, and over 90 have been found! Find Clune Hill by taking the B9077 between Aberdeen and Banchory. Turn south towards Woodlands of Durrie at the crossroads seven miles east of Banchory. Follow your nose and you'll be there. Park by the Forestry Commission track, climb to the summit of the hill, and there you are!

Crathie Church at Crathie, near Ballater, is where the Royal family attend church when they are at Balmoral. Open April to October, daily from 9.30 a.m. to 5.30 p.m., Sunday from 2 p.m. to 5 p.m. Tel: 013397 844525

Crimond Kirk possesses an incredible clock: it makes every hour a minute longer than real time! The clock-maker cut an extra notch into the face of the clock! Crimond is between Fraserburgh and Peterhead.

Cullykhan has an ancient fortified site at Castle Point, a good natural defensive position. Find it about ten miles west of Fraserburgh, signposted Fort Fiddes. There is a carpark and an information board.

Dunnideer is an ancient hill fort, similar in design to many others in Grampian, such as Little Conval at Dufftown (Moray), Knockargetty Wood at Cromar and Durn Hill at Portsoy. To get up to Dunnideer, park at the Belts, a clump of trees near Insch, and walk up the west side of the hill.

Fraserburgh. The *Mercat Cross* in Saltoun Square is seventeenth century.

Fyvie Parish Church has a pretty Tiffany window. The church is a nineteenth-century one. Tel: 01651 891230

Gamrie, near Gardenstown, has the ruins of *St John's Chapel*, an eleventh-century chapel.

Garlogie is on the B9119 west of Aberdeen and has the *Cullerlie Stone Circle*, where eight stones encircle eight small cairns.

Inverurie is where you will find the *Brandsbutt Stone*, a restored Pictish symbol stone with an inscription. Also look out for the *Easter Aquhorthies Stone Circle* nearby, apparently 4,000 years old.

Loanhead of Daviot Stone Circle is also near Inverurie. It is a 'recumbent' stone circle – in other words, it's laid back! So would you be after 4,000 years! Daviot is five miles north-west of Inverurie. From the carpark follow the path through the wood for 100 yards over the wicket gate and there you are.

Kildrummy Castle is near Kildrummy, west of Alford. Just the ruins of this thirteenth-century courtyard castle remain. It is owned by Historic Scotland, so they may charge for admission. Open April to September, Monday to Saturday from 9.30 a.m. to 6.30 p.m., Sunday from 2 p.m. to 4.30 p.m. Tel: 01975 571331

Kinneff Old Kirk, near Inverbervie, was the hiding place of the Scottish crown jewels, from 1651 to 1660. Now they are hidden in Edinburgh Castle!

Kintore Kirkyard is the place to look for Pictish symbol stones; there are two here, carved on two faces.

Laurencekirk. *Capo Long Barrow* is about six miles south-west of town, off a minor road signposted for RAF Edzell. Just think of it, burying the dead in communal graves!

Lumphanan, on the A980 south of Alford, has the *Peel Ring*, a twelfth-century 'motte' or castle mound. Open at all times.

The Maiden Stone is beside the unclassified road that runs south from the A96 to Chapel of Garioch north-west of Inverurie. The Maiden Stone was carved 1,200 years ago by a Pictish mason. An immense, 3.2-metre carving. Truly amazing.

Macduff. The *Parish Church* was formerly known as Doune Church and was transformed in 1865 by James Matthews into a magnificent Italianate landmark.

Memsie Burial Cairn, south-west of Fraserburgh, is a bronze-age cairn approximately 4,000 years old.

Monymusk. *St Mary's Church* has a display of local seventh–ninth-century Pictish stones. Find it in the village square. Open Easter to November during daylight hours. The church is twelfth-century. Tel: 01467 651470

Old Deer, near Mintlaw, is where you may see the *Loudon Wood Stone Circle* – a bunch of recumbent stones again, but this time in a woodland setting.

The Picardy Stone was set up nearly 1,400 years ago, and has intriguing symbols cut into three of its surfaces. Find the stone in a field to the south of a minor road about two miles north-west of Insch. Just hop over the stile.

Rhynie, south of Huntly, still has some Pictish sculptures stones in the square, although the most famous, the Rhynie Man, now stays in Aberdeen!

Nearby is Auchindoir, with *St Mary's Kirk*, a ruined medieval parish church.

Also near Rhynie is the *Tap o' Noth*, the highest hill fort in Scotland, built by the Picts.

Rosehearty. Just to the south is *Pitsligo Castle*, the ruins, now partly renovated, of a Forbes family stronghold. Also near Rosehearty is the *Mounthooley Doocot*, which is a splendid nineteenth-century doocot with great coastal views, too.

Sandend is near *Findlater Castle*, the clifftop ruin of a fifteenth-century Ogilvie stronghold. Open all year.

Slains Castle is at Cruden Bay, near Aberdeen. These ruins are perched on the clifftops – not ancient, but romantic, anyhow.

Strathdon is near Glenbuchat, where you will see the castle of the same name (*Glenbuchat Castle*). It is a ruin, and an eighteenth-century one at that.

Strichen is south of Fraserburgh on the A981. Take the B9093 and you should be able to see the *White Horse of Mormond*, which was cut into the hillside over 200 years ago.

This is a great area for ancient sites. Look for the *Strichen Stone Circle* about a mile south of the village on the A981. Turn down a track past a house and farm buildings to the west of the road, first turning on the right, then left and you can park outside Gardener's Cottage.

Tarland, north of Aboyne, is close to the *Culsh Earth House*, which was built more than 2,000 years ago. This is an underground chamber, a 'souterrain'. There are over 100 of these round Scotland! Find it off the B9119, two miles east of Tarland. There is an information board at the site, but you will need a torch to see inside! Tel: 0131 668 8600 (Historic Scotland)

Tomnaverie Stone Circle is another bronze-age recumbent stone circle, off the B9094 Aboyne–Tarland road. Open at all times.

Tullich Kirk once belonged to the Knights Templar. Look for a Pictish symbol stone built into the wall, and some simple cross-marked stones nearby. Tullich Kirk is about two miles east of Ballater on the A93.

Whitehill Stone Circle is at Tillyfourie, on the A944 south-east of Alford. It is another recumbent stone circle surrounded this time by small cairns.

Angus

Auchterhouse has an ancient church in *St Mary's*. This place of worship dates from 1275. As well as a lovely old font, there are beautiful stained-glass windows.

Fowlis Church is at *Fowlis Easter*. Take the A923 road to Liff from Dundee. This is a mid-fifteenth-century church, with parts of its rood-screen still extant and medieval paintings.

THE HIGHLANDS

Moray

The Bridge of Avon was built in 1754. This original has been superseded by one to cope with modern traffic, but from the picnic site you can still get a good view of the renovated old bridge.

Bridgend of Glenlivet doesn't only have the distillery of that famous name, it also has *Blairfindy Castle*. The castle was built in 1586 by the Earl of Huntly. Sadly it is now pretty dangerous, so you have to peer in from the surrounding fence.

Packhorse Bridge is a beautiful bridge over the Livet, where the river rushes through the gorge. The bridge may have been built at the same time as the castle. A good spot, with a carpark and picnic site.

About four miles south-west of the village along the B9136 you could discover the *Knock Earth House*. This is a stone-lined underground chamber, perhaps once used as an illicit whisy still. It is also possibly an underground food store from the Bronze Age. To get there, take the lovely walk along Strathavon, starting at the carpark either at Mains of Inverurie, or at Altnaglander.

Buckie has a *Seaman's Memorial*, in New Street. This is a chapel, opened in 1982, to commemorate all those who have lost their lives in the seas around since 1945. The lovely stained-glass windows are by a local artist.

Burghead Well has an obscure origin. Clearly immensely old, it is a chamber cut from 'living' rock, with a pool of water that could be either a well or a place of baptism.

Burghead was once a Pictish citadel, the evidence is in the fort that you can see the vague remains of behind the harbour. The *Burghead Bulls* were Pictish stone carvings found when the fort was destroyed to build the harbour. You can see one in the local library; others are in Elgin Museum, the Royal Museum in Edinburgh and in the British Museum!

Burghead is a place of great mystery. Look out for the *Clavie Stone* on Doorie Hill. Every year on 11 January the 'Clavie', a burning barrel of tar, is carried in a procession through the village. After all the pagan business the Clavie is placed on this ancient stone pedestal.

Cullen (or Old Cullen) has the *Cullen Auld Kirk*, which dates from the fourteenth century at least. A laird's gallery, beautiful sacrament house and a monument. What more could you ask for?

Drummuir is a village near Keith, and it boasts *Drummuir Castle*. The castle dates from 1848, and has a wonderful lantern tower, as well as great gardens. Castle tours are available only for a few weeks a year, usually in September, so call before you go. Expect a charge. Tel: 01542 810225 (Estate office)

Dufftown Castle probably dates from the thirteenth century. Although it is now but a ruin, it has had a glamorous history, including the last occupation by government forces, in 1746.

Mortlach Parish Church is one of the oldest places of Christian worship in Scotland. Parts of this old building survive, but much is now reconstructed. Legend links the church with Malcolm II, who apparently extended the church three spears' lengths as thanksgiving for defeating the Danes.

About a mile south-east of Dufftown you will see *Auchindoun Castle* (from the A941 or A920). The castle is on a steep hillside above the River Fiddich. Visit it via a rough track from the A941; the track, incidentally, isn't recommended for cars. Good Pictish earthworks, but it is all a bit unsafe, so just look from the outside.

Duffus Castle is two miles south of the village of Duffus, near Burghead, and overlooks the flat farmland of the area. This is a Norman motte and bailey castle – the remains of one at least. The keep and bailey wall date from about 1300. The castle was once the seat of the de Moravia family.

St Peter's Church is about a quarter of a mile east of Duffus. The ruined church dates from 1226, with bits and pieces added later.

Elgin. The remains of the hilltop site of Elgin's royal castle can easily be seen at *Lady Hill*. The castle was occupied by King Edward of England in 1296 during the Wars of Independence.

Birnie Kirk is an ancient church, built around 1140, and at one time the seat of the Bishopric. One of the few Norman churches in Scotland still in use. It has a Pictish symbol stone in the graveyard.

Pluscarden Abbey is six miles south-west of Elgin. Founded as a priory in 1230, Pluscarden is now home to a Benedictine community, and was elevated to the status of an abbey in 1974. Open all year, daily from 4.45 a.m.(!) to 8.45 p.m. Tel: 01343 890257

Fochabers is home to the *Tugnet Ice House*, which is well worth a visit (see Days Out).

Forres is the site of *Sueno's Stone*. This standing stone is at least 1,000 years old and has warlike scenes and a wheel cross carved onto it. There is now a protective building around the 23-foot-high stone.

Inveravon, south-west of Aberlour, is the site of *St Peter's Church*, where you can see the *Inveravon Stones*, Pictish symbol stones with enigmatic messages.

Keith has an interesting church in *St Thomas Church*, Chapel Street. Built in the Roman Doric style in 1831–32, it has a beautiful dome, a painting by Dubois gifted by Charles X of France in 1828, and exquisite stained glass.

Auld Brig is actually a rather picturesque packhorse bridge, just off Regent Street, which was built in 1609.

Holy Trinity Church is another church in Keith worth seeing. In the sanctuary is the 'Seabury Chair' on which Bishop Kilgour sat when he consecrated Bishop Seabury as the first Bishop of the American Episcopal Church.

Preshome is a village two miles south of Portgordon. *St Gregory's Church* was the first Catholic church built after the Roman Catholic Relief Act removed penalties – including banishment and death – for public celebration of mass. Heavy . . .

Scalan on the Braes of Glenlivet, was once the home of a Roman Catholic college for the priesthood. From 1717 to 1799 the college played a vital role in keeping the faith alive in northern Scotland. The priests have since moved to Aquhorthies near Inverurie.

Tomintoul is close to the *Lecht Mine*, which you will find a few miles south of town just off the A939. Between 1730 and 1737 iron was mined in these hills. Nothing going on today, of course; but there is an interpretative display, and a lovely walk along the burn.

Tomnavoulin is the site of *The Old Mill Visitor Centre*. This building is an old carding mill. The centre has an audio-visual display about the history of whisky-making, and all manner of similar temptations. Open April to October. Tel: 01807 59042/590432

Kirkmichael Church dates from 1807, and is at least the third church on the site. Look for the old market cross in the churchyard.

Church of the Incarnation, Tombae, was built in 1929 to replace the original – washed away by the 'Muckle Spate' of that year!

Tynet is a village to the north of the A98 between Fochabers and Portgordon. *St Ninian's Chapel* is the oldest post-Reformation Catholic church still in use in Scotland. It was originally a sheep shelter, and was given to the local Catholic community by the laird in 1755 to use as a clandestine church during that anti-Catholic period.

Highland Heartlands

Culloden Battlefield is naturally popular with visitors. Why not go a bit further to the south-east, to *Clava Cairns*? This is a much quieter place, without the tourist trappings, and has a really eerie feel to it. No wonder, when you consider that they are, after all, prehistoric tombs. You will find the site along an unclassified road, follow the few signs or ask a local.

Glenfinnan Monument is set amid beautiful Highland scenery, at the head of Loch Shiel. The monument was erected in 1815 by Alexander Macdonald of Glenaladale as a tribute to the Jacobites. A sad story is told at the visitor centre, so if the sorrowful inevitability of Scottish history becomes too much for you, you can pop into their snack bar or spend your pennies in the shop. Tel: 01397 722250

Inverness has that all-imposing castle, but why not venture into the streets and look for some other buildings? There are plenty of churches, and a couple of cathedrals too. *Ness Bank Church* in Ness Bank was built by William MacIntosh in 1900 in the Gothic revival style. *Free North Church* in Bank Street is the Free Church 'cathedral in the north'. *Old High Church* in Church Street (unsurprisingly) dates from 1772, with an even older tower. Look out for *St Andrews Scottish Episcopal Cathedral* in Ardross Street, built by Alexander Ross in 1866–69; there is a touch of the Gothic revival here, too. There is also *St Mary's RC Church* in Huntly Street, built by William Robertson in 1836–37.

Churches not for you? Look at *Abertarff House* in Church Street, the oldest secular building in Inverness; it was built by the Frasers of Lovat as their town house in 1593.

The Northern Highlands

Borve Castle at Bettyhill is a ruined medieval castle stronghold of Clan Mackay; it stands on an isthmus with a natural arch, through which small boats can pass.

Camster Cairns are one of the most famous ancient sites in Caithness – very spooky and in impeccable condition considering their age. Take a torch. Near Watten.

Canisbay Church dates from the fifteenth century, although there are references to a church in the area in 1222.

Croick Church is at the end of a lonely road west from Bonar Bridge. During the Clearances the names of the evicted were scratched on the window.

Culrain is the site of *Carbisdale Castle*, which was completed in 1914 by the Dowager Duchess of Sutherland. It is a youth hostel now (see Accommodation).

Dornoch Cathedral is the former cathedral of the bishop of Caithness.

Durness is close to *Balnakeil Church*, now a ruin which was built in 1619 as a monument to Rob Don, the Gaelic bard.

Forss. Just to the north is *Crosskirk,* where you will see *St Mary's Chapel*, which, it is believed, dates back to the twelfth century; it is now a ruin.

Golspie is the place to see *Dunrobin Castle and Gardens*. The castle is not free – it is after all an ancient seat, so who can blame them? But, if you come here when the castle is closed, from the end of October to Easter, you can wander freely round the gardens for nowt. Obviously wear your woollies!

Find the castle on the A9, half a mile north of Golspie. Tel: 01408 633177

Loch Assynt is where you will see *Ardvreck Castle*, now a ruin. The castle dates from 1591. Montrose was held prisoner here after the Battle of Carbisdale.

Rosal is a village that was sorted in the Clearances. You will find it about 14 miles south of Bettyhill in Naver Forest.

Skelpick, south of Bettyhill, has plenty of historical sites to choose from – an iron-age broch, neolithic chambered cairn or a ruined Clearance village.

Thurso has *Old St Peter's Church*, which is a ruin. It was built in the thirteenth century and was in use until 1832.

Tongue is the home of *Castle Varrick*, a ruined fourteenth-century MacKay stronghold. You can get a great view over the Kyle of Tongue from here.

Wick has *Old Parish Church*, which is worth a look. More exciting is *Sinclair and Girnigoe Castle* on the clifftop, battered by the elements. A sad place, and quite tricky in bad weather. Another ruin in Wick is *Oldwick Castle* which dates from the Norse occupation.

ISLANDS

Inner Hebrides

MULL
Find **Duart Castle** near Craignure. It is a beautiful thirteenth-century castle. As is often the case, the grounds are free but the castle isn't, so have a wander all around. The long walk to the castle is well worth it, as it stands on a promontory on the east of the island, with good views across to the mainland.

IONA
You must take the opportunity to visit the island if you can. The *Abbey* is glorious. The peace is something else.

RAASAY
To get to Raasay, you take the ferry from Sconser on Skye. Once you are over, you can see *Brochel Castle* which is at the far end of an unmarked road leading north on the island. It is a ruin, although it was once a Clan MacLeod stronghold.

The Western Isles

BARRA
Borve Castle is on a croft at Borve on the B892.

The **Church of St Barr** dates from the twelfth century. One of the ruined churches on this site has been restored and the Norse runes on the grave slab inside are well worth a look. Compton MacKenzie, the author of *Whisky Galore!*, is buried here.

On a tiny island in Castlebay you will see *Kisimul Castle*. You will have to pay to go over on the ferry, so you might prefer to admire it from a distance. Tel: 01871 810336

HARRIS

St Clement's Church at Rodel has the sculptured tomb of Alexander Macleod which he prepared before his death in 1547. Find the church right at the end of the A859.

Nisabost. The standing stone is to be found not far from Horgabost.

LEWIS

Aignish is the site of *St Columba's Church*, a ruined very early chapel and the ancient graveyard of the Macleods. On the A866.

This is the island of the famous *Callanish Standing Stones*. You will find the stones about 12 miles west of Stornoway, off the A859. This is a cross-shaped setting of standing stones, dating from about 3000 BC and is unique in Scotland. Well worth visiting for spookiness alone. There is a new visitor centre, too. Open all year, daily from 10 a.m. to 7 p.m. (till 4 p.m. in winter). Tel: 01851 621422

Dun Carloway is an iron-age dry-stone broch. It is really well preserved and worth seeing. Find it off the A858, about 16 miles from Stornoway.

Gress Mill dates from the eighteenth century, when it was used for milling barley.

Great Bernera is reached via a bridge 'across the Atlantic' and the B8059. There are plenty of standing stones, as well as a lovely beach at Bostadh which is the site of a recently excavated iron-age village.

Ness. At *Clach an Truiseil* you will see the largest single standing stone monolith in the north of Scotland. *Ballantrushal* stands at 5.7 metres high! On a side road off the A857.
   Also in the Ness area is Steinacleit, where you can see Shader (or Siadar in Gaelic), ancient stone sets and a village site. It is close to the A857.

St Moluag's Church was built on a very early chapel site. The current church is in use. Close beside the B8014.

Stornoway Churches include *St Columba's* on Lewis Street, which is the town's main parish church (built in 1794). *St Peter's Episcopal Church* has a sandstone front brought here from the hermit's chapel on the remote Flannan Isles. Look out for David Livingstone's bible in the vestry. The *Free*

Church on Kenneth Street attracts 1,500 people to its Sunday evening services!

Uig Sands. What are they doing in the 'Historical Sites' section you ask? Well, this is the place where they found the Lewis Chessmen. Bring them back British Museum!

NORTH UIST

Cairinis (or Carinish) is the site of *Teampull na Trionaid*, the ruins of an early religious site founded by Beatrice, Somerled's daughter, in about 1203. Even so, it was built on top of an earlier site. Close to the A865.

Dun an Sticir is at Port nan Long (Newton Ferry) and is said to be the remains of the last inhabited dun in North Uist. It was a home to Hugh MacDonald until 1602.

Langass has the *Barpa Langass*, which is a 5,000-year-old chambered cairn on the slopes of Ben Langass. You can see it from the A867, but don't go in whatever you do!
  Nearby is the *Pobull Fhinn*, a circle of standing stones, romantically named after 'Fingal's People'.

Scolpaig Tower is on a small island in a loch just west of the A865 in the north-west. This is the only folly in the Western Isles, and was built in the nineteenth century. (What does that say to you?)

SOUTH UIST

Howmore is a great site for old chapels and burial grounds, which date back from the twelfth or thirteenth centuries. The ancient burial ground of the Clan Ranald chiefs. Some brilliant thatched cottages too! Just off the A865.

Milton has the birthplace of Flora MacDonald, and is marked with a commemorative cairn beside the A865 (what a road!). No humming of the 'Skye Boat Song' now!

Ormacleit House and Castle is also just off the A865. The castle took seven years to build, for the Clan Ranald chief in 1708, and was destroyed by fire seven years later – by a spooky coincidence on the same night that the Clan Ranald chief was killed.

Pollachar is at the end of the B888, a standing stone with attitude that has a great view across the Sound of Barra.

Orkney

EGILSAY

Egilsay is a smaller island, where you will come across *St Magnus Church*. This is a round-tower chapel, which might suggest links with the Irish in the Viking ages. The tower makes the church unique in Scotland.

HOY

Hoy is one of the smaller islands, famous for the incredible rock stack – the Old Man of Hoy. If you visit the island, go along the glen that leads to Rackwick Bay to see the *Dwarfie Stane*. This stone was hollowed out of a block of red sandstone, and is a tomb some 5,000 years old. It has a passage and two compartments, but no one can say who lived here . . .

MAINLAND

Brough of Birsay is a tidal island off Mainland. Watch out on the causeway and don't get trapped by the tide! The island has the remains of early Christian and Norse settlements.

The Churchill Barriers are a historical site in their own right. They now form part of the road network, and connect Burray and South Ronaldsay to Mainland (the largest Orkney island). Constructed in the 1940s by POWs for defence reasons.

At Deerness you will find the ruins of a Norse chapel and village. Take a walk through the Mull Head Nature Reserve, and look at the amazing natural arch 'the Gloup' whilst you are here.

Dounby has *Click Mill*, the last horizontal water wheel of its kind in Orkney.

Haston is at Kirkwall, and this is where the *Grain Earth-house* can be seen. This is an iron-age underground chamber, or 'souterrain' – torches at the ready. You need to get the key to get in, there's a challenge! Tel: 0131 668 8600 (Historic Scotland, Edinburgh)

Holm (pronounced 'Ham') is the site of the Italian Chapel, which was built by Italian POWs during the construction of the Churchill Barriers in the Second World War. It doesn't look much from outside, but the interior is quietly spectacular.

Kirkwall has the beautiful *St Magnus Cathedral*, which was founded in 1035 by Earl Rognvald Kolson in memory of his uncle, Saint Magnus. Open Monday to Saturday; services are held on Sunday.

Orphir has the remains of Scotland's only circular church, *Round Church*, which dates from the early twelfth century. Also take a look at the *Earl's Bu* – the remains of a village drinking hall. An ancient pub!

Stenness is a must, for the amazing *Ring of Brodgar*, the *Barnhouse Neolithic Village* and the *Standing Stones of Stenness*. The stone circle was originally made up of 60 stones, but now only 36 remain, either as upright stones, or as broken stumps in the earth. Close by are the standing stones, a small circle from the third millennium BC. Barnhouse is a partly reconstructed village from around 3000 BC, perhaps once the home of those who built Maes Howe and the standing stones themselves. It has been suggested that the site is a complicated lunar observatory! Pretty spooky place.

Stromness is Orkney's second seaport. Look out for *Login's Well*, which supplied water to the ships of the Hudson Bay Company and the Cook Expedition to name a few. *The Canon* is said to be from the American privateer, *The Liberty*, captured in 1813.

PAPA WESTRAY

Papa Westray is one of the smaller islands. Visit the *Knap of Howar*, which is the earliest standing dwelling-house in north-western Europe, and dates from before 3500 BC.

St Boniface Church is a medieval chapel, with a twelfth-century nave.

ROUSAY

Rousay has some excellent prehistoric sites, which are free. *Midhowe Broch* and *Stalled Cairn* on the west coast of the island are excellent examples. The Midhowe broch is the best example of a broch in Orkney. Three brochs were originally built here in different stages, for defence purposes. The adjacent cairn – Midhowe Stalled Cairn – has 12 compartments, and has been described as 'The Great Ship of Death'. This often makes quite an impact on those who visit it. Visit during summer.

Also on Rousay is the *Taversoe Tuick Chambered Tomb*. This is an unusual two-storeyed monument, with two chambers one above the other.

SANDAY

Sanday, another small island, has the *Quoyness Chambered Tomb*, which dates from around 2900 BC, and contained artefacts similar to those found at Skara Brae.

SHAPINSAY

Shapinsay is an island north of Mainland. Look out for *Burroughston Broch*, a reconstructed Pictish broch featuring a cell and well. It shows the history of its occupation and the excavations that brought its history to light.

WESTRAY

Westray, an island north of Mainland, is the site of *Noltland Castle*, which was designed by Gilbert Balfour as a fortress, in a Z-shaped defensive form. It would have provided all-round visibility for the totally paranoid, but sadly it was never finished.

Also on the island is *Crosskirk*, at Tuquoy. This is a mid-twelfth-century parish church.

WYRE

Wyre is one of the islands north of Mainland. The incredibly named *Cubbie Roo's Castle* is the remains of Scotland's oldest stone castle. Its design is Norse, from the mid-twelfth century.

Shetland

MAINLAND

Scalloway Castle was once the stronghold of Earl Patrick, and Scalloway itself is the ancient capital. Ask for the key to the castle at the Shetland Woollen Company, which sits virtually in the shadow of the castle. Open Monday to Friday from 9 a.m. to 5 p.m.; also Saturday from 9 a.m. to 5 p.m. from May to September. In other words, if the shop is open then you will be able to get access to the ruined castle.

MUSEUMS

When is a museum not a museum? When it's a heritage centre!

As far as we are concerned, the two are one and the same, and they all add up to a free few hours in the company of plenty of old stuff. The more adventurous have audio-visual and interpretative displays, some even push the bounds of reality to their limits with the use of wax models and period costumes. Museums in the cities are generally larger, with more extensive collections and extravagant displays. It would take me about a week to make it round the National Museum of Scotland in Edinburgh's Chambers Street, probably a month if I took both my kids and my husband (he likes to linger amongst the mummies).

There are some delightful specialist museums, such as the Thimble Museum in Biggar and the Archie Sinclair Fossil Centre in Spittal. There are even two separate contenders for the title of 'Scotland's Noisiest Museum' which both have to be worth a visit. You will find some overlap with the Days Out section, because so many museums are really a great 'day out' and vice versa! Let me know how you get on.

THE WEST

Argyll and Bute

Dunoon is the home of the *Castle House Museum* which is in Castle Gardens. This is a new museum, which is due to open in the summer of 1997. A good collection of memorabilia, including a video of Clyde steamers from 1900 to 1989. For opening times, contact Mrs Paterson. Tel: 01369 703040

East Ayrshire

Auchinleck, near Cumnock, has a *Boswell Museum*. It can be viewed only by appointment. If you're into Boswell, give a call to Mrs Wilson on 01290 420931. (Mrs Wilson can usually be found in Chrissie's Shop in the village.)

Cumnock has the *District Heritage Centre and Baird Institute*. This baronial building houses a permanent Keir Hardie Room, as well as temporary exhibitions throughout the year. Open Monday, Tuesday, Thursday and Friday from 10 a.m. to 1 p.m. and 1.30 p.m. to 4.30 p.m., Saturday from 11 a.m. to 1 p.m. Tel: 01290 421553

Dalmellington is the home of the *Cathcartston Visitor Centre*, which really brings to life those poor Ayrshire weavers' lives. Audio-visuals and everything. Open all year, Monday to Friday from 10 a.m. to 4.30 p.m.; also Sunday from April to October from 2 p.m. to 5 p.m. Tel: 01292 550633

Fenwick, north of Kilmarnock, is a lonely spot. Here you will find the *Loch Goin Museum*, an isolated farmhouse that was a safe house for Covenanters in the Killing Times.

Kilmarnock has a wonderful museum, at the *Dick Institute*. Go and see their geological, archaeological and natural history collections particularly. Open April to September. Tel: 01563 526401

Waterside. Here, on the A719 near Kilmarnock, you will find *Chapel Row Cottage*, an iron-worker's cottage from 1913, which is a musuem too. Open by appointment. Tel: 01292 531144/550633

East Renfrewshire

Barrhead Community Museum is a local interest museum showing Barrhead through the ages. Open April to October, Monday, Wednesday and Friday afternoons, Tuesday and Thursday from 1 p.m. to 8 p.m., and Saturday from 10 a.m. to 5 p.m. Find the museum on Main Street. Tel: 0141 876 1994

City of Glasgow

The Burrell Collection. If you go to no other museum in Scotland, go to this one. It has over 8,000 exhibits from ancient civilisation to oriental art. In a beautiful setting, this is a unique experience. Open Monday to Saturday from 10 a.m. to 5 p.m., Sunday from 11 a.m. to 5 p.m. Get to the Burrell at Pollok Country Park, 2060 Pollokshaws Road. Tel: 0141 649 7151

Haggs Castle is at 100 St Andrew's Drive. The castle is now a museum specially designed for kids. The gardens are wonderful too, with a 'knot garden'. Open Monday to Saturday from 10 a.m. to 5 p.m., Sunday from 11 a.m. to 5 p.m. Tel: 0141 427 2725

The Hunterian Museum is at the University of Glasgow. This is the oldest museum in Scotland, in a Gothic setting! Lots of archaeology, ethnography and geology. (That's bones and rocks mostly!) Open Monday to Saturday from 9.30 a.m. to 5 p.m., Sunday from 11 a.m. to 5 p.m. Tel: 0141 330 5431/0141 330 4221

Kelvingrove Art Gallery and Museum are in the leafy splendour of Argyle Street, by Kelvingrove Park. Displays include natural history and more archaeology and ethnography . . . Open Monday to Saturday from 9.30 a.m. to 5 p.m., Sunday from 11 a.m. to 5 p.m. Tel: 0141 287 2000

Museum of the 603 (City of Glasgow) Squadron is a little way out of the centre, at Queen Elizabeth Avenue, Hillington. It tells the story of this air squadron from 1925 to 1957. Open Wednesday and Friday from 7.30 p.m. to 9.30 p.m.; also the first Sunday of every month, from 2 p.m. to 5 p.m. Tel: 0141 810 6455

Museum of Transport is at Kelvin Hall on Burnhouse Road. Look for the great reconstruction of a typical 1938 Glasgow street. All kinds of transport feature, including the once-great Glasgow trams. Open Monday to Saturday from 10 a.m. to 5 p.m., Sunday from 11 a.m. to 5 p.m. Tel: 0141 221 9600

The People's Palace is a great museum for all ages, with wonderful reconstructions of the social and industrial history of the city from 1175. Once you've visited it, take a stroll around the *Winter Gardens*. Find the People's Palace in Glasgow Green. Open Monday to Saturday from 10 a.m. to 5 p.m., Sunday from 11 a.m. to 5 p.m. Tel: 0141 554 0223

The Piping Centre at McPhater Street, Cowcaddens, is close to the Theatre Royal and the RSAMD. Here you will find the *National Museum of Piping* and all that it entails! For those new to the pipes, as well as the knowledgeable. Tel: 0141 353 0220

If you are daring and book in advance, you could visit the **Police Museum** at

Strathclyde Police, 173 Pitt Street. Ring them up for an appointment, and don't let them show you the cells! Tel: 0141 204 2626

Regimental Museum of the Royal Highland Fusiliers is a must for regimental history enthusiasts. Find it at 518 Sauchiehall Street. Open weekdays from 8.30 a.m. to 4.30 p.m. (till 4 p.m. on Friday). Tel: 0141 332 0961

St Mungo Museum of Religious Life and Art is unique. Faiths from around the world are represented. Look for Salvador Dali's *Christ of St John of the Cross*. St Mungo's is at 2 Castle Street. Open Monday to Saturday from 10 a.m. to 5 p.m., Sunday from 11 a.m. to 5 p.m. Tel: 0141 553 2557

Scotland Street School Museum of Education is in a school that was designed by Charles Rennie Mackintosh, so expect a thoroughly educational, as well as an aesthetic experience. Open Monday to Saturday from 10 a.m. to 5 p.m., Sunday from 2 p.m. to 5 p.m. It is at 225 Scotland Street, opposite Shields Road underground station. Tel: 0141 429 1202

Springburn Museum is at Atlas Square, Ayr Street, in the Springburn area of Glasgow. A social history museum centring on the north of the city. This is an Independent Community Museum. Open Monday to Friday from 10.30 a.m. to 5 p.m., Saturday from 10 a.m. to 4.30 p.m. Tel: 0141 557 1405

Inverclyde

Greenock has the *McLean Museum and Art Gallery* on Kelly Street. Exciting natural history exhibits – watch for the Indian insects and the stuffed tiger – are on a gallery floor. Egyptian relics will go down well with small people. There is a great deal about the past of Inverclyde; primarily boatbuilding and engineering. A building beautifully restored. Open all year, Monday to Saturday from 10 a.m. to 5 p.m. Tel: 01475 723741

Greenock Custom House Museum is at Custom House Quay. Displays focus on the Customs and Excise Service – not forgetting their most famous employee, Rabbie Burns. Open Monday to Friday from 10 a.m. to 4 p.m. (with an hour for lunch). Tel: 01475 726331

North Ayrshire

Irvine has the *Glasgow Vennel Museum*, in the old part of the town. Set in a cobbled street that harks back to the nineteenth century, look out for the eighteenth-century Burns reminders. The museum also has a gallery that houses temporary exhibitions. Tel: 01294 275059

Kilbirnie. The *Stables Museum*, which shows Kilbirnie over 150 years, is housed in the historic Walker Hall. The entrance is through the gate beside Dr Walker's statue. Open June to September. Tel: 01505 683445

Largs features a *Christian Heritage Museum*, which shows the history of Christian monastic life in Britain. Open April to September. Tel: 01475 687320

Saltcoats. The *North Ayrshire Museum*, housed in a former church, is a local history museum that centres on the Three Towns: Saltcoats, Stevenston and Ardrossan. Open all year. Tel: 01294 464174

West Kilbride Museum Society have displays including dresses, Ayrshire lace, trade and craft implements, dolls and toys.

CUMBRAE

Millport has a *Museum of the Cumbraes*, a small local history museum with changing displays, housed in a former garrison house. Open June to September, Monday to Saturday from 11 a.m. to 5 p.m.

The *Museum and Marine Biological Station*, also in Millport, has an excellent aquarium. Open all year. Tel: 01475 530581

North Lanarkshire

Airdrie is the home of the *Weavers' Cottages Museum*. This is an excellent reconstruction of a weaver's house, which dates from the nineteenth century. Open daily except Wednesday and Sunday, from 10 a.m. to 1 p.m. and 2 p.m. to 5 p.m. Tel: 01236 747712

Coatbridge is the home of *Summerlee Heritage Trust* which happily promotes itself as 'Scotland's Noisiest Museum'. History here means the iron, steel and engineering industries. There are some great machines here, including the giant Garratt steam engine, as well as reconstructions of a Co-op shop, an Edwardian photographer's studio and even a bicycle and radio shop. The only things that cost money are the tram rides, which are just 25 pence for children and 50 pence for adults. Look out for special events at Summerlee throughout the year. Find Summerlee at West Canal Street. Open all year, daily from 10 a.m. to 5 p.m. Tel: 01236 431261

Cumbernauld Museum stands in *Palacerigg Country Park* (see Days Out). It has a permanent exhibition on the origins and development of the village of Cumbernauld. Open Monday to Friday from 10 a.m. to 4.30 p.m., Saturday and Sunday from 11 a.m. to 4 p.m. Tel: 01236 735077

Kilsyth. The *Colzium Lennox Estate* is nearby. Look for a local history museum in this glorious environment. The museum is open by appointment, so ring before you go. Tel: 0141 304 1800 (North Lanarkshire Leisure)

Motherwell Heritage Centre is an ambitious new local history centre telling the story of the district. Tel: 01698 266166 (Department of Cultural Services)

Shotts Heritage Centre. When is a museum not a museum? When it's a Heritage Centre! Local history from the Covenanters to the present day (see Days Out). Open weekdays from 9.30 a.m. to 7 p.m. (till 12 noon on Wednesday), Saturday from 9.30 a.m. to 5 p.m. Tel: 01501 821556

Renfrewshire

Lochwinnoch Community Museum is a fine local history museum, Scotland's first in fact, as it opened in 1984. In the main street of the town. Open Monday, Wednesday and Friday from 10 a.m. to 1 p.m., 2 p.m. to 5 p.m. and 6 p.m. to 8 p.m.; Tuesday and Saturday from 10 a.m. to 1 p.m. and 2 p.m. to 5 p.m. Tel: 01505 842615

Paisley is the home of *Paisley Museum and Art Galleries* in the High Street. As you would expect, there is a huge selection of Paisley Pattern material. Open all year, Monday to Saturday from 10 a.m. to 5 p.m. Tel: 0141 889 3151

Sma' Shot Cottages are in Shuttle Street. They are, in truth, eighteenth-century weavers' cottages restored to their former 'glory'. Open May to end September, Wednesday and Saturday from 1 p.m. to 5 p.m. Tel: 0141 889 1708

Renfrew Community Museum plans to open in 1997 in the former Brown Institute building in Canal Street.

South Ayrshire

Girvan has the *McKechnie Institute* on Dalrymple Street, a museum and community arts centre which features local history and material about the Ailsa Craig. Tel: 01465 713643

South Lanarkshire

Biggar Gasworks Museum is a bit different. This is the only remaining gasworks in Scotland, now preserved as a museum. Open end May to end September, daily from 2 p.m. to 5 p.m. Tel: 01899 21070

If that wasn't enough for you, try the *Thimble Museum* – Britain's only museum devoted to these handy little thumb protectors (no kidding!). Over 5,000 of them, some from the thirteenth century! Open Monday to Saturday from 9.30 a.m. to 5.30 p.m., Sunday from 12.30 p.m. to 4.30 p.m. Tel: 01899 221581

Douglas is the site of the *Douglas Heritage Museum*, in the former dower-house of the old Castle of Douglas. Many artefacts surrounding the Cameronians and other local historical material. Donations are welcome. Open Easter to October, weekends from 2 p.m. to 5 p.m. It is wise to telephone in advance as admission is by arrangement only. Tel: 01555 851442

Hamilton has the *Low Parks Museums*, which comprises the former District Museum and the Cameronians (Scottish Rifles). A new complex with an excellent local history collection. Open Monday to Saturday from 10 a.m. to 5 p.m., Sunday from 12 noon to 5 p.m. Tel: 01698 283981

Lanark Museum is a local history museum with changing exhibitions. Open

May to September, Friday and Saturday from 10.30 a.m. to 4.30 p.m. Tel: 01555 664226

Strathaven is home to *The John Hastie Museum,* a small local history museum in Strathaven Park. Displays from the Covenanters to beautiful ceramics. Tel: 01355 261261

THE EAST

East Lothian

Dunbar Town House Museum in the High Street is the home of an exciting archaeology and local history centre. 'Dunbar Underground' even offers you a chance to make your own prehistoric pot! Open end March to October, daily from 12.30 p.m. to 4.30 p.m. Tel: 01368 863734

Gullane is the site of the *Heritage of Golf Museum.* Visits are by appointment only, so give them a call first! The exhibition shows how the game developed since arriving from Holland in the fifteenth century. The museum is at West Links Road. Tel: 01875 870277

Haddington has the *Jane Welsh Carlyle Museum* at Lodge Street. This is a Regency-period home, styled as of the period, dedicated to the memory of the woman herself (yes, Jane). Open April to September. Tel: 01620 823738

North Berwick Museum tries hard to appeal to all ages, and succeeds. There is a Bass Rock room, with stuffed stuff, and an exhibition of pastoral art from the late nineteenth and early twentieth centuries. Young children will enjoy the Scottish Discovery Room, where the hands-on experience extends to grinding your own oats or making nets. The museum is on School Road and is open from the end of March to October, daily from 11 a.m. to 5 p.m. Tel: 01620 895457

North Berwick Lifeboat Station is a musuem of another kind. Here, at 1 Melbourne Road, you can see a variety of lifeboat memorabilia, in a station which houses the only *Blue Peter* lifeboat in Scotland! Open April to September, daily from 10.30 a.m. to 5 p.m. Tel: 01620 892418

Prestonpans. The *Prestongrange Industrial Heritage Museum* tells the tale of the many local industries and those who worked in them. Guided tours are available from the visitor centre – look particularly for the enormous Cornish beam engine, which pumped water out of the mine. The first Sunday of the month they hold steam days, when you can go along and see locomotives in action, and even have a ride. Great events programme too. Open end March to October, daily from 11 a.m. to 4 p.m. You will find the Heritage Museum at Morrison's Haven. Tel: 0131 653 2904

City of Edinburgh

Bank of Scotland Museum is at the stunning Bank building on the Mound. One to visit, if only to have a look at some forgeries! They won't mention your overdraft! Open July to September, Monday to Friday from 10 a.m. to 4.40 p.m. Tel: 0131 243 5467

The Fire Museum is at the Central Fire Station at Lauriston Place. Here you can see vintage fire engines and, if you phone in advance you might get to chat about fires gone by with an expert. Open Monday to Friday, from 9 a.m. to 4.30 p.m. Tel: 0131 228 2401

Huntly House Museum is one of many museums on the Royal Mile. This is a restored sixteenth-century mansion, its collection focusing on Edinburgh's past. Open Monday to Saturday from 10 a.m. to 6 p.m. (till 5 p.m. in winter); also Sunday at Festival-time, from 2 p.m. to 5 p.m. Tel: 0131 529 4143

The **Museum of Childhood** on the Royal Mile isn't just for kids. This 'noisiest museum in the world' is jam-packed with childhood memories. Open Monday to Saturday from 10 a.m. to 6 p.m. (till 5 p.m. from October to May); also Sunday afternoon at Festival-time. Tel: 0131 529 4142

Newhaven Heritage Museum is at 24 Pier Place, beside the harbour. Reconstructed and spooky sets of fisher-folk from the village of Newhaven. Hands-on exhibits and spoken accounts of people's lives. Open daily from 12 noon to 5 p.m. Tel: 0131 551 4165. If you get peckish, you won't be able to resist fish and chips at Harry Ramsden's next door.

The People's Story is in the Canongate Tolbooth, on the Royal Mile (what a great area for museums!). The stories of ordinary Edinburgh folk give this museum its charm. Open all year, Monday to Saturday from 10 a.m. to 6 p.m. (till 5 p.m. in winter); also Sunday at Festival-time, from 2 p.m. to 5 p.m. Tel: 0131 529 4057

Queensferry Museum specialises in the history of the wildlife on the shores of the Forth Estuary. Look out, too, for the local history displays. The museum is between the two Forth bridges, on the High Street at the water's edge. Open Monday, Thursday, Friday and Saturday from 10 a.m. to 1 p.m. and 2.15 p.m. to 5 p.m., and Sunday afternoon. Tel: 0131 331 5545

Royal Museum of Scotland – this has to be one of the most extensive and enjoyable museums to take your children to, anywhere. Seriously, it is a museum for all ages, from stuffed animals to engineering, Ancient Egypt to science and technology. A lovely environment too, ideal for a rainy, or equally a sunny, day. Spend some time in the Bio Dome, one of the latest exhibits, that looks at the ecology of the planet. Big stuff! Find the museum on Chambers Street (parking is tricky round here). Open all year, Monday to Saturday from 10 a.m. to 5 p.m., Sunday from 12 noon to 5 p.m. Tel: 0131 225 7534

The **Scottish Agricultural Museum** is located in the unlikely-seeming area beside the airport, some seven miles west of the city centre. If you love the countryside and rural farming history, this is the place for you. What the hell is a mooldie-koose anyhow? Open April to September, daily from 10 a.m. to 5 p.m.; October to March, Monday to Friday from 10 a.m. to 4 p.m. The only time this museum charges for admission is during the Highland Show at next-door Ingliston Showground. Tel: 0131 333 2674

Scottish United Services Museum is in Edinburgh Castle. Tel: 0131 225 7534. The only problem here is that you have to pay to get into the castle, although the museum itself is free. If you do choose to go into Edinburgh Castle – it is well worth it I must say, friends of mine recently spent *five hours* there – then stretch those pennies a bit further with a trip round the Scottish regalia. Open all year, Monday to Saturday from 9.30 a.m. to 4.45 p.m. and Sunday afternoon.

The Writers' Museum is in the glorious Lady Stair's House, just off the Royal Mile. This is a real treasure-trove for the literary, with many items associated with Scotland's finest writers, such as Burns, Scott and Stevenson. Open all year, Monday to Saturday from 10 a.m. to 6 p.m. (till 5 p.m. in winter); also Sunday at Festival-time from 2 p.m. to 5 p.m. Tel: 0131 529 4901

Midlothian

Dalkeith. To the east of town is the small village of Cousland and the *Cousland Smiddy*. It is a working smiddy, but with a museum element, too. Ring in advance to make sure of your timing. Tel: 0131 663 1058

West Lothian

Bathgate is home to *Bennie Museum*, the Bathgate Heritage Museum in the oldest row of cottages in the town. Open all year, Monday to Saturday from 10 a.m. to 4 p.m. (11 a.m. to 3.30 p.m. in winter). Find it at Mansfield Street. Tel: 01506 634944

Linlithgow is on the Edinburgh and Glasgow Union Canal. What better place to discover the *Canal Museum*, run by a group of volunteers in the shape of the Linlithgow Union Canal Society. The museum is in a former canal stable row (those horses must have been pretty hefty by any reckoning), full of photographs and artefacts associated with this famous canal. The museum is open only at weekends from Easter to September, from 2 p.m. in the afternoon; this coincides with their canal boat trips (see Days Out).

THE BORDERS

Dumfries and Galloway

Carsphairn Heritage Centre is a small rural centre with changing local exhibitions as well as 'time span' interpretation of the surrounding area. Open June to September daily, and over the Easter holidays. Carsphairn is on the New Galloway to Dalmellington road.

Dumfries houses the *Crichton Royal Museum* which takes an in-depth look at 200 years of hospitals. Look out for the operating theatre! Find it at Easterbrook Hall, Crichton Royal Hospital. Open all year, Thursday and Friday from 1.30 p.m. to 4.30 p.m.; also Saturday in summer. Tel: 01387 255301 ext 2360

Dumfries Museum is the largest museum in south-west Scotland, tracing the history of the people of Dumfries and Galloway. The museum is centred around the eighteenth-century windmill tower which stands above the town. Check out the prehistoric footprints! Open Monday to Saturday from 10 a.m. to 1 p.m. and 2 p.m. to 5 p.m.; also Sunday afternoons in summer. (Closed Mondays in winter too!) Tel: 01387 253374 (At the same location you will find the Camera Obscura, 80 pence for adults and 40 pence for concessions – see Days Out.)

Old Bridge House Museum is the oldest house (1660) in Dumfries, and a 'people's story' type of museum. Open April to September from 10 a.m. to 1 p.m. and 2 p.m. to 5 p.m., Sunday from 2 p.m. to 5 p.m. Tel: 01387 256904

Moffat Museum possibly shouldn't be here – there is a charge of 50 pence for adults and 20 pence for kids. Not much to pay, though, for the story of this sheep and spa town. Open Easter to end September, weekdays (except Wednesday) and Saturday from 10.30 a.m. to 1 p.m. and 2.30 p.m. to 5 p.m.; also Sunday afternoon. Tel: 01683 220868

Ruthwell. The *Duncan Savings Bank Museum* is seven miles to the west of Annan in the village of Ruthwell. Who would have thought that the TSB started here! You don't have to show your bank book for entry (thank goodness!). Open all year, daily from 10 a.m. to 1 p.m. and 2 p.m. to 5 p.m.; closed on Sunday and Monday from October to March. Tel: 01387 870640

Sanquhar Tolbooth Museum in the High Street looks at the story of 'Upper Nithsdale', like Sanquhar knitting and mines and miners. Open April to September, Tuesday to Saturday and Sunday afternoon. Tel: 01659 50186

Stranraer Museum is another fine local history museum, with good archaeology and farming stuff. Watch for the Ross Room, dedicated to Arctic explorer Sir John Ross and his nephew. Open all year, Monday to Saturday. Tel: 01776 705088

Wigtown Museum has lots of interest on the 'Wigtown martyrs', together with local history material.

Scottish Borders

Coldstream has *The Hirsel*, which houses a museum of the estate's past and present. There is also an arts and crafts centre, walks and a nice tea-room (see

Days Out). Open Monday to Friday from 10 a.m. to 5 p.m., weekends from 12 noon to 5 p.m. The grounds are open all the time during daylight hours. Tel: 01890 882834

Galashiels has the *Galashiels Museum and Exhibition* in the Peter Anderson Mill Complex, which is primarily a local history display, focusing on the woollen trade. Open April to October, Monday to Saturday from 9 a.m. to 5 p.m.; also Sunday in summer from 12 noon to 5 p.m. Tel: 01896 2091

Old Gala House and Christopher Boyd Gallery has a painted ceiling dating from 1635. Beautiful. Open late March to October, Monday to Saturday from 10 a.m. to 4 p.m., Sunday from 2 p.m. to 4 p.m. Tel: 01750 20096

Innerleithen is home to *St Ronan's Well*, which has a small museum telling the fascinating story of the well itself. Open Easter to October, daily from 2 p.m. to 5 p.m.

Peebles has two interesting museums. The *Tweeddale Museum and Picture Gallery* is at the Chambers Institute in the High Street. An unusual collection here, which includes the collection of William Chambers, the publisher who gave the building to Peebles in 1859. Look for the 'Secret Room' which contains an incredible plasterwork frieze copied from the Parthenon. Open all year, Monday to Friday; also Saturday and Sunday afternoon from Easter to October. Tel: 01721 720123

The Cornice Museum of Ornamental Plasterwork seems to continue a theme! A small but award-winning museum which creates an ornamental plasterer's workshop from around 1900. You can even try your hand at plasterwork – don't panic, they'll give you some wellies and a pinny! Find this museum at Innerleithen Road. Open all year, Monday to Friday from 10 a.m. to 12 noon and 2 p.m. to 4.30 p.m. A small charge in the form of a donation. Tel: 01721 720212

Selkirk has *Halliwell's House Museum and Robson Gallery* at Halliwell's Close, off Market Place. At one time the building was an ironmongers, and part of it has been reconstructed in museum form. Open April to October, Monday to Saturday from 10 a.m. to 5 p.m., Sunday from 2 p.m. to 4 p.m. In November and December it is open daily from 2 p.m. to 4 p.m. Tel: 01750 20096

Visit *Sir Walter Scott's Courtroom* also in Market Place. Exhibitions focus on Sir Walter Scott's time as Sheriff of Selkirk. Open from April to October, Monday to Saturday from 10 a.m. to 4 p.m. Tel: 01750 20096

CENTRAL, TAYSIDE AND FIFE

Clackmannanshire

Alloa Museum and Gallery has an excellent local history collection. Look out for their reconstruction of a Victorian Christmas – totally spooky! The bald guy in the ill-fitting suit is an alien! An excellent series of lectures (charges for these) and even a 'History and Heritage Week' annually, with events to spark a historical interest. The museum is at The Spiers Centre, 29 Primrose Street. Tel: 01259 213131

Dundee City

Barrack Street Museum has been a natural history centre since 1980. Great collection on wildlife and geology, including the skeleton of the famous Tay Whale. Open Monday from 11 a.m. to 5 p.m., Tuesday to Saturday from 10 a.m. to 5 p.m. Tel: 01382 432020

Broughty Castle Museum is at Castle Green in Broughty Ferry. The building was once a fifteenth-century fort. Lots of local history exhibits, alongside an interesting seashore life gallery. Wonderful views from the top of the castle. Open Monday from 11 a.m. to 1 p.m. and 2 p.m. to 5 p.m., Tuesday to Thursday and Saturday from 10 a.m. to 1 p.m. and 2 p.m. to 5 p.m.; also Sunday afternoon in summer. Tel: 01382 776121

Falkirk

Bo'ness is where you will find the *Kinneil Museum*, at Duchess Anne Cottages on the Kinneil Estate. This is an interpretative centre telling the story of the estate from Roman times to the present. Open April to September, Monday to Friday from 10 a.m. to 5 p.m. (with an hour for lunch); October to March, Saturday from 10 a.m. to 5 p.m. Tel: 01506 778530

Falkirk itself is the place for *Callendar House*, where you can experience life in an 1820s working kitchen and generally see the house at work through the ages. Get interactive with the computers, too. Open all year, Monday to Saturday from 10 a.m. to 5 p.m.; also Sunday from April to September, from 2 p.m. to 5 p.m. Tel: 01324 503770

Grangemouth Museum on Bo'ness Road occupies the top floor of the Grangemouth Library building. A local history museum, open all year, Monday to Saturday from 10 a.m. to 12.30 p.m. and 1.30 p.m. to 5 p.m. Tel: 01324 504699

Fife

Buckhaven Museum is on College Street above the library, and features a lively fishing display, as well as temporary exhibitions throughout the year. Opening hours are complicated, but are basically Monday to Friday afternoons, evenings too on Monday and Tuesday. On Saturday they open from 10 a.m. to 12.30 p.m but they are closed all day on Wednesday. Confused? Tel: 01592 712192

Burntisland Museum is above the library, at 102 High Street. The central exhibit is of Burntisland Edwardian Fair. Open weekdays from 10 a.m. to

1 p.m. and 2 p.m. to 5 p.m. (till 7 p.m. on Tuesday and Thursday). Tel: 01592 872781

Crail Museum and Heritage Centre is in an eighteenth-century house, and shows the history of the Royal Burgh of Crail. Lots about fishing. Open Easter; June to mid-September, Monday to Saturday from 10 a.m. to 1 p.m. and 2 p.m. to 5 p.m., Sunday from 2 p.m. to 5 p.m. Tel: 01333 450869

Dunfermline Museum and Small Gallery has local history collections, including a special linen damask collection. (For serious interior decor buffs.) Temporary displays, too. Open all year, Monday to Saturday from 11 a.m. to 5 p.m. Tel: 01383 721814

Dunfermline is also home to *Pittencrieff House Museum* which is in Pittencrieff Park. Local history and costumes. Look out for a model of the seven-foot Dunfermline 'Giant'! Open April to October, daily except Tuesday from 11 a.m. to 5 p.m. Tel: 01383 722935/721814

Dysart gives a home to the *John McDougall Stuart Museum*. The museum depicts the life of this seventeenth-century explorer. He was the first man to cross Australia from south to north via the central desert (at least, presumably he was the first white European guy to do so . . .) Open June to August, Monday to Saturday from 2 p.m. to 5 p.m. Tel: 01592 260732

Inverkeithing Museum is situated within a medieval friary on Queen Street. Spooky or what? Actually, local history with an industrial/social slant. Open all year, Wednesday to Sunday from 11 a.m. to 5 p.m. Tel: 01383 410495/721814

Kirkcaldy Museum and Art Gallery is in the War Memorial Gardens. Here they have local, as well as wider displays, and also events throughout the year. Open all year, Monday to Saturday from 10.30 a.m. to 5 p.m. Tel: 01592 260732

Newburgh has the *Laing Museum*, with its displays on Victorian Scotland, including that all-important self-help ethic. (The story of our times reflected indeed!) Open Easter; June to September, Monday to Saturday from 10 a.m. to 12.30 p.m. and 2.30 p.m. to 5 p.m., Sunday from 2.30 p.m. to 5 p.m. Tel: 01337 840223

St Andrews Museum is in Kilburn House, Kilburn Park. The exhibits, naturally, tell the tale of the town. Open April to September, daily from 10 a.m. to 5 p.m.; October to March, Monday to Friday from 10 a.m. to 4 p.m., Saturday and Sunday from 12.30 p.m. to 5 p.m. Tel: 01334 477706

Museum of St Andrews Preservation Trust on North Street has displays including a nineteenth-century grocer's shop. Open Easter; June to September from 2 p.m. to 5 p.m. Tel: 01334 477629

Perth and Kinross

Alyth Museum is on Commercial Street, Alyth, and features folk history and farming, with local material. Open May to September, Wednesday to Sunday from 1 p.m. to 5 p.m. Tel: 01738 632488

Auchterarder Heritage is an exhibition within Auchterarder Tourist Information Centre on the High Street. Open Monday to Friday from 9.30 a.m. to 1.30 p.m. Tel: 01764 663450

Blair Atholl has a small folk museum, the *Atholl Country Collection*, with displays of village and country life. Open Easter; end May to mid-October from 1.30 p.m. to 5.30 p.m. (from 9.30 a.m. in July, August and September). Come off the A9 for Blair Atholl and turn in at the White House. Tel: 01796 481232

Errol. Just one mile north-east of the village is *The Old Railway Station*, a restored country station from the 1920s with lots of historical items. A bit different too! Open Easter to end September, Sunday from 12 noon to 5 p.m. Tel: 01575 540222 (Errol Estates Office)

Kinross Museum is in the High Street. Displays centre on the local history of the area. Open May to September, Tuesday to Saturday from 1 p.m. to 5 p.m. Tel: 01738 632488 (Perth Museum and Art Gallery)

Perth Museum and Art Gallery covers the wildlife and, of course, the social history of the area. Catch the glass and silver exhibits. Look for the most awe-inspiring building in George Street. Open Monday to Saturday from 10 a.m. to 5 p.m. Tel: 01738 632488

Black Watch Regimental Museum is at Balhousie Castle, Hay Street, Perth, and is free, although a donation to museum funds is appreciated. Two hundred and fifty years of history of this famous regiment. Open Monday to Saturday from 10 a.m. to 4.30 p.m. (till 3.30 p.m. from October to April). Tel: 01738 621281 ext 8530

Stirling

Smith Art Gallery and Museum is on Dumbarton Road (see Galleries). Open Tuesday to Saturday from 10.30 a.m. to 5 p.m., Sunday from 2 p.m. to 5 p.m. Tel: 01786 471917

GRAMPIAN

Aberdeen City

Aberdeen Maritime Museum is in one of the oldest parts of the city, on Shiprow. A great collection of all things of the sea. Open Monday to Saturday from 10 a.m. to 5 p.m. Tel: 01224 585788

James Dun's House is on Schoolhill, almost directly opposite the Art Gallery. This is a fine, restored eighteenth-century town house, featuring special exhibitions and almost covering the museum/gallery borders. Open Monday to Saturday from 10 a.m. to 5 p.m. Tel: 01224 646333

Marischal Museum is at Marischal College, Broad Street. This place has some great exhibits, like an Egyptian mummy and shrunken heads. There are prehistoric Scots, too! Open Monday to Friday from 10 a.m. to 5 p.m., Sunday from 2 p.m. to 5 p.m. Tel: 01224 273131

Provost Skene's House is a gloriously renovated and refurbished town house. Look out for the Regency Parlour, beautiful plaster ceilings and the Painted Gallery. Open Monday to Saturday from 10 a.m. to 5 p.m. Find it at Guestrow, off Flourmill Lane. Tel: 01224 641086

The Tolbooth is Aberdeen's museum of civic history. Some nicely gruesome touches, as you would expect of a building that was a prison in the seventeenth century. Open April to September, Tuesday to Saturday from 10 a.m. to 5 p.m. (till 8 p.m. on Thursday), Sunday from 2 p.m. to 5 p.m. Tel: 01224 621167

The Zoology Museum can be found on Tillydrone Avenue. There are plenty of Scottish birds, as well as exhibits of all sizes. Open Monday to Friday from 9 a.m. to 5.30 p.m. Tel: 01224 272857

Aberdeenshire

Banchory Museum is in Bridge Street. It only opened in 1994 but has good local history displays, as well as travelling exhibitions that add a bit of variety. Open Easter to end June and October, weekends and public holidays from 11 a.m. to 1 p.m. and 2 p.m. to 5 p.m.; June to September, daily from 11 a.m. to 1 p.m. and 2 p.m. to 5 p.m. Tel: 01779 477778

Banff Museum is in the High Street, entry is via the library door, the museum is on the top two floors. Good bird displays, as well as lots of silver. Look out for the unique Boar's Head Carnyx. Open June to September, daily except Thursday from 2 p.m. to 5.15 p.m. Tel: 01779 477778

Fordyce Joiners Workshop and Visitor Centre, near Portsoy, gives an insight into the life of a rural, Victorian carpenter. Open Easter to end October, daily from 10 a.m. to 5 p.m.; in winter at weekends and in the evening by arrangement. Tel: 01779 477778

Garlogie Mill Power House Museum is a recent addition to the North-East of Scotland Museums' Service. The museum centres on the engine house of the former Garlogie Mill, which houses the only beam engine of its type in Scotland to have survived intact in its original situation. Displays on the workings of the mill and an audio-visual presentation complete the experience. Open Thursday to Monday from 12.30 p.m. to 5 p.m. Garlogie is at Skene, beside the junction of the B9119 and B9125. Call 01779 477778 for details.

Huntly Brander Museum is in the Square at Huntly. There are various displays, mainly on local history. Open all year, Tuesday to Saturday from 10 a.m. to 12 noon and 2 p.m. to 4 p.m. Tel: 01779 477778

Inverurie Musuem is on the first floor of the library, a local history museum with occasional travelling exhibitions. Open all year, weekdays except Wednesday from 2 p.m. to 5 p.m., Saturday from 10 a.m. to 1 p.m. and 2 p.m. to 4 p.m.

Maud Old Station Museum is at the old railway station. Plenty of memorabilia for railway fans. Tel: 01779 477778

Peterhead. The *Arbuthnot Museum*, on St Peter Street, is also the headquarters of the local museums' service, and very good they are too! This museum was founded in 1850 and is based on the collections of Adam Arbuthnot. An excellent maritime section, too. Open all year, Monday to Saturday from 10.30 a.m. to 1.30 p.m. and 2.30 p.m. to 5 p.m. (till 1 p.m. on Wednesday). Tel: 01779 477778

Sandhaven Meal Mill Visitor Centre shows off 200 years of meal-milling history. The last miller retired in 1981. You can gawp at the working model, or take a guided tour. You will find the Meal Mill opposite Sandhaven harbour, on the left as you enter the village from Fraserburgh on the B9301. Open May to end September, weekends from 2 p.m. to 4.30 p.m. Tel: 01771 622857

Stonehaven Tolbooth Museum is at the Harbour, on the quay. The maritime collection has lots of fishing boat models and there are some very good reconstructed rooms too (a coopers' workshop and Victorian sitting-room). Open June to end September, Monday and Thursday to Saturday from 10 a.m. to 12 noon and 2 p.m. to 5 p.m.; on Wednesday and Sunday 2 p.m. to 5 p.m. Tel: 01779 477778

Angus

Arbroath Museum is actually situated in the signal tower of the Bell Rock Lighthouse, which was built by the grandfather of Robert Louis Stevenson. Naturally the museum has great exhibits relating to the lighthouse itself, alongside excellent local history material. As you would expect, this quaint museum is strong on fish. You can even *smell* Arbroath smokies in one display! Open all year, Monday to Saturday from 10 a.m. to 5 p.m.; also Sunday in July and August, from 2 p.m. to 5 p.m. Tel: 01241 875598

   St Vigean's Museum is north of the town centre, a cottage museum containing some good Pictish gravestones. Tel: 01241 872433

Brechin Museum is fairly small, and situated within the library in St Ninian's Square, with a strong local history collection. Tel: 01356 622687

Forfar houses the *Meffan Museum* inside the Meffan Institute on the West High Street. This exciting museum has some fine Pictish stones and an unusual 'walk-through-street' exhibit. Look out for the witch-burning re-enactment, which is sure to put the fear of God into the kids. The Meffan Gallery is under the same roof, which makes this a great rainy afternoon spot. Tel: 01307 464123

Montrose Museum is on Panmure Place. This is one of Scotland's oldest museums, and has some particularly effective displays around the Baltic-made ships that formed the backbone of the port's growth. Watch out for more exciting Pictish stones, an art gallery and a wildlife gallery – with lots of stuffed stuff. What beady eyes they have! Tel: 01674 673232

RFC/RAF Montrose Museum is at Waldron Road. Open Sunday only, April and end October, from 11 a.m. to 5 p.m. For details call Montrose Museum. Tel: 01674 673107

Also in the care of Montrose Museum is the *William Lamb Memorial Studio* in Market Street. Open July to mid-September, Tuesday to Sunday from 2 p.m. to 5 p.m. Once again, if in doubt contact Montrose Museum.

For a museum with a real difference, visit the *Sunnyside Museum* at Sunnyside Royal Hospital, Montrose. The exhibits centre on psychiatric care! Open Easter to end September, Wednesday from 2 p.m. to 3 p.m. Tel: 01674 830361

THE HIGHLANDS

Moray

Dufftown Museum is in the Clock Tower on the Main Square. A collection of local interest, with some unusual whisky industry pieces.

Elgin Museum has some Pictish carvings, dinosaur footprints and bones of an ancient inhabitant of Moray, to say the least! Open Monday to Friday from 10 a.m. to 5 p.m., Saturday from 11 a.m. to 4 p.m. and Sunday from 2 p.m. to 5 p.m. Find it all in the High Street. Tel: 01343 543675

Fochabers Folk Museum is in the old Pringle Church in the village High Street. Look out for their collection of horse-drawn vehicles, and the local history material, too. An antiques shop – Pringles Antiques – is in the same building. Open all year, from 9.30 a.m. to 1 p.m. and 2 p.m. to 5.30 p.m.

Forres has the *Falconer Museum*, in Tolbooth Street. Good local history material, including geological items. Look out for Roy Williamson's instruments (he of Corries fame). Open April and May, from 10.30 a.m. to 12.30 p.m. and 1.30 p.m. to 4 p.m.; May to September opening half an hour earlier and later (Monday to Saturday) and Sunday from 12 noon to 5 p.m. In winter they open from 10 a.m. to 5 p.m., Monday to Saturday. Confused? Tel: 01309 673701

Lossiemouth has a *Fishery and Community Museum* on Pitgaveny Street.

Great scale models of fishing boats, as well as a reconstruction of James Ramsay MacDonald's study. (The first British Labour Prime Minister was born nearby at Seatown.) Tel: 01343 813772

Tomintoul Museum is in the Square. Some good reconstructions to make you glad you're a twentieth-century boy (or girl). Local interest temporary exhibitions in the summer, too.

Highland Heartlands

Fort William is the home of the *West Highland Museum*, which houses several thousand artefacts illustrating West Highland life. Excellent Jacobite collections. Find it at Cameron Square. Tel: 01397 702169

Ionad Nibheis Visitor Centre is in Glen Nevis, and has an exhibition and audio-visual diplay on the natural history and social history of Glen Nevis, and Ben Nevis. Tel: 01397 700774/01397 705922

Inverness Museum and Art Gallery has wonderful exhibits on the natural history of the Highlands. There are special events and even performances during the year. Open all year, Monday to Saturday from 9 a.m. to 5 p.m. Find the museum at Castle Wynd – very central. Tel: 01463 237114

Kingussie is in a wild bit of the country. You won't even be able to get indoors at the open-air *Highland Folk Museum* on Duke Street. Get an insight with a tableau, that's my motto. Events in summer. Open all year. Tel: 01540 661307

Nairn Museum is in Viewfield House, off King Street. This is an outstanding example of a local community museum, with a rich and varied collection on display. Open June to September, Monday to Saturday from 10 a.m. to 4.30 p.m. Tel: 01667 456798

Invernairn Mill Visitor Centre is just east of Nairn on the main A96. This is a heritage museum and exhibition centre, with a working millwheel. Open all year, closed on Monday from October to April. Tel: 01667 455273

Newtonmore houses the *Clan MacPherson Museum*. If you are one of them, this is for you. If you're not, well, adopt one. In the Main Street, open May to September only. Tel: 01540 673332

The Northern Highlands

Dunbeath Heritage Centre has a great exhibition on Caithness, including an audio-visual programme. Good archives and they are even willing to help you trace your ancestors (providing, of course, they actually came from the area!). Tel: 01593 731233

Dunnet Bay Pavilion is an ever-changing local natural history exhibition. Close to the beautiful Dunnet Head. Open April to September, Tuesday to Friday from 2 p.m. to 5 p.m., weekends from 2 p.m. to 6 p.m. Tel: 01847 821531

John o' Groats is, naturally, the place to find the *Last House in Scotland*. They actually have a free museum here, on the history of John o' Groats and the surrounding area. Tel: 01955 611250

Latheron is the home of Clan Gunn. Also the home of the *Clan Gunn Heritage Centre*. A member of the clan even discovered America. Open June to September, Monday to Saturday from 11 a.m. to 5 p.m.; also Sunday afternoon in July and August.

Spittal, near Thurso, has the interesting *Archie Sinclair Fossil Centre*, in Spittal Village Hall. Exhibitions on local and natural history, particularly fossils. Tel: 01847 841266 or 01955 621257

ISLANDS

The Western Isles

BARRA
Look for the *Craigston Museum,* a thatched cottage museum.

BENBECULA
Here you will find the second museum of the *Museum nan Eilean* (see Stornoway, Lewis below). This 'branch' was set up in 1988 in *Sgoil Lionacleit*, a six-year-old community school. On the B892. Ring the Stornoway number for details.

HARRIS
You might come across the *South Harris Historical Society* which has an exhibition on local and natural history at Leverburgh.

LEWIS
Shawbost School Museum is on the A858, 19 miles north-west of Stornoway. This museum shows life the way it was on Lewis. Open April to November from 10 a.m. to 6 p.m. Donations are welcome. Tel: 01851 710213

Stornoway is home to the *Museum Nan Eilean.* You will find it on Francis Street. The museum has all kinds of things relating to the archaeology, history and social history of the Western Isles. Open Monday to Saturday from 10 a.m. to 1 p.m. and 2 p.m. to 5 p.m. until the end of August, then Monday to Friday only from September. Tel: 01851 703773

NORTH UIST
The *Taigh Chearsabhagh Museum and Arts Centre* is in Lochmaddy. Exhibitions feature local and natural history and arts. They also have a café.

SOUTH UIST

Here you might find the *Kildonan Museum*, which has local history exhibitions. It also has a tea-room. Let me know about it.

Orkney

Museums. There are a number of museums on the islands, but many of them carry an admission charge! They include *Stromness Museum*, *The Smiddy Museum* and the *Wireless Museum* in Kirkwall.

Kirkwall has *Tankerness House Museum and Gardens*, which occupies one of Scotland's finest town houses. Great archaeology material. Open all year, Monday to Saturday; also Sunday afternoon from May to September. Free admission from October to March!

GALLERIES

Looking around you is the key to enjoying this book and enjoying your leisure time, whether it is in your own home town, or visiting a new area. This whole section, purely about galleries, more or less takes it for granted that you, dear reader, are one of the converted. You are the kind of person who wants to experience life to the full, to have images and memories and thoughts and words filling your waking hours. You are one of the converted who can look at the new as well as the old, and take away real pleasure. This is surely what the gallery experience is about. Some of the galleries listed here are new, specialising in modern and contemporary Scottish art. There are other galleries which have older paintings and sculpture, masterpieces and treasures that are valuable parts of Scotland's great artistic heritage. All of these are a sheer joy to behold!

There are also a number of superb craftspeople working in Scotland, who have workshops and studios all over the country. For space reasons alone these have not made it into the book, perhaps they might next time. If there are any others that you think should be included please write and tell me, and let me know why and what you enjoyed most.

How difficult it is to talk about galleries, let alone the experience of appreciating art! My favourite? The Fruitmarket Gallery in Edinburgh is always a challenge, and I have loved it ever since I first came to the city.

Wherever *you* choose, relax and take a deep breath; you just breathed in Art.

THE WEST

Argyll and Bute

Tighnabruaich (pronounced Tie-na-broo-ich) has the *Kyles-Side Painting Centre*. There is a gallery, studio and an Art Club. Open all year, Wednesday to Saturday from 10 a.m. to 4 p.m.; also Monday in July and August and Tuesday from May to October. Tel: Mrs J. Marshall 01700 811716/811681

East Ayrshire

Kilmarnock has a gallery at the *Dick Institute*. Go and see their exhibitions by Scottish painters in particular. Open April to September. As prior notice is required to view the gallery, give them a call. Tel: 01563 526401

East Dunbartonshire

Milngavie has the *Lillie Art Gallery* in Station Road, which exhibits many local artists. Tel: 0141 943 3247

City of Glasgow

Aldessan Gallery and Batik Studio can be found at Clachan of Campsie. This is a collection of craft workshops which are open for public viewing. Open May to September, Monday to Friday from 11 a.m. to 5.30 p.m., weekends from 11 a.m. to 8 p.m.; in winter, daily from 11 a.m. to 5 p.m. Tel: 01360 313049

The Annan Gallery is at 164 Woodlands Road in the city. Paintings and prints here are mostly traditional. Lots of photos, too. Open Monday to Friday from 10 a.m. to 5 p.m., Saturday from 10 a.m. to 12.30 p.m. Tel: 0141 332 0028

The Burrell Collection. If you only have time to visit one place whilst in Glasgow, make it the Burrell. This gallery has an exquisite collection, not only of paintings, but also of *objets d'art* from all over the world. Look out for the Impressionist works. A proportion of the collection changes from time to time. It is a must! Open Monday to Saturday from 10 a.m. to 5 p.m., Sunday from 11 a.m. to 5 p.m. Get to the Burrell at Pollok Country Park, 2060 Pollokshaws Road. Tel: 0141 649 7151

Centre for Contemporary Arts (CCA) is at 350 Sauchiehall Street, and has a changing programme of free exhibitions in two galleries. Often controversial, usually modern, it is always worth seeing what's on show at the CCA. Great café-bar too. Open Monday to Saturday from 11 a.m. to 6 p.m., Sunday from 12 noon to 5 p.m. Tel: 0141 332 7521

Collins Gallery is at the University of Strathclyde at 22 Richmond Street. They have 12 exhibitions here a year, from fine art to photography and design. Usually unusual. Open Monday to Friday from 10 a.m. to 5 p.m., Saturday from 12 noon to 4 p.m. Tel: 0141 552 4400

Compass Gallery is at 178 West Regent Street. This is the oldest established contemporary gallery in the west of Scotland. Even their window display is to die for. They have discovered some of Britain's most successful artists, too! Open Monday to Saturday from 10 a.m. to 5.30 p.m. Tel: 0141 221 6370

Fringe Gallery Castlemilk might seem a bit out of the way, as it is some miles from the centre of town. In many ways that is the point. Visit it and you will have experienced some of the real Glasgow, just on the way there. Castlemilk is an area with a reputation for real innovation in the arts, community arts, and the arts with a capital A. Find the gallery at Castlemilk Shopping Centre, 18 Castlemilk Arcade, Castlemilk. Open Monday to Saturday from 10 a.m. to 5 p.m. Tel: 0141 634 2603

Gallery of Modern Art (GOMA) at Queen Street, offers four floors of challenging material! Most material is by living artists. Open Monday to Saturday from 10 a.m. to 5 p.m., Sunday from 11 a.m. to 5 p.m. Tel: 0141 331 1854

Glasgow Print Studio and the Original Print Shop are at 22 and 25 King Street. They have monthly exhibitions of contemporary material, international and Scottish. At the workshop you can see how prints are made. Open Monday to Saturday from 10 a.m. to 5.30 p.m. Tel: 0141 552 0704

Cyril Gerber Fine Art is a cosy basement gallery in the centre of town, specialising in British, mainly Scottish, nineteenth- and twentieth-century work. Open Monday to Saturday from 9.30 a.m. to 5.30 p.m. Tel: 0141 221 3095/0141 204 0276

The Hunterian Art Gallery is at 82 Hillhead Street. A real variety of works, from Rembrandt to Whistler, together with the recently refurbished Mackintosh House. Open Monday to Saturday from 9.30 a.m. to 5 p.m. Tel: 0141 330 5431

Kelvingrove Art Gallery and Museum are on Argyle Street, by Kelvingrove Park. An outstanding collection and selection of art. There is also a good café and shop. Open Monday to Saturday from 10 a.m. to 5 p.m., Sunday from 11 a.m. to 5 p.m. Tel: 0141 287 2000

St Mungo Museum of Religious Life and Art is an unusual gallery. Their most splendid painting is certainly Salvador Dali's *Christ of St John of the Cross* (very controversial in its time). St Mungo's is at 2 Castle Street. Open Monday

137

to Saturday from 10 a.m. to 5 p.m., Sunday from 11 a.m. to 5 p.m. Tel: 0141 553 2557

Street Level is at 26 King Street. This gallery has a reputation for showcasing photography, mixed media, and other forms of unusual art. Open Tuesday to Saturday from 10 a.m. to 5.30 p.m. Tel: 0141 552 2151

Tramway is an amazing venue – it was once an enormous tram depot, and now has a range of performance spaces and a café, as well as a large gallery space. Expect to be challenged. A lot of work that has been on display here has caused dismay amongst the city's 'worthies'! (The same goes for the CCA.) Open Wednesday to Sunday from 12 noon to 6 p.m. Tel: 0141 422 2023

Transmission Gallery is at 28 King Street, just along from Street Level. New material, usually by local artists, always on the verge of being difficult! (In other words, excellent.) Open Tuesday to Saturday from 11 a.m. to 5 p.m. Tel: 0141 552 4813

Inverclyde

Greenock has the *McLean Museum and Art Gallery* on Kelly Street. This beautifully restored building has many examples of Scottish painting. Even a café. Open all year, Monday to Saturday from 10 a.m. to 5 p.m. Tel: 01475 723741

North Ayrshire

Irvine. The *Glasgow Vennel Museum*, in the old part of the town, has temporary art exhibitions throughout the year. Call for details at the time. Tel: 01294 275059

North Lanarkshire

Airdrie Arts Centre has temporary art exhibitions. For opening hours and news of what is on currently, give them a call. Tel: 01236 755436

Bellshill Cultural Centre at John Street, Bellshill, is a similar type of venue. It is a multi-purpose place, with exhibitions and a café for starters. Ring to see what's going on. Tel: 01698 841831

Renfrewshire

Lochwinnoch is where you'll find *The Bluebird Gallery*. This could be described as an 'intimate' gallery. Changing exhibitions and crafts, too, on sale; even a tea-room. Open daily from 10.15 a.m. to 5 p.m.; closed Monday in winter. Tel: 01505 842225

Paisley is the home of *Paisley Museum and Art Galleries*, in the High Street. Visit the Paisley shawls as well as the gallery. Open all year, Monday to Saturday from 10 a.m. to 5 p.m. Tel: 0141 889 3151

Paisley Arts Centre is in a renovated kirk on New Streeet. Here the pictures jostle with the café. Open from 10 a.m. till pretty late, as the venue is chiefly a theatre. Tel: 0141 887 1010

South Ayrshire

Ayr has the *Maclaurin Art Gallery*, at Rozelle Park, Monument Road, Alloway. The gallery has changing exhibitions all year round. Tel: 01292 445447

Girvan. The *McKechnie Institute* doubles as an arts centre and has displays by local artists. Tel: 014654 713643

South Lanarkshire

Strathaven has the *Town Mill Arts Centre* at Stonehouse Road. This is a former mill, renovated as an arts centre. You can arrange a guided tour of the mill if there aren't any art exhibitions on when you visit. Tel: 01357 540339

THE EAST

East Lothian

Stenton, near Dunbar, is the unlikely venue for the *Macaulay Gallery*. This gallery has an ongoing programme of temporary exhibitions, often by women. Open Monday, Tuesday, Friday and Saturday from 12 noon to 5 p.m., Sunday from 12.30 p.m. to 5 p.m. Tel: 01368 850256

City of Edinburgh

Bourne Fine Art is an established gallery with a record of important and enjoyable exhibitions. Find them at 6 Dundas Street. Open Monday to Friday from 10 a.m. to 6 p.m., Saturday from 10 a.m. to 1 p.m. Tel: 0131 557 4050

Calton Gallery is another one in an expensive part of the town. Particularly good for fine Scottish art. Open Monday to Friday from 10 a.m. to 6 p.m., Saturday from 10 a.m. to 1 p.m. Find the gallery at 10 Royal Terrace. Tel: 0131 556 1010

City Art Centre has at least two gallery spaces. Occasionally they have a big exhibition – recently they had a Star Trek one – for which there is an admission charge. Mostly though, their exhibitions are free, and the gallery is airy and light with a good café. The City Art Centre is at 2 Market Street, near Waverley Station. Open Monday to Saturday from 10 a.m. to 5 p.m. Tel: 0131 529 3993

Collective Gallery is on Cockburn Street and, as its name implies, is run by an artists' co-operative. A diverse range of art. Open Tuesday to Saturday from 11 a.m. to 5 p.m. Tel: 0131 220 1260

Contact Gallery specialises in work by Scottish artists and by local artists associated with the gallery and workshops held at the centre. They are at Grindlay Court Centre, Grindlay Street Lane, near the Lyceum Theatre. Open Monday to Thursday from 10 a.m. to 4 p.m., Friday from 10 a.m. to 2.30 p.m. Tel: 0131 221 0721

Dundas Street Gallery is a small gallery, with exhibitions usually by local artists. Open Monday to Friday from 10 a.m. to 6 p.m., Saturday from 10 a.m. to 1 p.m. Tel: 0131 558 9363

The Dunedin Gallery is at 6 Hillside Street and features Scottish work, including sculpture. Open Tuesday to Friday from 11 a.m. to 6 p.m., Saturday from 11 a.m. to 4.30 p.m. Tel: 0131 557 3753

The Edinburgh Gallery is at 18a Dundas Street, and is another small selling gallery with some good material. Open Monday to Friday from 11 a.m. to 5 p.m., Saturday from 10 a.m. to 1 p.m. Tel: 0131 557 5227

Edinburgh Printmakers Workshop is an exciting little gallery on Union Street. Open Tuesday to Saturday from 10 a.m. to 6 p.m. Tel: 0131 557 2479

The Firth Gallery is at 35 William Street, a selling gallery specialising in Scottish work. Open Monday to Friday from 11 a.m. to 5 p.m., Saturday from 11 a.m. to 4 p.m. Tel: 0131 225 2196

The Fruitmarket Gallery is opposite the City Art Centre on Market Street. (You could easily spend an arty afternoon down here!) This is my favourite of all the Edinburgh galleries. A huge variety of often challenging exhibitions, with a contemporary slant. Also a trendy café and bookshop. Open Tuesday to Saturday from 10.30 a.m. to 5.30 p.m., Sunday from noon to 5 p.m. Tel: 0131 225 2383

Hanover Fine Arts is another one in the New Town area, at 22a Dundas Street (what a street this is for small selling galleries). Open Monday to Friday from 10.30 a.m. to 6 p.m., Saturday from 10 a.m. to 4 p.m. Tel: 0131 556 2181

Inverleith House – was once the Gallery of Modern Art. It sits on a hill in the Royal Botanic Garden, and the statues at the pond in front seem to beckon you in. Temporary, changing exhibitions nowadays, still with the accent on the contemporary. Open daily from 10 a.m. to 5 p.m. Tel: 0131 556 8921

Judith Glue Gallery is on the High Street, right beside the Scandic Crown Hotel. The gallery is a new 'craft-based' gallery, within a succesful little shop complex. Open Monday to Saturday from 9.30 a.m. to 6 p.m., Sunday from 10 a.m. to 6 p.m. Tel: 0131 556 5443

Kingfisher Gallery is at 5 Northumberland Street Lane NW, and I bet you have difficulty finding it! Another gallery in the golden triangle of the New Town. Open Tuesday to Saturday from 11 a.m. to 4.20 p.m. Tel: 0131 557 5454

The Leith Gallery is at 65 The Shore, Leith. Here you can see Scottish contemporary art in a very up-and-coming-young-ad-agency-man area. (Less up-and-coming for many who have lived, or dare I say worked, here for many years.) Tel: 0131 553 5255

The National Gallery of Scotland is *the* gallery. Large rooms, high ceilings, vast canvases, famous international names. Awe-inspiring. Sometimes they have 'paid for' exhibitions too. If you only have time to do one gallery, you probably ought to make it this one. Open Monday to Saturday from 10 a.m. to 5 p.m., Sunday from 2 p.m. to 5 p.m. The gallery is at the foot of the Mound – yes, the enormous one, that's it. Tel: 0131 556 8921

National Library of Scotland seems a peculiar thing to include here, but they do have a fairly big exhibition space, often dedicated to art. The library is on George IV Bridge, you can't miss it! Open Monday to Saturday from 10 a.m. to 5 p.m., Sunday from 2 p.m. to 5 p.m. Tel: 0131 226 4531

The Open Eye Gallery is at 75–79 Cumberland Street. In this part of town you will trip over a gallery wherever you go. Everything here, from paintings to jewellery, in a changing programme. Open Monday to Friday from 10 a.m. to 6 p.m., Saturday from 10 a.m. to 4 p.m. Tel: 0131 557 1020

The Portfolio Gallery is an established gallery with a record of challenging photographic exhibitions. Another one of my own favourites. Find it at 43 Candlemaker Row. Open Tuesday to Saturday from 12 noon to 5.30 p.m. Tel: 0131 220 1911

Rogues Gallery is at 58 St Stephen Street. This is a good street for browsing anyway, so go and spend some time in the second-hand shops before checking out the gallery's cartoons. (They specialise in caricatures/cartoons, anything irreverent.) Open Tuesday to Saturday from 11 a.m. to 6 p.m. Tel: 0131 225 5558

Royal Museum of Scotland in Chambers Street has art exhibitions, usually going alongside a theme that they are concentrating on with a temporary exhibition. Tel: 0131 225 7534

Royal Overseas League. I know it seems unlikely, but there is a gallery in there! The gallery is called the 'Landings Gallery' and it has exhibitions from time to time through the year. Call them for details. Find the League at 100 Princes Street. Tel: 0131 225 1501

The Scottish Gallery is at 16 Dundas Street. Handy area for another ten galleries too! Revolving exhibitions, everything from silverwork to fine art. Open Monday to Friday from 10 a.m. to 6 p.m., Saturday from 10 a.m. to 4 p.m. Tel: 0131 558 1200

Scottish National Gallery of Modern Art is at Belford Road, just outside the city centre. This is an awe-inspiring gallery, from the Moore on the lawn to the café in the basement. They have some paying exhibitions too. Open Monday to Saturday from 10 a.m. to 5 p.m., Sunday from 2 p.m. to 5 p.m. Tel: 0131 556 8921

Scottish National Portrait Gallery is on Queen Street in a beautiful pink sandstone building. There are some wonderful portraits here; it is worth visiting just to see the Scottish history frieze around the walls of the foyer and gallery of the stairs. A very nice café too. Open Monday to Saturday from 10 a.m. to 5 p.m., Sunday from 2 p.m. to 5 p.m. Tel: 0131 556 8921

Stills Gallery is on Cockburn Street, and specialises in photographic art. Excellent. Open Tuesday to Friday from 11 a.m. to 6 p.m., Saturday from 11a.m. to 5 p.m. Tel: 0131 225 9876

Talbot Rice Gallery is up at Edinburgh University, at the corner of the quad of the Old College. A real variety of temporary exhibitions are held here. It is well worth investigating. Open Tuesday to Saturday from 10 a.m. to 5 p.m. Tel: 0131 650 2211

The Torrance Gallery is another at Dundas Street, at 29b this time. Can you tell them all apart? Local artists, with an annual exhibition programme. Open Monday to Friday from 11 a.m. to 6 p.m., Saturday from 10.30 a.m. to 4 p.m. Tel: 0131 556 6366

WASPS Gallery – here you are guaranteed to find new and innovative work. WASPS is an artists' co-operative, and this is where they showcase their art. Find it at Patriothall, off Hamilton Place in Stockbridge. Open daily from 12 noon to 6 p.m. Tel: 0131 225 1289

West Lothian

Linlithgow has *The Line Gallery*, at 222a High Street. Modern art, from overseas as well as closer to home. They take a few risks, so it is worth a visit if you are in Linlithgow. Open Monday to Saturday from 10 a.m. to 6 p.m., Sunday from 12 noon to 4 p.m.; closed Wednesday. Tel: 01506 670268

THE BORDERS

Dumfries and Galloway

Dumfries has the *Gracefield Arts Centre* with its collection of over 400 paintings and regular exhibitions by local artists. Tel: 01387 262084

Kirkcudbright is the place to visit the *Waterfront Workshop and Gallery*. Here you can even watch a local sculptor and woodcarver at work. Tel: 01557 331649

Palnackie, near Dalbeattie, is the place for the truly alternative. Go into the *North Glen Gallery* to see an American glass-blowing wizard. He may engage you in discussion whilst he gives you a demonstration, be prepared to get philosophical! Tel: 01556 600200

Scottish Borders

Broughton Gallery in Broughton, ten miles west of Peebles on the A701, is in a tower house designed by Basil Spence. They sell and show contemporary work. Open 24 March to 15 October, then 17 November to 22 December, daily except Wednesday from 10.30 a.m. to 6 p.m. Tel: 01899 830234

Galashiels has the *Old Gala House and Christopher Boyd Gallery*, which is run by the Museum Service. They have occasional art exhibitions here too. Tel: 01750 20096

Hawick has the *Scott Gallery* at the Hawick Museum in Wilton Lodge Park. Interesting exhibitions. Tel: 01750 20096 (Museums Service)

Jedburgh has the small *Mainhill Gallery* at Ancrum, just up the A68. Open Monday to Friday from 11 a.m. to 5.30 p.m., Saturday and Sunday from 10 a.m. to 4 p.m. Call in advance to check whether there is an exhibition on. Tel: 01835 830518

Melrose has the *Martin Gallery*, which is open all year daily from 10 a.m. to 6 p.m. It has a permanent exhibition of Border landscapes by John F. Martin. Tel: 01896 822739
   There is also the *Melrose Station Artists Studio and Gallery* at Palma Place, which displays the work of local artists and craftspeople. Open all year, daily from 10 a.m. to 5 p.m. Tel: 01896 823631

Peebles is where you will find *Tweeddale Museum and Picture Gallery*, at the Chambers Institute in the High Street. Take in the plasterwork frieze too. Open all year weekdays; also Saturday and Sunday afternoon from Easter to October. Tel: 01721 720123

Selkirk is home to the *Halliwell's House Museum* which often has art on show. Tel: 01750 20096

St Abbs, on the coast ten miles north of Berwick-upon-Tweed, has the *Kittiwake Gallery* with changing local exhibitions. Open Monday to Friday from 12 noon to 4 p.m.; daily in summer from 10 a.m. to 6 p.m. Tel: 018907 71504

Stichill Smithy Gallery is at Ednam Road, Stichill, on the B6364 north of Kelso. This gallery is set in the shoeing end of an old smithy! Changing

143

exhibitions. Open Easter; July to end August. During other months open only at weekends. Tel: 01573 470346

CENTRAL, TAYSIDE AND FIFE

Clackmannanshire

Alloa Museum and Gallery has art by local and Scottish artists. Find the gallery at The Speirs Centre, 29 Primrose Street. Tel: 01259 213131

Dundee City

McManus Galleries are in Albert Square. The art gallery is on the first floor (above the museum), with a further exhibition gallery and costume gallery on the second floor. Look particularly for the Victoria Gallery, with works by Rossetti, McTaggart and Millais. Open Monday from 11 a.m. to 5 p.m., Tuesday to Saturday from 10 a.m. to 5 p.m. Tel: 01382 432020

Seagate Gallery and Printmakers Workshop is also worth a visit. They have a broad range of exhibits, from printmaking and photography to performance art and video! Find the gallery at 36–40 Seagate. Open from Tuesday to Saturday from 10 a.m. to 5 p.m. Tel: 01382 226331

Fife

Dunfermline Museum and Small Gallery hosts temporary displays on a variety of subjects, including art, craft and photography. Open all year, Monday to Saturday from 11 a.m. to 5 p.m. Tel: 01383 721814

Dunfermline is also home to *Pittencrieff House Museum* which is in Pittencrieff Park. Art exhibitions are held here. Open April to October daily except Tuesday, from 11 a.m. to 5 p.m. Tel: 01383 722935/721814

Kirkcaldy Museum and Art Gallery is in the War Memorial Gardens. It has a superb collection of Scottish paintings, as well as temporary exhibitions. Open all year, Monday to Saturday from 10.30 a.m. to 5 p.m. Tel: 01592 260732

Leven is the venue for *Silverburn Arts and Craft Centre*, which is on the Silverburn Estate. Local crafts, from knitwear to wood-turning. Open May to September, Saturday and Sunday from 1 p.m. to 5 p.m.; also Wednesday in July and August, from 1 p.m. to 5 p.m.

Markinch has the *Balbirnie Craft Centre* at Balbirnie Park. This incorporates workshops of a furniture-maker, a glass-blower, a jewellery-maker, a leather-worker and a gallery of watercolours. Open daily. Contact the gallery for more details. Tel: 01592 756016

Perth and Kinross

Perth Museum and Art Gallery has some great art, as well as interesting glass and silver exhibits in the museum. In the biggest-looking building in George Street. Open Monday to Saturday from 10 a.m. to 5 p.m. Tel: 01738 632488

The Fergusson Gallery is in a stunning round building at Marshall Place and houses a large number of works by J.D. Fergusson himself (Impressionist/post-Impressionist influence/era). Open Monday to Saturday from 10 a.m. to 5 p.m. Tel: 01738 441944

Stirling

Aberfoyle. The *Green Gallery* is in the Main Street, and often features wildlife and nature exhibitions. Tel: 01877 382873

Stirling. The *Smith Art Gallery and Museum* has an excellent record for staging unusual temporary exhibitions throughout the year. The Smith is in an imposing building on Dumbarton Road, close to the city centre. Open Tuesday to Saturday from 10.30 a.m. to 5 p.m., Sunday from 2 p.m. to 5 p.m. They also have occasional events here. Tel: 01786 471917

The *MacRobert Arts Centre* at the University of Stirling has a tremendous variety of exhibitions during the year. Tel: 01786 467163

GRAMPIAN

Aberdeen City

Aberdeen Art Gallery is a large municipal gallery with a brilliant series of high-quality touring exhibitions, and excellent facilities too. Find the gallery on Schoolhill. Open Monday to Saturday from 10 a.m. to 5 p.m. (till 8 p.m. on Thursday), Sunday from 2 p.m. to 5 p.m.

Gallery Heinzel exhibits paintings and drawings by European artists. The gallery is in Spa Street. Tel: 01224 625629

Peacock Printmakers have a reputation that has spread far and wide. They sometimes display at the large municipal gallery. Find Peacock Printmakers at 21 Castle Street. Tel: 01224 639539

Aberdeenshire

Banff has the unusual *Colleonard Sculpture Garden and Gallery* on Sandyhill Road, with an abstract figurative selection in a five-acre garden. Open March to September, from 9 a.m. to 7 p.m. Tel: 01261 818284

Angus

Forfar is the place for the *Meffan Institute*, on West High Street. A good local gallery, with a museum attached for full value! Tel: 01307 464123

Montrose Museum and Art Gallery is on Panmure Place. A lively little gallery space. Open Monday to Saturday from 10 a.m. to 5 p.m. Tel: 01674 673232
  The Stables Art Centre might need a call before you go, to see what they have currently on display. It is at 113 High Street. Tel: 01674 677223

THE HIGHLANDS

Moray

Buckie has the *Peter Anson Gallery* at Town House West. The gallery is beside the library in Cluny Place. Watercolours of scenes around Buckie by a local artist. Tel: 01309 673701
  Also try the *Baranoff Studio and Gallery* at 6 Seafield Street, Cullen, near Buckie. Open May to October, Monday to Saturday from 10 a.m. to 5 p.m., Sunday from 2 p.m. to 5 p.m.; in winter closed Wednesday afternoon and Sunday. Tel: 01542 841410

Highland Heartlands

Inverness Museum and Art Gallery is well worth a visit. There are special events and even performances during the year. Open all year, Monday to Saturday from 9 a.m. to 5 p.m. Find the gallery at Castle Wynd. Tel: 01463 237114

The Highland Printmakers Workshop is beside the River Ness in the centre of Inverness, and you should pop in to see whether you can view someone at work. They run printmaking courses, too, and have some beautiful things on sale.

The Northern Highlands

Durness has a *Printmakers Gallery* which you will find at 15 Balnakeil Craft Village, Durness. Bold and colourful prints by artist-printmaker Ishbel MacDonald. Open April to October, Monday to Saturday from 10 a.m. to 6 p.m. The other workshops in the 'craft village' may be worth exploring. Tel: 01971 511277

Elphin has the *Swallow Gallery* on Church Brae. In a renovated croft house, spot the resident artist. Open April to September, Monday to Saturday from 2 p.m. to 4 p.m. Tel: 01854 666247

Lochinver has *The Clashmore Gallery*, at Clashmore, Stoer. Stoer is one of the villages to the north of Lochinver on the coast road. The artist (who also takes commissions) has drawings and prints of local scenery, wildlife and crofting. Open May to September.

Lybster Gallery is at Quatre Bras, Lybster, and has changing displays by northern Scottish artists. Tel: 01593 721325

Lyth has an *Arts Centre*, which functions as a gallery from 1 July to 31 August. Mostly contemporary fine art, with a variety of temporary exhibitions, too. Tel: 01955 641270

Thurso has the *Swanson Art Gallery* at Thurso Library, Davidson's Lane. A changing programme of visual arts from local and Highland-wide artists. Open all year. Tel: 01847 896357

Wick has the *Harbour Gallery* at 14b Harbour Terrace, overlooking the harbour. A continuous and changing exhibition, which features lots of work by Caithness and Sutherland artists. Tel: 01955 604992
  St Fergus Art Gallery at Wick Library, Sinclair Terrace, has a varied and exciting programme of changing exhibitions. Open all year. Tel: 01955 603489

ISLANDS

The Inner Hebrides

SKYE
Broadford Gallery has work by resident artist. Local landscapes. Open Monday to Saturday from 10.30 a.m. to 5.30 p.m. Tel: 01471 822011

Dunvegan is near the *Orbost Gallery* which has paintings and prints of Skye by professional artists. Open April to October, daily from 10 a.m. to 6 p.m. Tel: 01470 511240

Kilmaluag, by Duntulm, in the north of the island is where you will find the *Trotternish Art Gallery*. A variety of landscapes. Open all year. Tel: 01470 552302

Portnalong in the Minginish area has *The Little Gallery*. Etchings and watercolours by resident artist, and others. Open daily in summer from 9.30 a.m. to 6 p.m. Check during the winter. Tel: 01478 640254

Portree. The *An Tuireann Arts Centre* is on Struan Road. Their exhibitions change monthly and there are performances and workshops, even a café, on site. Tel: 01478 613306

The Western Isles

LEWIS

Lewis and Stornoway should immediately prompt you to visit *An Lanntair*. Much of the best from artists resident in the Outer Isles is displayed here in a series of temporary exhibitions during the year. They also have a lively bookshop and a coffee shop (which also has its own exhibits). Open Monday to Saturday from 10 a.m. to 5.30 p.m. Tel: 01851 703307

SOUTH UIST

In Lochmaddy is the *Taigh Chearsabhagh Museum and Arts Centre*. Exhibitions feature local art and artists. They also have a café.

Orkney

If you are in Stromness, don't miss the *Pier Arts Centre* – modern art housed in an eighteenth-century building. The centre holds the best collection of the St Ives School outside St Ives itself. Look out for work by Barbara Hepworth, Ben Nicholson, Patrick Heron and Alfred Watts. There are also changing exhibitions throughout the year. Open Tuesday to Saturday from 10.30 a.m. to 5 p.m. Tel: 01856 850209

While you are about it, don't forget to visit *Stromness Books and Prints*. A gem of a bookshop, gallery, café, social centre, you name it! What an atmosphere.

FESTIVALS

What a weird and wonderful selection of events happen in the course of a Scottish year. Wherever you happen to be, you can bet your life there will be something happening soon somewhere near you (particularly if you happen to be reading this in the height of the summer). Many of the festivities are of a local nature, which means that the whole village or town will be out in the streets around you. I can't think of a better way to get to know somewhere!

There are a number of Highland Games too, and not just in the Highlands! These are bizarrely entertaining, with a flavour of the unchanging nature of the countryside about them. Gala days usually begin with street parades, followed by festivities that involve races, competitions and stalls at the local park. Expect much fancy-dress rivalry. There are even some local flower shows and agricultural shows, which will really introduce you to Scotland!

There are a number of highly acclaimed festivals in Scottish cities during the year. The various Edinburgh Festivals are obvious examples, but Glasgow's Mayfest and the Aberdeen Alternative Festival also have their devotees.

Sporting events of various kinds have been included, not to excess, but the most important should be here. The Scottish Grand National is good for a flutter and the various regattas at sailing Meccas around our coastline have been included for their spectacle.

For anyone looking for accommodation, it might be wise to check the dates of your trip with the timings of any major festivals, as this could affect the availability of a bed for the night. You would be well advised to book extremely early, for example, if you hope to get a place to stay in Edinburgh during the Festival. Prices have been known to soar at less reputable establishments (and some of the more reputable too!) for that three-week period. You will also struggle to get a space in the most rudimentary B&B on Barra during the Feis. There. Sermon over! Make the most of your wild days with a bit of pre-planning. Enjoy!

ALL OVER SCOTLAND

1 Jan	Ne'er Day
25 Jan	Burns Day
27 Jan	Start of National Tea Drinking Week
29 Jan	Start of National Gargling Week (nothing to do with the above!)
11 Feb	Shrove Tuesday (Pancake Day)
Apr–May	National Tell-a-Story Week
23 Apr	World Day of the Book
31 Apr	Beltane Fire Festival
17 May	International Museums Day
17–25 May	Museums Week
23 May–7 Jun	Highland Festival – events all over the Highlands and Islands
Jun	Scottish Canal Week
Jul	International Women's Day
Sep	Doors Open Day
Oct	National Poetry Day
Oct	Royal National Mod (*Gaelic Music Festival – venue changes each year*)
Oct/Nov	Scottish International Storytelling Festival
18 Oct–1 Nov	Scottish Book Fortnight
30 Nov	St Andrew's Day
31 Dec	Hogmanay

1997 is . . .

1400th Anniversary of St Columba of Iona
1600th Anniversary of St Ninian of Whithorn
700th Anniversary of the Battle of Stirling Bridge

THE WEST

Argyll and Bute

1 Jan	*Rhu*	New Year Swim
26 Apr	*Oban*	Fiddlers' Rally

3–4 May	*Oban*	Highlands and Islands Music and Dance Festival
4 May	*Lochgilphead*	Half Marathon
Jun	*Kilmore*	Kilmore and Kilbride Highland Games
Jun	*Kintyre*	Kintyre Music Festival
Jun	*Oban*	Raft Race
7 Jun	*Lochgair*	Fun Run
14 Jun	*Cove*	Cove Regatta
21 Jun	*Campbeltown*	Highland Games
Jul	*Knapdale*	Sheepdog Trials
Jul	*Southend*	Highland Games
15 Jul	*Inveraray*	Highland Games
19 Jul	*Taynuilt*	Highland Games
20 Jul	*Rosneath*	Rosneath and Clynder Highland Games
23 Jul	*Luss*	Highland Gathering
26 Jul	*Strachur*	Strachur Carnival
31 Jul–2 Aug	*Tarbert*	Loch Fyne Fair
Aug	*Campbeltown*	Agricultural Show
Aug	*Helensburgh*	Helensburgh and Gare Loch Annual Flower and Vegetable Show
Aug	*Oban*	Lorn Show
8–10 Aug	*Inveraray*	Classic Boat Festival
29–30 Aug	*Dunoon*	Cowal Highland Gathering
27–28 Aug	*Oban*	Argyllshire Gathering (Oban Games)
Sep	*Tarbert*	Rigid Inflatable Boat Grand Prix
19–21 Sep	*Tarbert*	Music Festival
10–12 Oct	*Dunoon*	Jazz Festival

BUTE

1–5 May	*Various venues*	Jazz Festival
17–21 Jul	*Various venues*	International Folk Festival
22–25 Aug	*Bute*	International Country Music Festival
23 Aug	*Rothesay*	Bute Highland Games

East Ayrshire

Apr	*Kilmaurs*	Agricultural Show
Apr	*Ochiltree*	Agricultural Show
May	*Stewarton*	Agricultural Show
Jun	*Mauchline*	Gala Day
Jun	*Fenwick*	Gala Day
Aug	*Fenwick (Marchbank)*	Fenwick Show
Aug	*Muirkirk*	Agricultural Show
Sep	*Mauchline*	Mauchline Flower Show
5 Nov	*Kilmarnock (Dean Park)*	Fireworks Display

City of Glasgow

Jan	*Various venues*	Celtic Connections (Arts Festival)
May	*Various venues*	Mayfest (International Arts Festival)
Jul	*Various venues*	International Jazz Festival
Aug	*Glasgow*	World Pipe Band Championships
Aug	*From Glasgow*	RSAC Veteran, Vintage and Classic Car Run

Inverclyde

Jan/Feb	*Greenock*	Inverclyde and Renfrew Music Festival
Feb	*Greenock*	Inverclyde District One-Act Play Festival
May	*Gourock*	Highland Games
May	*Kilmacolm*	Kilmacolm and Port Glasgow Agricultural Show
June	*Gourock Park (The Walled Garden)*	Garden Party
Nov	*Greenock (Battery Park)*	Fireworks Display

North Ayrshire

Apr	*Largs*	Clyde Cruising Club Spring Weekend
26 and 27 Apr	*Fairlie (Kelburn Country Centre)*	Woodcraft and Forestry Fair
May	*Dalry*	Dalry Farmers Society Annual Open Show
10–11 May	*Fairlie (Kelburn Country Centre)*	Country Fair and Gymkhana
24 May	*Kilbirnie*	Garnock International Highland Games
24–26 May	*Fairlie (Kelburn Country Centre)*	Festival of Flight
31 May–7 Jun	*Various venues*	North Ayrshire Expo (District Arts Festival)
Jun	*Saltcoats*	Ardrossan Highland Games
1–7 Jun	*Largs*	Brisbane Queen Festival
20 Jul	*Irvine (Eglinton Country Park)*	Ayrshire Vintage Tractor and Machinery Fair
25–27 Jul	*Irvine*	Irvine Harbour Festival
Aug	*Dalry*	Dalry Flower Show
14–25 Aug	*Irvine*	Marymass Music Festival (and Folk Festival)
16–17 Aug	*Fairlie (Kelburn Country Centre)*	New Zealand Festival
22–25 Aug	*Fairlie (Kelburn Country Centre)*	International Rocket Weekend
22–31 Aug	*Largs*	Largs Regatta Week
30 Aug–7 Sep	*Largs*	Viking Festival

31 Aug	*Largs*	Viking Day
Oct	*Irvine*	Ayrshire Scottish Music Festival

ARRAN

May	*Various venues*	Festival of Music
May	*Arran*	Dramafest
May	*Arran*	Jazz and Blues Festival
11–15 May	*Arran*	Arran Festival of Music
17 May	*Arran*	Goatfell Race
9–15 Jun	*Arran*	Festival of Folk
29 Jun	*Arran*	Shiskine Valley Half Marathon
Jul	*Arran*	Arran Fleadh (Musical weekend with a Celtic flavour)
12–19 Jul	*Lamlash*	Lamlash Gala Week
14–20 Jul	*Kildonan*	Kildonan Fun Week
16–20 Jul	*Lochranza*	Lochranza Gala Weekend
2–9 Aug	*Corrie*	Corrie Capers
6 Aug	*Blackwaterfoot*	Arran Farmers Society Show
9 Aug	*Brodick*	Highland Games

CUMBRAE

14–21 Jun	*Millport*	Cumbrae Week
20 Jul	*Millport*	Gala Day
1–4 Aug	*Millport*	Millport-Nashville Country and Western Festival
3 Aug	*Millport*	Raft Race
10 Aug	*Various venues*	Gala Day
7 Sep	*Cumbrae*	Round Island Race
27 Sep	*Millport*	Millport Illuminations (and Fireworks)

North Lanarkshire

5 Nov	*Strathclyde Country Park (Watersports Centre)*	Fireworks Display and Bonfire Night

Renfrewshire

Feb	*Paisley*	Paisley Book Fair
May	*Paisley*	Paisley Writers Festival
17–25 May	*Paisley (Museum and Art Galleries)*	Museums Week
Sep–Dec	*Renfrewshire Libraries*	Children's Book Festival

South Ayrshire

29–31 Mar	*Girvan*	Girvan Cycle Race
Apr	*Dundonald*	Dundonald Farmers Society Show
19 Apr	*Ayr*	Scottish Grand National

30 Apr–1 May	*Ayr*	Agricultural Show
3–5 May	*Girvan*	Folk Festival
14–15 May	*Troon*	10K Race
Jun	*Ayr (Rozelle Park)*	Holy Fair
Jun	*Ayr*	Ayr Arts Festival
1 Jun	*Girvan*	Carrick Lowland Gathering
22–29 Jun	*Girvan*	Civic Week
Jul	*Dundonald*	Highland Games
28–30 Aug	*Ayr*	Ayr Flower Show
Sep	*Ayr*	Ayr Gold Cup (Horseracing)
26–28 Sep	*Girvan*	Jazz Festival
17–19 Oct	*Girvan*	Mini Folk Festival

South Lanarkshire

Jul	*Hamilton*	'T in the Park'
Sep	*New Lanark*	Victorian Fair
31 Dec	*Biggar*	The Biggar Bonfire

West Dunbartonshire

7–12 Jul	*Loch Lomond Golf Club*	World Invitational Golf Championship
18–27 Jul	*Loch Lomond*	Loch Lomond and Clyde Festival
19 Jul	*Balloch Castle Country Park*	Balloch Highland Games
26 Jul	*Dumbarton*	Fun Day and Pipe Band Competition
Nov	*Dumbarton*	Torchlit parade

THE EAST

East Lothian

May	*Haddington*	Festival Week
Jul	*Musselburgh*	Honest Toun Festival Week
Jul	*Dirleton*	Archers Games and Fete
Aug	*Dunbar*	Vintage Vehicle Rally
Sep	*Dunbar*	Flower Show

City of Edinburgh

17 Mar–19 Apr	*Various*	Puppet and Animation Festival
21–30 Mar	*Edinburgh*	Folk Festival
22 Mar–6 Apr	*Edinburgh*	International Science Festival
31 Apr	*Calton Hill*	Beltane Fire Festival
19–25 May	*Inverleith Park*	Scottish International Children's Festival

155

19–22 Jun	*Edinburgh*	Royal Highland Show
2–10 Aug	*Edinburgh*	Jazz Festival
4–30 Aug	*Edinburgh*	Great West End Craft and Design Fair
10–24 Aug	*Edinburgh*	Drambuie Edinburgh Film Festival
1–23 Aug	*Edinburgh*	Military Tattoo
9–25 Aug	*Edinburgh*	Book Festival
10–30 Aug	*Edinburgh*	International Festival
10–30 Aug	*Edinburgh*	International Fringe Festival
Oct	*Edinburgh*	Beer Festival
29 Dec–1 Jan	*Edinburgh*	Edinburgh's Hogmanay

Midlothian

Mar	*Various venues*	Puppet and Animation Festival
Mar	*Penicuik*	Scottish Country Dance Festival
May (first Sunday)	*Ratho*	Pumpathon (vintage fire engine event)
Jun (third Sunday)	*Ratho*	Annual Scottish Canal Jump Competition
Aug	*Dalkeith (Vogrie Park)*	Vogrie Festival Day
Oct	*Midlothian Libraries*	Festival

West Lothian

Apr	*Almond Valley Heritage Trust, Livingston*	Vintage Vehicle Rally
May	*Bathgate*	Highland Games
Jun	*Linlithgow*	The Marches (Town Carnival)
Aug	*Almond Valley Heritage Trust, Livingston*	Family Fun Day
Sep	*Almond Valley Heritage Trust, Livingston*	Traditional Harvest Festival

THE BORDERS

Dumfries and Galloway

4–6 Apr	*Gatehouse of Fleet*	Spring Festival of Music, Arts and Crafts
23 May–1 Jun	*Various venues*	Dumfries and Galloway Arts Festival
24–25 May	*Wanlockhead*	British Gold Panning Championships
24–25 May	*Drumlanrig Castle, near Thornhill*	Drumlanrig Fair
25 May	*Dumfries*	Vintage Rally and Vehicle Run
5–6 Jun	*Whithorn*	Pilgrims Way 1997

7–14 Jun	Lockerbie	Riding of the Marches and Gala Day
14–22 Jun	Dumfries	Guid Nychburris Festival
Jun/Jul	Penpont	Penpont Gala Week
5 Jul	Annan	Riding of the Marches (Traditional processions)
11–13 Jul	Drumlanrig Castle, near Thornhill	Horse Driving Trials
14–19 Jul	Moffat	Moffat and District Gala Week
18–19 Jul	Moniaive	Gala Days
18–21 Jul	Kirkcudbright	Civil War Weekend
23 Jul	Ruthwell	Brow Well Service
25 Jul	Langholm	Common Riding (Traditional procession)
26 Jul	Palnackie	World Flounder Trampling Championships
26 Jul	New Luce	Gala Day
27 Jul–2 Aug	Portpatrick	Lifeboat Week
27 Jul–3 Aug	Gatehouse of Fleet	Gala Week
30 Jul	Stranraer	Agricultural Show
Aug	Creetown	Gala Week
Aug	Samye Ling Centre, Eskdalemuir	Open Day
2 Aug	Dumfries and Lockerbie	Agricultural Show
2–10 Aug	Port William	Carnival Week
2–10 Aug	Galloway Forest	Park Fun Week
3 Aug	Parton	World Alternative Games, including World Gird 'n' Cleek Championships
6 Aug	Wigtown	Agricultural Show
7 Aug	Castle Douglas	Stewartry Agricultural Show
9–10 Aug	Dumfries	Border Gathering
9–16 Aug	Sanquhar	Riding of the Marches (Traditional procession)
22–31 Aug	Langholm and Eskdale	Music and Arts Festival
23 Aug	Kirkcudbright	Grand Parade
24 Aug	Kirkcudbright	Historic Vehicle Rally
25 Aug	Kirkcudbright	Floodlit Tattoo
30 Aug	Gatehouse of Fleet	Horticultural Society Show
30 Aug	Moffat	Agricultural Show
31 Aug	Whithorn	Annual Pilgrimage
Sep	Wanlockhead (Museum of Lead Mining)	Scottish Festival
Sep	Dumfries	Highland Dance Championships
6 Sep	Whithorn	Ninian to Now
15–20 Sep	Dumfries	Nithsdale Burns Festival
27 Sep	Eskdale	Agricultural Show
4 Oct	Cardoness Castle, near Gatehouse of Fleet	Oktober Musical Beerfest and Barbecue
27 Oct	Wanlockhead	Halloween Party

157

Scottish Borders

13 Feb	*Jedburgh*	Ba' Games
3–5 May	*The Hirsel Coldstream*	May Fair
11 May	*Melrose*	Spring Teddy Fair
18 May	*Newtown St Boswells*	Vintage Agricultural Rally
23–26 May	*Allanton*	Beer and Blues Festival
24–25 May	*Traquair House, Innerleithen*	Beer Festival
25–31 May	*Chirnside*	Civic Week
6–7 Jun	*Hawick*	Common Riding
6–14 Jun	*West Linton*	Whipman
13–14 Jun	*Selkirk*	Common Riding
13–14 Jun	*Eyemouth*	Seafood Festival
14 Jun	*Swinton*	Gala Day
15–21 Jun	*Peebles*	Beltane Festival
15–22 Jun	*Melrose*	Melrose Festival
22–28 Jun	*Galashiels*	Braw Lads Gathering
28 Jun–4 Jul	*Greenlaw*	Festival Week
28 Jun–11 Jul	*Jedburgh*	Jethart Callants Festival
4–6 Jul	*Newcastleton*	Traditional Music Festival
5 Jul	*Duns*	Jim Clark Rally
6 Jul	*Kelso*	Kelso Games
6–12 Jul	*Duns*	Summer Festival
6–13 Jul	*Earlston*	Civic Week
12 Jul	*Jedburgh*	Border Games
13 or 20 Jul	*Eyemouth*	Herring Queen Festival
3rd week in Jul	*Innerleithen*	St Ronan's Border Games Week
Sat of 3rd week in Jul	*Caerlee Hill, Innerleithen*	St Ronan's Bonfire and Procession
13–19 Jul	*Kelso*	Civic Week
19 Jul	*Newtown St Boswells*	Farmers Show
19 Jul	*Innerleithen*	Scottish Border Games
25–26 Jul	*Kelso*	Border Union Show (includes Craft Fair)
2 Aug	*Duns*	Berwickshire Agricultural Show
2–3 Aug	*Traquair House Innerleithen*	Traquair Fair
3–9 Aug	*Coldstream*	Civic Week
9–24 Aug	*Hawick*	Summer Festival
9–10 Aug	*Ayton Castle, Ayton*	Kite Festival
16–17 Aug	*Thirlestane Castle, Lauder*	Scottish Championship Horse Trials
17 Aug	*Melrose*	Summer Teddy Fair
23 Aug	*Melrose*	Pipe Band Concert
24 Aug	*Newcastleton*	International Sheepdog Challenge
27 Aug–2 Sep	*Lauder*	Common Riding
30 Aug	*Newcastleton*	Liddesdale Agricultural Show
30 Aug–14 Sep	*Peebles*	Arts Festival

6–8 Sep	*Melrose*	Music Festival
7–14 Sep	*Peebles*	Highland Games
12 Sep	*Kelso*	Ram Sales
12–14 Sep	*Hawick*	Borders Festival of Jazz and Blues
13–14 Sep	*Selkirk*	Vintage Classic and Veteran Vehicle Show
18–26 Oct	*Various*	Borders Food and Restaurant Week
18 Oct–1 Nov	*Various*	The Borders Festival

CENTRAL, TAYSIDE AND FIFE

Clackmannanshire

May	*Alloa*	Mayfest Parade and street entertainment
May	*Alloa*	Real Ale Festival
16–25 May	*Various venues*	Clackmannanshire May Festival
25 May	*Alva, Cochrane Park*	Family Fun Day
July	*Alva*	Highland Games
17–26 Oct	*Alloa*	Octoberfest

Dundee

17–24 May	*Dundee*	Country Music Festival
Jun	*Dundee*	Jazz and Blues Festival
Jun	*Dundee*	Folk Festival
Jul	*Dundee*	Summer Festival
19–25 Jul	*Dundee*	East Coast Sailing Week
Aug	*Dundee*	Water Festival
5–7 Sep	*Camperdown Park*	Dundee Flower Show
Nov	*Dundee University*	Mountain Film Festival
31 Dec–2 Jan	*Dundee*	City Centre Carnival

Falkirk

10–25 May	*Falkirk*	Tryst – The Festival
27 Jun	*Bo'ness*	Children's Fair Festival
Jul	*Falkirk*	International Food and Drink Festival
20 Jul	*Falkirk*	Children's Festival
26 Jul	*Airth*	Highland Games
16–17 Aug	*Falkirk*	Falkirk Family Show

Fife

Apr	*Kirkcaldy*	Links Market (Largest Street Fair in Europe)
May	*St Andrews*	Ecurie Ecosse Tour (Vintage cars travelling to Skye)
May	*Balcormo, by Leven*	Fife Show
May	*St Andrews (Craigtoun Park)*	Craigtoun Country Fair
Jun	*Cupar*	Cupar Festival
Jun	*Strathmiglo*	Highland Games
Jun	*Markinch*	Highland Games
Jun	*Newburgh*	Highland Games
Jun	*Ceres*	Highland Games
Jun	*Largo*	Largo Festival
Jul	*Auchtermuchty*	Auchtermuchty Festival
Jul	*St Andrews (Craigtoun Park)*	Vintage Car Rally
Jul	*Anstruther*	Life Boat Gala Day
Jul	*Cupar*	Highland Games
Jul	*Crail*	Crail Festival
Jul	*Thornton*	Highland Gathering
Jul	*Burntisland*	Highland Games
Jul	*St Andrews*	Highland Games
Jul	*Elie*	Elie Fayre Day
Jul	*St Monans*	St Monans Civic Week
Jul	*Anstruther*	Anstruther Fair
Aug	*Inverkeithing*	Highland Games
Aug	*Pittenweem*	Pittenweem Arts Festival
Aug	*Pittenweem*	Pittenweem Fish Festival
Aug	*St Andrews*	Lammas Market
Sep	*Leuchars*	RAF Leuchars Air Show
Oct	*Dunfermline*	Arts Festival
Oct	*St Andrews*	Dunhill Cup (golf)
30 Nov	*St Andrews*	St Andrew's Day Celebrations

Perth and Kinross

23 Mar	*Pitlochry*	Festival of Choirs
25 Apr–5 May	*Perth*	Food Festival
May–Oct	*Pitlochry*	Events at the Festival Theatre
May	*Blair Atholl*	Atholl Gathering, Atholl Highlanders Parade
23 May–1 Jun	*Perth*	Festival of the Arts
31 May	*Blackford*	Highland Games
18–22 Jun	*Dunkeld and Birnam*	Arts Festival
Jul	*Blair Atholl*	Blair Atholl Festival
2 Jul	*Kenmore*	Highland Games
Jul/Aug	*Comrie*	Comrie Fortnight

31 Jul–4 Aug	*Strathearn*	Summer Music Festival
Aug	*Perth*	Highland Games
Aug	*Crieff*	Highland Games
Aug	*Aberfeldy*	Atholl and Breadalbane Highland Gathering
Aug	*Kinross*	Kinross Show
Aug	*Blairgowrie*	Glenisla Highland Games
Aug	*Kirkmichael near Blairgowrie*	Strathardle Highland Gathering
Aug	*Birnam, near Dunkeld*	Highland Games
Aug	*Kinloch Rannoch*	Highland Games
1–2 Aug	*Perth*	Agricultural Show
21–24 Aug	*Blair Castle, Blair Atholl*	International Horse Trials
Sep	*Pitlochry*	Highland Games
7 Sep	*Blairgowrie*	Highland Games
31 Dec	*Comrie*	Flambeaux Procession

Stirling

Throughout 1997: Battle of Stirling Bridge 700th Anniversary

23–25 May	*Doune and Dunblane*	Fling – music, street parades, Doune castle open day
31 May	*Drymen*	Agricultural Show
14 Jun	*Stirling*	Agricultural Show
20–22 Jun	*Killin*	Traditional Music and Dance Festival
5 Jul	*Doune and Dunblane*	Agricultural Show
13 Jul	*Stirling (Kings Park)*	Highland Games
18–27 Jul	*Callander, Aberfoyle*	Trossachs Highland Festival
26 Jul	*Lochearnhead*	Balquhidder, Strathyre and Lochearnhead Highland Games
26–27 Jul	*Callander*	World Highland Games
Aug	*Callander*	Sheepdog Trials
Aug	*Crianlarich*	Flower Show
Aug	*Stirling*	Tartan Festival
3 Aug	*Bridge of Allan*	Highland Games
6 Aug	*Killin*	Highland Games
16 Aug	*Killin*	Agricultural Show
6 Sep	*Drymen*	Flower and Vegetable Show
12–13 Sep	*Stirling*	700th Anniversary of the Battle of Stirling Bridge

GRAMPIAN

Aberdeen City

6 May	*Aberdeen*	Beltane Fair
26 May	*Aberdeen*	10K Run
Jun	*Aberdeen (Hazlehead Park)*	Scottish Pipe Band Championship
1 Jun	*Dyce*	Dyce Gala
8 Jun	*Cove Bay*	Cove Bay Gala
15 Jun	*Aberdeen*	Cycle Race
15–16 Jun	*Old Meldrum*	Old Meldrum Sports and Highland Games
16 Jun	*Aberdeen*	City of Aberdeen Highland Games
21–22 Jun	*Aberdeen*	Steam Engine Rally
12–15 Jul	*Aberdeen*	Cutty Sark Tall Ships' Race
14 Jul	*Aberdeen (Union Street)*	Aberdeen Live Festival Parade
15–20 Jul	*Aberdeen*	Aberdeen Live
15–20 Jul	*Aberdeen*	International Football Festival
26–27 Jul	*Aberdeen*	Classic Car Rally
31 Jul–10 Aug	*Aberdeen*	International Youth Festival
3 Aug	*Aberdeen*	Gallowgate Fair
30–31 Aug	*Aberdeen*	Clydesdale Horse and Pony Show
12–22 Sep	*Aberdeen*	TechFest 97, Science and Technology Festival
9–18 Oct	*Aberdeen*	Alternative Festival (Arts Festival)
Nov/Dec	*Aberdeen*	Winter Festival
31 Dec	*Aberdeen*	New Year Spectacular

Aberdeenshire

19 Apr	*Inverurie*	Garioch Fiddlers' Rally
25–26 Apr	*Banff*	Spring Show
4 May	*Kemnay, by Inverurie*	Don Raft Race
10 May	*Banchory*	Festival of Scottish Music
17 May	*Strichen*	Buchan Heritage Festival
Jun	*Drumtochty Castle, Auchenblae*	Drumtochty Highland Games
Jun	*Alford*	Alford Cavalcade (Vintage vehicle show)
7 Jun	*Stonehaven*	Feein' Market
8 Jun	*Kildrummy*	Vintage Car Rally
8 Jun	*Turriff*	Pipe Band Contest
14 Jun	*Monymusk*	Sheepdog Trials
21 Jun	*Drumtochty*	Highland Games
21–22 Jun	*Stonehaven*	Vintage Vehicle Rally
Jul	*Aboyne and Deeside*	Aboyne and Deeside Festival

1–30 Jul	*Braemar*	Gala Month
5–6 Jul	*Portsoy*	Scottish Traditional Boat Festival
11–13 Jul	*Stonehaven*	Folk Festival
12 Jul	*Echt, Skene and Midmar*	Agricultural Show
18–19 Jul	*New Deer*	New Deer Show
20 Jul	*Stonehaven*	Highland Games
20 Jul	*Alford*	Alford Cavalcade
26 Jul	*Fraserburgh*	Fish Festival
2 Aug	*Aboyne*	Highland Games
2–8 Aug	*Ballater*	Gala Week
4–5 Aug	*Turriff*	Turriff Show
9 Aug	*Tarland*	Agricultural Show
14 Aug	*Ballater*	Highland Games
14–17 Aug	*Castle Fraser, Sauchen, Inverurie*	Clan Fraser Gathering
16 Aug	*Peterhead*	Harbour Open Day
16 Aug	*Old Rayne*	Lourin' Fair
23 Aug	*Strathdon*	Lonach Highland Gathering and Games
6 Sep	*Braemar*	Braemar Royal Highland Gathering
Oct	*Various venues*	The Doric Festival
31 Dec	*Stonehaven*	Fireball Festival

Angus

Mar	*Glenisla*	British Cup Sled Dog Race
May	*Arbroath*	Country Music Festival
May	*Arbroath*	Angus Show
Jun	*Monifieth*	Lowland Games
Jun	*Forfar*	Highland Games
Jun	*Forfar*	Gala Day
Jul	*Carnoustie*	Gala Day
Jul	*Carnoustie*	Scottish Open Golf Championship
Jul	*Kirriemuir*	Kirriemuir Show
Jul	*Arbroath*	Highland Games
Jul	*Glamis*	Grand Scottish Proms (Outdoor picnic and fireworks)
Aug	*Montrose*	Highland Games
Aug	*Glenisla*	Highland Games
Sep	*Kirriemuir*	Kirriemuir Music Festival
Nov	*Clova*	Clova Road Race

THE HIGHLANDS

Moray

2 Jan	*Dufftown*	Boys' Walk and Ball
11 Jan	*Burghead*	Burning of the Clavie (Traditional Ceremony)
1 Mar	*Aberlour*	Spring Flower Show
22 Mar	*Lossiemouth*	Spring Bulb Show
Apr	*Keith*	Spring Flower Show
Apr	*Millbuies Country Park, Elgin*	Easter Bonnet Parade
29–30 Apr	*Elgin*	Great North of Scotland Model Railway Show
Jun	*Aberlour*	Theme Day
Jun	*Keith*	Festival of Country and Western Music
Jun–Jul	*Dallas*	Dallas Gala
13–15 Jun	*Keith*	Festival of Traditional Music and Song
19–22 Jun	*Elgin*	Science Festival
23 Jun	*Keith*	Grange Highland Games
28 Jun	*Garmouth*	Maggie Fair
Jul	*Buckie*	Gala Day
6 Jul	*Forres*	Highland Games
19–21 Jul	*Lossiemouth*	Folk Festival
20 Jul	*Tomintoul*	Tomintoul Highland Games
20 Jul	*Elgin*	Highland Games
26 Jul	*Dufftown*	Highland Games
Aug	*Aberlour*	Summer Flower Show
Aug	*Buckie*	Flower Show
Aug	*Deskford*	Flower Show
Aug	*Duffus*	Gala Day and Horticultural Show
Aug	*Fochabers*	Speyfest (Traditional Music and Arts Festival)
2 Aug	*Aberlour*	Aberlour and Strathspey Highland Games
10–11 Aug	*Keith*	Agricultural Show
Sep	*Forres*	Flower Show
Sep	*Keith*	Summer Flower Show
Sep	*Rothes*	Flower Show
Sep	*Fochabers*	Flower and Honey Show
Sep	*Elgin*	Moray Marathon
Sep	*Elgin*	Flower Show
20 Sep	*Lossiemouth*	Summer Flower Show
20 Sep	*Elgin*	Fiddlers' Rally
2 Nov	*Forres*	Fireworks Display and Bonfire
2 Nov	*Elgin*	Fireworks Display and Bonfire
26 Dec	*Burghead*	Boxing Day Swim

Highland Heartlands

Jan	*Aviemore*	Spillers Bonio/Siberian Husky of GB Sled Dog Race
Feb	*Strathspey*	Cross Country Ski Championships
Feb	*Inverness*	Snowman Motor Rally
Mar	*Inverness*	Music Festival
Mar	*Glencoe*	Downhill Speed Skiing World Cup Race
Mar	*Aviemore*	International Curling
Mar	*Kingussie*	Badenoch and Strathspey Music Festival
Mar	*Cairngorm Ski Centre*	Snow Festival Weekend
Mar	*Fort William*	Annual Fiddlers' Rally
Apr	*Inverness*	Folk Festival
Apr	*Newtonmore*	Easter Bunny Festival
Apr	*From Fort William*	Four Tops Fell Running Race
Apr	*Fort William*	Lochaber People's Marathon
Apr	*Strathspey*	Steam Railway Enthusiasts Display, Strathspey Railway
May	*Strathspey*	Thomas the Tank Engine Weekend, Strathspey Railway
May	*Fort William*	Scottish Six Day Trial (International Motorbikes)
May	*Fort William*	Caol and Lochaber Music Festival
May	*Roybridge*	Feis Brae Lochaber (Traditional Festival)
Jun	*by Fort William*	Aonach Mor Hill Race (from Nevis Range)
Jun	*Kyle*	Kyle Mod (Traditional Festival)
Jun	*Beauly*	Highland Games
Jun	*From Aviemore*	Tour of Speyside Cycle Race
Jun	*Kirkhill*	Gala Week
Jun	*Maryhill*	Gala Week
Jun	*Kintail to Beauly*	Highland Cross Biathlon
Jun	*Auldearn, near Nairn*	St Colms Fair
Jun	*Grantown-on-Spey*	Highland Games
Jul	*Acharacle*	Feis Nan Garbh Chriochan (Traditional Festival – Festival of the Rough Boundaries)
Jul	*Lochaline (Knock Park)*	Morvern Games
Jul	*Lochaline area*	Morvern Gala Week
Jul	*Arisaig*	Highland Games
Jul	*Invergarry*	Glengarry Highland Games
Jul	*Inverness*	Highland Games
Jul	*Kilchoan*	Kilchoan Show
Jul	*Kincraig*	Kincraig Fete
Jul	*Boat of Garten*	Gala Day
Jul	*Inverness*	Inverness Tattoo
Jul	*Inverness*	Annual Three-Day Antiques Fair

165

Jul	Fort William (An Aird)	Lochaber Highland Games
Jul	by Muir of Ord, Black Isle	Strathconon Games
Jul	Great Glen to Strathspey	The Corrieyairick Challenge (Biathlon)
Jul	Beauly	Gala Week
Jul	Nairn	Vintage Vehicle Rally
Jul	Kilchoan	Kilchoan Regatta
Jul	Nairn	Gala Week
Jul	Nairn	Agricultural Show
Jul	Rothiemurchus Estate, near Aviemore	Rothiemurchas International Highland Games
Aug	by Fort William	Glen Nevis River Race
Aug	Nairn	Highland Games
Aug	Mallaig	Mallaig and Morar Highland Games
Aug	Newtonmore	Clan MacPherson Rally
Aug	Glenfinnan	Glenfinnan Highland Gathering and Games
Aug	Drumnadrochit	Glenurquhart Highland Gathering and Games
Aug	Strontian	Sunart and District Agricultural Show
Aug	Muir of Ord	Black Isle Show
Aug	Nethybridge	Abernethy Highland Games and Clan Grant Gathering
Aug	Inverness	Marymas Fair
Aug	Torlundy, by Fort William	Lochaber Agricultural Show
Aug	Grantown-on-Spey	Agricultural Show
Sep	Carrbridge	Festival of Music
Sep	Carrbridge	World Porridge Making Championships
Sep	Inverness	Northern Meeting Piping Competition
Sep	Fort William	Ben Nevis Race (Fort William to top of Ben Nevis)
Oct	Badenoch and Strathspey	Feis Spey (Cultural Festival)
Oct	Glentruim, by Newtonmore	Decathlon Weekend
Nov	From Fort William	Lochaber People's Half Marathon
Dec	Grantown-on-Spey	Torchlight Procession
24 Dec	Aviemore	Torchlight Procession with Santa and his Reindeer
31 Dec	Newtonmore	Hogmanay Celebrations
31 Dec	Fort William	Hogmanay Party

The Northern Highlands

Feb	Dornie	Traditional Music Festival
May	Alness	Vintage Car Rally
Jun	Strathpeffer	Victorian Events

Jun	*Dingwall*	Highland Traditional Music Festival
Jun	*Golspie*	Sutherland Triathlon
Jul	*Thurso*	Caithness Highland Gathering and Games
Jul	*Dunbeath*	Dunbeath Highland Games
Jul	*Durness*	Highland Gathering
Jul	*Halkirk*	Highland Games
Jul	*Wick (Riverside)*	Caithness Agricultural Show
Jul	*Dornoch*	Sutherland Agricultural Show
Jul	*Lochcarron*	Highland Games
Jul	*Lairg*	Gala Week
Jul	*Dingwall*	Highland Games
28 Jul–2 Aug	*Plockton*	Plockton Regatta
Aug	*Golspie*	Gala Week
Aug	*Lochinver*	Assynt Highland Games
Aug	*Dornoch*	Highland Gathering
Aug	*Tain, near Dornoch*	Highland Gathering
Aug	*Mey*	Royal British Legion Games
Aug	*Helmsdale*	Helmsdale and District Highland Games
Aug	*Strathpeffer*	Highland Gathering
Aug	*Invergordon*	Highland Games
Aug	*Portmahomack*	Gala Week
Aug	*Fortrose*	St Boniface Fair
Aug	*Lairg*	Crofters Show
Aug	*Dunrobin Castle, Golspie*	Vintage Motor Rally
Sep	*Bonar Bridge*	Invercharron Traditional Highland Games
Sep	*Thurso/Wick*	Northlands Festival

ISLANDS

The Inner Hebrides

May	*Mull, Jura, Arran*	Isle of Jura Scottish Peaks Race (begins at Oban)

SKYE

Apr	Easter Events (Armadale, Clan Donald Centre)
May	Classic and Vintage Car Rally
Jun	Skye Live (organised by the local Round Table)
Jun	Piping Competition (Armadale)
7 Jun	Half Marathon – begins at Portree
7 Jun	Clan Donald Sheepdog Trials (Ostaig, Sleat)
21 Jun	Elgol Gala Day

Jul	Dunvegan Castle Music Festival (Dunvegan)
1–5 Jul	National Archery Tournament (Armadale)
7–19 Jul	Feis an Eilein – Skye and Lochalsh Festival
12 Jul	Glamaig Hill Race (Sligachan)
28 Jul–2 Aug	Folk Festival
2 Aug	Portree Show
5 Aug	Piping Competitions (Portree)
6 Aug	Skye Highland Games (Portree)
6 Aug	Silver Chanter – piping recital at Dunvegan Castle
8 Nov	Dunvegan Castle Fireworks Spectacular

MULL

25–27 Apr	Mull Music Festival
Jul	Round Mull Race
17 Jul	Mull Highland Games (Tobermory)
18 Jul	Lifeboat Show
14 Aug	Salen Show and Dance
Sep	Fiddlers' Rally
Oct	Tour of Mull Car Rally

ISLAY

Jun	Islay Festival
13–14 Jun	Islay Mod
Aug	Raft Race
14 Aug	Agricultural Show

TIREE

5–12 Jul	Tiree Festival
Oct	Tiree Wave Classic

The Western Isles

May	*Barra to Lewis*	Western Isles Challenge (Adventure Sport Race)

BARRA

Early Jul	Feis Bharraigh (Barra Festival)
Early–mid Jul	Highland Games (Borve)
Jul–Aug	Blasad den Iar (A Taste of the West)

BENBECULA

Jun	Benbecula Half Marathon
Early Aug	Feis Tir a Mhurain (Lionacleit)

HARRIS

Apr to Sep	Feis na Hearadh events
Early Jun	Harris Mod (Mod na Hearadh)
Mid–late Jul	Harris Gala (2 weeks)

2nd week Jul	Harris Children's Feis
Jul	Harris Half Marathon
Jul–Aug	Blasad den Iar (A Taste of the West) (Leverburgh)

LEWIS

Late Mar	Feis nan Coisir (Stornoway)
Early Apr	Piping Competition (Stornoway)
May	Lewis Half Marathon
Early-mid Jun	Lewis Mod (Mod Leodhais)
Mid-late Jun	Hebridean Celtic Music Festival (Stornoway)
Early-mid Jul	North Lochs Summer Fair (Leurbost)
Mid-Jul–early Aug	Lewis Carnival (2 weeks)
Mid–late Jul	Lewis Highland Games (Tong)
Late Jul	West Side Agricultural Show (Barvas)
Early Aug	Carloway Agricultural Show (Carloway)
Early Aug	Feis Eilean an Fhraoich (Stornoway)
Early Aug	Fish Festival (Stornoway)

NORTH UIST

Mid-Jul	North Uist Highland Games (Hosta)
Early–mid Jul	Feis Tir an Eorna (Paible – 1 week)
Mid-Jul	Berneray Week (Berneray, South Uist)
Late-Jul–early Aug	North Uist Agricultural Show (Hosta)
Jul–Aug	Blasad den Iar (A Taste of the West) (Carinish)
Early Aug	Twin Peaks Hill Race

SOUTH UIST

Mid-Jun	Uist Mod (Mod Uibhist)
Early Jul	Ceolas Music School
Mid–late Jul	Highland Games (Askernish)
Late Jul	South Uist Agricultural Show
Jul–Aug	Blasad den Iar (A Taste of the West)

Orkney

1 Jan	*Kirkwall*	New Years Day Boys' and Men's Ba' Game
1–4 May	*Various*	Country and Irish Festival
17 May	*Kirkwall*	Norway Constitution Day Parade
22–25 May	*Stromness*	Traditional Folk Festival
7–8 Jun	*Longhope*	St Columba Remembers (St Columba's Church)
15 Jun	*Hoy*	Half Marathon
Mid-Jun	*Finstown*	Gala Day
20–25 Jun	*Kirkwall and Stromness*	St Magnus Festival

28 Jun	*Stronsay*	Stronsay Regatta
5 Jul	*Longhope*	Longhope Regatta
12 Jul	*Holm*	Holm Regatta
19 Jul	*Stronsay*	Stronsay Regatta
26 Jul	*Westray*	Westray Regatta
26 Jul	*Hoy*	Hoy Gala Day
1 Aug	*Sanday*	Sanday Show
2 Aug	*Kirkwall*	Kirkwall Regatta
2 Aug	*East Mainland*	Agricultural Show
5 Aug	*Shapinsay*	Agricultural Show
6 Aug	*South Ronaldsay and Burray*	Annual Show
7 Aug	*Dounby*	West Mainland Show
9 Aug		County Show
10 Aug		Riding of the Marches
10 Aug	*Kirkwall*	Orkney Vintage Vehicle Rally
13 Aug	*St Magnus Cathedral*	St Magnus Fair
16 Aug	*South Ronaldsay*	Festival of the Horse and Boys' Ploughing Match
12–18 Sep	*Various venues*	Science Festival
25 Dec	*Kirkwall*	Christmas Day Ba'
31 Dec	*Kirkwall*	Ba'

Shetland

10 Jan	*Scalloway*	Fire Festival
28 Jan	*Lerwick*	Up-Helly-Aa (Traditional Viking Fire Festival)
7 Feb	*Uyeasound*	Up-Helly-Aa
7 Feb	*Nesting and Girlsta*	Up-Helly-Aa
21 Feb	*Northmarine*	Up-Helly-Aa
28 Feb	*Cullivoe*	Up-Helly-Aa
28 Feb	*Bressay*	Up-Helly-Aa
14 Mar	*Brae*	Up-Helly-Aa
3–6 Apr	*Various*	Shetland Folk Festival
May	*Lerwick*	Lifeboat Open Day
17 May	*Lerwick, various venues*	Norwegian Constitution Day Parade
Jun	*Lerwick*	Gala Day (Gilbertson Park)
1 Jun	*Aith*	Lifeboat Gala Day
6–7 Jun	*Burra*	Burra Regatta
14–15 Jun	*Whiteness and Weisdale*	Gala and Regatta
21 Jun	*Foula*	Round Foula Yacht Race
21 Jun	*Lerwick*	Mid Summer Carnival
28 Jun	*Sandwick*	Gala and Regatta
1–2 Jul		Vikingkonvoien 97
5 Jul	*Noss*	Scottish Natural Heritage – Noss Open Day

5 Jul	*Brae*	Brae Regatta
5 Jul	*Sandwick*	Sandwick Gala
12 Jul	*Fetlar*	Sheepdog Trials
12 Jul	*Aith*	Aith Regatta
19 Jul	*Walls*	Walls Regatta
19 Jul	*Northmarine*	Sheepdog Trials
21 Jul	*Fetlar*	RSPB Open Day
22–24 Jul	*Lerwick Harbour*	Vikingkonvoien
26 Jul	*Skeld*	Skeld Regatta
26 Jul	*Yell*	Sheepdog Trials
27 Jul	*Sumburgh Head*	RSPB Open Day
Aug	*Uyeasound*	Sheepdog Trials
2 Aug	*Voe*	Agricultural Show
6 Aug	*Tingwall*	Sheepdog Trials
9 Aug	*Scalloway*	Scalloway Regatta
13 Aug	*Cunningsburgh*	Agricultural Show
16 Aug	*Unst*	Sheepdog Trials
20 Aug	*Walls*	Agricultural Show
30 Aug	*South Mainland*	Sheepdog Trials
31 Aug	*Nesting and Girlsta*	Nesting and Girlsta Show
6 Sep	*East Yell*	East Yell Show
6–7 Sep	*Skeld*	Flower Show
20 Sep	*Tingwall, outside Lerwick*	County Sheepdog Trials
Oct	*Various venues*	Shetland Accordion and Fiddle Festival

SPORTS

Scotland is one big sportsground. With so many beaches, wide open spaces, mountains, lochs and rivers, the whole country is a paradise for healthy activity. You have only to step out, stout shoes and strong heart (or is that vice versa?) and let your limbs do the rest.

There are so many places to walk, ramble and climb in Scotland that a book of this nature could never do them justice. Walkers will find Scotland the place of their dreams.

There are a number of sports that are popular in Scotland and attract many visitors, but are actually hugely expensive. Golf is one, fishing another. Fishing for free is possible with a little ingenuity. It is free to fish in the sea anywhere! Orkney also offers free fishing. Golf is a different prospect, and I have yet to find a free (or cheap) course to include. (Please let me know if you come across any.)

This section doesn't touch on those sports for which a vast sum of money is required, and neither does it list all the sports centres and swimming pools up and down the country. There are charges attached to sports like these in these kind of places. Pools and sports centres you will find listed in any local phone book under the name of the local authority, or ask at the local Tourist Information Centre.

The kind of sport that is free is the knocking about a

ball in a park variety. Any size of ball, from tennis to rugby (you might pay a little for a tennis court). Plenty of parks and open spaces for running are all here.

Once again, take some deep breaths, and if that proves too exhausting, take a piece of Kendal Mint Cake.

THE WEST

Argyll and Bute

Helensburgh has tennis and putting at *Hermitage Park* on Sinclair Street.

Loch Awe. It is traditionally free to fish for trout (brownies), up to a certain distance from the bank, organise a free permit for full protection from the firm hand of the baillie's law.

East Ayrshire

Cumnock has an outdoor swimming pool, tennis and putting at *Woodroad Park* from Easter to mid-September.

Fishers should ask the Ayrshire Tourist Board for their 'Fishing in Ayrshire' booklet, which details the rivers and lochs, and the people and places to go for permits. It does not give any prices, but it does list two places that you don't pay for!

Golfers going anywhere in Ayrshire or Arran would be advised to pick up the Ayrshire and Arran Tourist Board's leaflet on golf courses. It does not give any details of the costs at each course, however. For further details phone the Tourist Information Centre at Ayr (see Days Out).

Kilmarnock has pitch and putt and trampolining at *Kay Park* as well as boats for hire. It is open from dawn to dusk. Along similar lines try *Annanhill Gardens* for their pitch and putt and golf.

Loch Doon has free fishing, mostly for trout. It is also excellent for windsurfing. Please don't confuse the two.

Watersports enthusiasts going anywhere in Ayrshire should get a copy of the Tourist Information booklet 'Water Sports in Ayrshire' from the Tourist Information Centre at Ayr (see Days Out).

East Dunbartonshire

Kirkintilloch has a park that is really more in Lenzie. At *Woodhead Park* there is basic putting, trampolines and room for a bit of DIY sport. Tel: 0141 776 2151

East Renfrewshire

Giffnock has *Rouken Glen Park*, with plenty of grass for sporty types to make the most of. Tel: 0141 620 2084

City of Glasgow

Alexandra Park, on Alexandra Parade, has a golf course.

Bellahouston Park, on Dumbreck Road, has plenty of space for football, running and the like. Open all year, daily from 8 a.m. to 9 p.m. Tel: 0141 649 2100

Glasgow Green, on the banks of the Clyde, has room for probably 100 football pitches, so it makes a good jogging and ball-sports park. Open all year, daily from 8 a.m. to 9 p.m. Tel: 0141 771 6372

Kelvingrove Park, near the University, has putting and tennis courts. Open all year, daily from dawn to dusk. Tel: 0141 287 5064

Linn Park is in Cathcart between Clarkston Road and Carmunnock Road. Serious sportspeople could attempt the assault course here!

Pollok Country Park is a beautiful environment for running, cycling, ball sports and anything else you fancy. Perhaps a spot of Tai Chi? Or isn't that a sport? Sorry . . . Tel: 0141 632 9299

Inverclyde

Clyde-Muirshiel Regional Park has sports such as archery and canoeing – there is a charge for these activities. Tel: 01505 842803 (Muirshiel Centre). For more information about the regional park itself get hold of Clyde-Muirshiel Park Authority, which is based at Barnbrock Farm, near Kilbarchan. Tel: 01505 614791

Gourock can offer sport recreation at the park at *Broomberry Drive*. Look out for the tennis courts, bowling and pitch and putt.

North Ayrshire

Ardrossan, Saltcoats and Stevenston have some good places for sea fishing from the shore. Try the south bay and around the harbours. Ardneil Bay, about three miles north, is good for cod.

Eglinton Country Park, two miles north of Irvine, caters for sports enthusiasts amongst all its other park users. There are attractive cycle paths and plenty of space and trails for running or jogging, whatever. Tel: 01294 551776

Irvine has *Beach Park* beyond the Magnum Leisure Centre, which sports a trim track and other frightening fitness hurdles along the route. The park is very good, the sporty interior of Magnum Centre has a great reputation but isn't free.

Kilbirnie Loch has space and costly facilities for water-skiing or canoeing. Why not go along and *watch*? It's sure to be hilarious.

Largs has *Douglas Park* where you can get a passable game of tennis – as long as your game is passable, if you get my drift.

CUMBRAE
Millport has good sea fishing at a bank between the south-east point of Millport Bay and Keppel Pier. Fintry Bay is also good fun for sea fishing.

North Lanarkshire

Fishing is not free, but it's cheap, at Drumpellier Country Park, near Coatbridge (see Days Out). Tel: 01236 422257. You could also try Hillend Reservoir, Caldercruix, Tel: 01236 425576, or Lily Loch, Caldercruix, Tel: 01236 769221

Kilsyth has a place to try for sport – *Burngreen Park* – with summer extras such as tennis and trampolines.

Strathclyde Country Park has so many sports I need a radox bath just thinking about it. There is curling for the true enthusiast, watersports like canoeing and other, faster stuff, as well as activities such as putting and bowling. There are tennis courts, too. If running or cycling is your thing, this is your place. They even have a reasonably priced 9-hole golf course. Tel: 01698 266155

Renfrewshire

Lochwinnoch has *Castle Semple Country Park*, with watersports facilities, like canoes, at a price. This is a part of the Clyde-Muirshiel Regional Park. Tel: 01505 842882

Paisley has a central park, *Barshaw Park* on Glasgow Road, where you could, at a push, get sporty. Tel: 0141 889 2908

Renfrew has *Robertson Park* (on Inchinnan Road and Paisley Road) with a cycle training track and space for jogging etc. Tel: 0141 886 2807

South Ayrshire

Ayr. Sea fishing off the shore is good along Newton Shore, around the harbour mouth and from the rocky coastline at the Heads of Ayr.
  Loch fishing at *Martnaham Loch* is by a free permit, but you must get permission by applying in writing. (Col Bryce Knox, Martnaham Lodge, by Ayr.) Bear in mind this is a conservation area.

Girvan is good for sea fishing from the pier for plaice and flounder. At night hope for rock cod. 'Horse Rock', a mile south of town, is very popular and only 50 yards from the Stranraer road.

Golfers in South Ayrshire should pick up the 'Golf in South Ayrshire' leaflet available from South Ayrshire Council, Tel: 01292 282842. This has prices in it, and Maybole is the cheapest course that they list.

Prestwick has sea fishing from the shore, particularly at night. Popular areas include the end of Maryborough Road and Monkton where the Pow Burn flows into the sea.

South Lanarkshire

Biggar has a park with sports spaces on Broughton Road. There is golf, swingball, tennis, putting, even a boating pond and bikes for hire. Open all year. Tel: 01899 20319

East Kilbride has a town-centre park off Westmains Road, near the railway station and the Dollan Aqua Centre. (The Dollan Aqua Centre is a lovely one, but not free, or even very cheap.) The sport here involves the boating pond. Tel: 01355 271200. The *James Hamilton Heritage Park* has a serious watersports centre for those with wetsuits. Tel: 01355 276611

Lanark has *Biggar Park and Lanark Loch*, off Hyndford Road. Plenty of open spaces, and that means SPORT. There is boating on the loch, tennis, pitch and putt, even fishing. Tel: 01555 661331

Stonehouse has the *Alexander Hamilton Memorial Park* where you could quite easily have a game of footie or even fly a kite.

Strathaven has a park between the Glasgow Road, Three Stanes Road and Lethame Road. Tel: 01357 21995

West Dunbartonshire

Balloch is where you will find *Balloch Castle Country Park*, with enough space to run until you drop. Fly your kite. Tel: 01389 758216

Dumbarton has *Levengrove Park* with the traditional putting or crazy golf. Perhaps crazy golf doesn't count as sport. Don't ask me, I'm crazy.

THE EAST

East Lothian

Beaches. *Gullane* is a great dune-bounded beach that is very popular with windsurfers. *Longniddry Beach* is another windsurfing spot.

Dunbar has the charm of *Lauderdale Park* for summer sports like table-tennis, trampolines, swingball, putting and crazy golf. Pay a small charge.

North Berwick. The *Lodge Grounds* has summertime fun like crazy golf and table-tennis, for a small charge.

City of Edinburgh

Blackford Hill and Pond, to the south-east of the city, could be the kind of place for a quick jog if the fancy takes you.

Bonaly Country Park, on Bonaly Road, has fishing in the reservoir. Room too for jogging, but it is pretty hilly so go slowly now. Tel: 0131 445 3383

The **Braid Hills,** off Comiston Road, have a golf course, which looks pretty exclusive to me. There is also a jogging track that gets used by horseriders too. Just listen out for cries of 'Fore!' and 'Giddy up, Neddy!' and you should be safe enough. You could fly kites or let off flares, as the fancy takes you.

Holyrood Park is always packed with sportspeople. I don't mean 'packed', it is such a wide open place it only gets busy on Fringe Sunday. It is popular though, with good reason. Good for jogging, football, rugby, anything with a ball and a few friends, even tennis courts near the palace. Sometimes they have wild kite-flying days here when you will see several in the sky at once. Not good for the neck muscles.

Inverleith Park is adjacent to the 'Botanics' and has large green spaces frequently dedicated to rugby, football and similar.

The Meadows is excellent for sport. Friends of mine even used to pretend to play football here on Sunday afternoons. They were all so poorly equipped that the pitch shrank ten metres every week. It was either that or some late-teenage heart attacks. Look out for tennis courts too.

Saughton Park and *Balgreen Park* have wide open spaces for sport and even the *Saughton Sports Complex*, I believe. Tel: 0131 444 0422

Midlothian

Vogrie Country Park, by Gorebridge, has a small golf course as well as great walks and jogs too (see Days Out). Tel: 01875 821990

West Lothian

Beecraigs Country Park has well-organised sport for those who are willing to pay. You can try archery or rock climbing. There is some fishing available too (see Days Out). Tel: 01506 844516

Linlithgow Loch is a haven for those keen on sailing, canoeing and windsurfing. A good bit of trout fishing too. You will pay of course – I prefer to watch from the bank.

Polkemmet Country Park by Whitburn has a golf course and putting green (there is a charge for these). Tel: 01501 743905

THE BORDERS

Dumfries and Galloway

Castle Douglas has *Lochside Park*, with bowling, putting, boating and even sailing, although there is a small charge for all of these.

Dalbeattie has *Colliston Park* with facilities available like trampolines, putting and boating. You will pay a little. In *Dalbeattie Forest* and at *Screel Hill* (both Forest Enterprise) there are mountain-bike trails (see Days Out).

Dumfries has *Dock Park* with putting, crazy golf, trampolines, a paddling pool and tennis. Look for these in summer, and expect to pay a small charge. *Ae Forest* has good mountain-bike routes (see Days Out).

Lockerbie has McJerrow Park with tennis courts available for hire.

Moffat has *Station Park* with boating, sailing and putting on offer, whilst *Beechgrove Park* has bowling and tennis. At Beechgrove you can try putting too, at the sports centre.

Sanquhar has *Lorimer Park*, which has a bowling green and putting too.

Stranraer has *Agnew Park*, which has crazy golf, putting, boating and sailing, even canoeing and windsurfing on Marine Lake, although there are charges (minimal for the simple things).

Scottish Borders

Duns Park has a trim track if you want to reduce your waistline.

Hawick has *Wilton Lodge Park* on Wilton Park Road, with crazy golf and more besides. Tel: 01450 375991

Kelso has *Sheddon Park* with tennis, putting, swingball and even table-tennis in the summer. *Croft Park* has a trim track.

Melrose has *Gibson Park* with pitch and putt for keen golfers.

CENTRAL, TAYSIDE AND FIFE

Clackmannanshire

Alloa has *Gartmorn Dam Country Park and Nature Reserve*. Fishing here is not free, but it isn't arm-and-leg variety when it comes to cost. Nice walking area too. Tel: 01259 214319

Dundee City

Baxter Park has a boating pond and, more importantly, tennis courts and bowling greens.

Caird Park has facilities for golf and athletics, as well as winter pitches. You can get more information on any Dundee park. Tel: 01382 434000

Camperdown Country Park is a wonderful place, with many activities, plus sport on the side. There is pitch and putt, for example, and a boating pond. Tel: 01382 432689

Clatto Country Park has excellent amenities for watersports enthusiasts, as it incorporates an old reservoir (see Days Out). Tel: 01382 436505 or 01382 889076

Lochee Park has space enough for ball-games and running about (or along).

Falkirk

Falkirk has *Dollar Park* with summertime sport laid on in the form of putting and tennis.
    Callendar Park on Callendar Road also has summer extras, with the emphasis perhaps on fun rather than exercise.
    Bantaskine Park is *the* Falkirk park for sports enthusiasts, as there is a trim track and plenty of room for serious athletic activity.

Grangemouth has *Zetland Park,* with tennis courts available in the summer.

Fife

Dunfermline Park has table-tennis and even trampolines in the summer.
    Townhill Country Park, by Dunfermline, is the place with the space for jogging, running, or (in my case) walking very slowly. Tel: 01383 725596

Kirkcaldy has good parks like *Beveridge Park* on Abbotshall Road. You could even play table-tennis here in the summer. It is open all year, although the facilities are available in summer only, from 12 noon to 8 p.m.

Dunnikier Park has putting. Check out the skateboard rink, too.
Ravenscraig Park has pitch and putt and tennis courts.

Markinch has the beautiful 415 acres of *Balbirnie Park* with its 18-hole golf course. Space here for any activity you desire (to pay for, except for the self-evidently free). The park stretches right to Glenrothes. Tel: 01592 645661

St Andrews has *Kilburn Park* with its tennis courts, bowling green and putting, which all carry a small charge. Tel: 01334 477706

Perth and Kinross

Coupar Angus has *Larghan Park* with facilities like putting, and pitch and putt. Tel: 01828 627394

Crieff has a brilliant park in *MacRosty Park*. There are activities like putting (80 pence), pitch and putt (90 pence), tennis (90 pence per half-hour, 50 pence to hire your stuff). These were 1996 charges, but they should give an indication of what you can expect to pay at civic parks all over.

Kinross has *Kirkgate Park* right beside Loch Leven, which offers putting, summer fun like trampolines and crazy golf! All this for a small charge from April to September. Tel: 01577 863161

Perth has a *North Inch* and *South Inch*. At the North Inch you can get into proper sport, or go for the kind described at MacRosty Park in Crieff (for the same kind of prices). The South Inch has boating, trampolines, putting and crazy golf, all for a small charge.

Stirling

Aberfoyle. The *Queen Elizabeth Forest Park* has cycle trails as well as excellent walking-type recreation (see Days Out).

Doune has *Moray Park* for footie, cricket, and even tennis in summer months. We tried kites, but it is a bit too small and it was utterly exhausting.

Loch Katrine has a long stretch of paved walkway along its bank, which cyclists think is great. Mad joggers might, too. You can also hire bicycles at the pier if you want to cycle the length of the loch.

Stirling Parks include *Beechwood Park*, off St Ninian's Road, which has putting, bike tracks and a mini road system with bikes for hire Tel: 01786 79000.
   A large municipal park is *King's Park*, which has room to run, play footie, a bit of rugby, a round of golf, and still be home in time for tea.

GRAMPIAN

Aberdeen City

Aberdeen has the *Queen's Links Park* with putting and tennis at the Esplanade. There is space for jogging, running, cycling all over the seafront area here. A glorious new swimming pool and sports centre too, beside the Beach Ballroom on the Esplanade.

Parks in Aberdeen include *Duthie Park and Winter Gardens*, with activities like tennis and putting. Tel: 01224 583155

Hazlehead Park has pitch and putt, table-tennis, trampolines and swingball in summer. Sports are available from 10 a.m. Tel: 01224 276276

Countesswells Forest is on Countesswells Road, and has lots of tracks for horses and runners with a sense of purpose and hearts of steel.

Aberdeenshire

Huntly has *Cooper Park* with a small charge for table-tennis, tennis and trampolines in summer, even (for a larger charge) cross-country skiing!

Peterhead beach is popular with watersports nutters.

Portsoy has a park at *Loch Soy* with pitch and putt.

Angus

Crombie Country Park has an orienteering course, and Animalteering, an easier form of orienteering for youngsters (see Days Out). Tel: 01241 860360

Forfar Loch Country Park has a Lochside Leisure Centre. Pay for the activities here, but many things in the park are free. Tel: 01307 464201

Monikie Country Park, on the B962 north of Dundee, has excellent paying watersports facilities, but it also has lots of free things to keep you going whilst you watch the waterbabes. Tel: 01382 370202

THE HIGHLANDS

Moray

Elgin has *Cooper Park* with space to run and throw a ball. *Millbuies Country Park*, five miles south of the town, off the A941 to Rothes, has wayfaring and fishing. Tel: 01343 860234

Forres has *Grant Park*, on Victoria Road, where you could catch a ball, or have a jog.

Lossiemouth has the fun of the *Burghead Fun Track*, with go-karts, putting and pitch and putt. *Marine Park* has croquet and trampolines in the summer.

Highland Heartlands

Nairn Leisure Park offers the lot. There is an outdoor games complex and a glorious swimming pool and steam room (a charge for these). Tel: 01667 453061

The Northern Highlands

Beaches. Some of the best surf in the country can be found around these shores. Try at Dunnet Bay for example, or round at Thurso. There is also a fair amount of sea fishing excitement to be had.

ISLANDS

The Inner Hebrides

Mull is the island for sea fishing. Just watch out for those whales and basking sharks, now!

Orkney

Fishing – all fishing on Orkney is free. It all dates back to an ancient Norse law! It is usual to join the Orkney Angling Association out of respect anyway.

Kirkwall has *Brandyquoy Park* with its putting green (there is a charge for this).

ACCOMMODATION

Accommodation of all sorts is included in this section, from hostels and camping, through bed and breakfast to hotels. Naturally the hotels and bed and breakfast places are of the cheap variety, and many of them are on the local tourist board lists, so they have some sort of recommendation behind them. If you are somewhere where there isn't anything listed, then you should try the nearest Tourist Information Centre; they are enormously helpful with accommodation, and (usually for a fee) can even book somewhere for you. (You can book in advance around the country in this way very easily.) In some areas I have suggested farmhouse B&Bs, which are occasionally a little dearer than town centres, but are often in far pleasanter situations. In general there is nothing dearer than £17–£18 for a single, most of the B&Bs coming in at around £14–£15 per person.

You certainly don't have to pay a lot of money for accommodation if you don't want to; there is plenty to chose from and, in most areas, competition keeps prices down. When it comes right down to it, of course, you will usually get what you pay for, and your standards are your own! If you are travelling with your family, you will want to phone ahead to youth hostels and the like to check that family rooms are available, whilst for a bunch of single or friendly folk it can be quite an adventure to go off hill-walking and camp *al fresco* on the hillside – remembering that where possible you should ask a farmer's permission to stay on his/her land. Hostels cost anything from £3 to £8 or £9 per person, whilst you can get a two-person tent bedded down on a nice campsite for somewhere around a fiver.

The local post office in my experience can often be a real help if you need to find somewhere to stay and have arrived utterly clueless. They usually know of B&Bs or accommodation nearby that can provide a place to take off your boots at the very least. Another suggestion from the heart: if you are on the camping route and you find yourself beginning to tire, try asking at sites whether they have any static caravans to let. There is a wonderful place at Sconser (near Sligahan) on Skye where the lady at the B&B also has a small and quite poorly equipped caravan to let, at a fiver a night. A real boon to a footsore camper in the height of midgie season.

Happily, Scotland is an easy place to camp within the sound of fresh running water, and there are lots of beautiful places to rest your weary bones on a thin camping mattress and stare up at a starry sky unpolluted by the orange glow of street lights. In Shetland they have absolutely no qualms about the 'camp where you fancy' attitude to life. There is something very satisfying about waking up with a coating of dewy dampness around you and a healthy chilly nose and roasting sleeping-bag-still-got-your-socks-on toes. The message here is: whenever you can, don't be restricted by the 'place to stay for the night' mentality that constricts us into mortgages and endowment policies. Get out and about and enjoy your days, and with just a little help from this section hopefully the nights will take care of themselves.

THE WEST

Argyll and Bute

Ardentinny

CAMPING
Glenfinart Park (Mr and Mrs Worters), Ardentinny, by Dunoon, is in the grounds of a ruined mansion. Open Easter to October. Priced from £2–£5. Tel: 01369 810256

Arrochar

HOSTEL
SYHA, Ardgartan, Arrochar is a standard hostel. Open February to December. Priced at £6–£7 per night per person. Tel: 01301 702362

B&B
The Road Man's Cottage, Glencrose, Rest and be Thankful, by Arrochar, is close to the A83, five miles from Arrochar. Open all year. Prices from £11.50. Tel: 01301 702557

Campbeltown

B&B
Ballygreggan Farm (Mrs Tracy Millar), Drumlemble, by Campbeltown, is open all year. Prices from £12–£13. Tel: 01586 810211

HOTEL
Dellwood Hotel, Drumore, Campbeltown, is family-run. Open all year. Prices from £15 per person sharing, £17–£25 for a single. Tel: 01586 552465

Carradale

CAMPING
Carradale Bay Caravan Park is on a sandy beach with lovely views of Arran. On the B8001/B842. Open Easter to September. Prices from £6–£11 per night for tents or caravans. Tel: 01583 431665

Connel

B&B
North Ledaig Caravan Park, Connel, by Oban, is a quiet beach-side park looking over to Mull. Great facilities. Open Easter to October. Prices from £6.30–£10.50, for caravans only. Tel: 01631 710291

Dalmally

B&B

'Trade Winds', Lochawe, Dalmally, has a large garden, and don't forget Loch Awe has free fishing! Open February to October. Prices from £14–£16 single, £14–£20 sharing. Tel: 01838 200248

Dunoon

CAMPING

Stratheck Caravan Park, Loch Eck, is by Dunoon. You can rent caravans here, too. Open March to October and December to January. Prices from £5–£10. Tel: 01369 840472

B&B

Larkfield (Mrs Glass), 41 George Street, Hunter's Quay, is a quiet place near the ferry. Open April to October. Prices from £13.50–£15. Tel: 01369 702247

Helensburgh

B&B

Eastbank (Mrs D. Ross), 10 Hanover Street, has a view of the Clyde estuary. Open all year. Prices from £16. Tel: 01436 673665

Inveraray

CAMPING

Argyll Caravan Park has plenty of amenities, even a bar! Open April to October. Prices from £6–£9.50, for tents and caravans. Tel: 01499 302285

HOSTEL

SYHA, Dalmally Road, Inveraray, is a standard hostel. Open mid-March to October. Price per night from £4.60–£5.60. Tel: 01499 302454

B&B

Lorona (Mrs D. Campbell), Main Street South, Inveraray, overlooks Loch Fyne. Open April to October. Prices from £14.50–£15.50. Tel: 01499 302258

Isle of Seil

B&B

The Bridge to the Atlantic at Clachan-Seil (check out the food and the view at the Willowburn Hotel) doesn't carry a toll, and there aren't any ferries.

Audrey's B&B, No 1 The Old Coach House, Ellenabeich, Isle of Seil, has an ocean view. Open April to October. Prices from £12.50–£15. Tel: 01852 300549

Kilberry

CAMPING

Port Ban Caravan Park, Kilberry, by Tarbert, is a secluded seaside park with great sunsets. The park is one mile north of Kilberry. Open April to October. Prices from £5.50–£6.90 per night for tents and caravans. Tel: 01880 770224

Kilmartin

B&B

Tibertich (Mrs Caulton), Kilmartin, is a working sheep farm just off the A816. Open March to October. Priced at £14. Tel: 01546 810281

Lochgilphead

CAMPING

Tara's Field, Tigh-Na-Glaic, Crinan, Lochgilphead, is in a great situation, by the Crinan Canal with views over Jura and Scarba. Open all year. Prices from £2.50–£8 for tents and caravans. Tel: 01546 830243

Lochgilphead Caravan Park, Bank Park, Lochgilphead, is a serious campsite with good amenities. Open April to October. Priced at £7 a night for a pitch. Tel: 01546 602003

Luss

B&B

Glemollochan Farm (Mrs K. Wragg), Luss. Open Easter to October. Rooms for £16–£19.50 per person for a double/twin for B&B. Tel: 01436 860246

Machrihanish

CAMPING

Camping and Caravan Club Site, East Trodigal, Machrihanish, is just a mile from the brilliant beach. Open March to September. Prices from £8.20–£10.40. Tel: 01586 810366

B&B

East Drumlemble Farm, Machrihanish, by Campbeltown, is in a beautiful area. Try the bay for example. Open April to October. Priced at £13. Tel: 01586 810220

Oban

CAMPING

Oban Divers Caravan Park is on Glenshellach Road and has excellent facilities. Open March to November. Priced at £7–£8 per pitch per night. Tel: 01631 562755

Oban Caravan and Camping Park, Gallanach Road, Oban, has glorious sea views two miles from the centre of town, towards Gallanach. Open April to mid-October. Price per pitch per night is £6–£8. Tel: 01631 562425

HOSTELS

SYHA, Esplanade, is a high standard hostel open daily till 2 a.m. Open 23 March to end November. Price per night is £6.60–£8. Tel: 01631 562025

Jeremy Inglis has budget accommodation at 21 Airds Crescent. Open all year. Sharing priced at £6.50–£7. Singles are £11–£12. Tel: 01631 565065

Oban Backpackers Hostel is at Breadalbane Street and sells itself as 'sensational'! Open all year. Prices from £8.50–£9.90 per person. Tel: 01631 562107

B&B

Invercloy Guest House, Ardconnel Terrace, is on the main Oban Hill with panoramic views. Open all year. Prices from £12–£20 per person. Tel: 01631 562058

Barranrioch Farm (Mrs Davidson), Glencruitten, Oban, is in a rural setting overlooking the tremendous (but not free, sadly) Rare Breeds Farm. Open all year. Prices from £12 per person either single or sharing. Tel: 01631 770223

Inver (Mrs McEwan), 32 Glencruitten Drive, Oban, is just five minutes' walk from the town centre. Open Easter to September. Prices are very reasonable, £11–£12 per person sharing. Tel: 01631 563472

Tarbert

CAMPING

West Loch Tarbert Holiday Park is a quiet place with lochside views. It is two miles south of Tarbert on the left of the A83. Open April to October. Prices from £5 per pitch per night. Tel: 01880 820873

HOTEL

Tarbert Hotel, Harbour Street, Tarbert, is well priced with good facilities. Open all year. Prices from £17.50. Tel: 01880 820264

Tayinloan

CAMPING

Point Sands Caravan Park, Tayinloan, by Tarbert, is beside a beautiful sandy beach. Open April to October. Prices from £6–£9.50 for tents or caravans. Tel: 01583 441263

Tighnabruaich

HOSTEL

SYHA, High Road, Tighnabruaich, is a standard hostel with 40 beds. Open end March to beginning October. Prices from £4.60–£5.60 per night. Tel: 01700 811622

B&B

Piermount (Ron and Liz Alexander), Kames, Tighnabruaich overlooks the Kyles of Bute. Open all year. Priced from £14. Tel: 01700 811218

BUTE

Rothesay

B&B

Guildford Court (Mr Williamson), Watergate, Rothesay, is just a minute from the ferry terminal, with great views over the harbour and bay. Open all year. Prices from £14–£17 per person. Tel: 01700 503770

East Ayrshire

Cumnock

CAMPING
Woodroad Caravan Park, Lugar, Cumnock, is open April to September. Prices from £3.25 for a tent on its own, to £5.35–£8 for a caravan and car (1996). Tel: 01290 422111/422318

B&B
Viewfield (E. Turnbull), 131 Glaisnock St, Cumnock, is priced at £12.50 per person (1996). Open April to October. Tel: 01290 421959

Kilmarnock

B&B
Hillhouse Farm (Mrs M. Howie), Graddyards Road, is open all year, and is actually a farmhouse. Priced at £14–£17 per person sharing, or £15–£18 per person single (1996). Tel: 01563 523370

Kilmaurs

B&B
Aulton Farm (A. Hawkshaw), Kilmaurs, near Kilmarnock, is open all year. The facilities here are very good. Priced at £13.50 per person sharing, or £15 single (1996). Tel: 01563 538208

Sorn

B&B
Templandshaw Farm (Mrs P. Poole), Sorn, is open all year. Priced from £12–£15 for singles or sharing (1996). Tel: 01290 551543

City of Glasgow

CAMPING
Balgair Castle Caravan Park, Overglinns, Fintry, G63 has pitches from £5.50–£8.95 per night, for two people plus caravan/tent. Open March to October. Tel: 01360 860283

Craigendmuir Park, Campsie View, Stepps, G33 has pitches from £6 per night for two people plus car/caravan/tent. Open all year. Tel: 0141 779 4159/2973

HOSTELS
SYHA, 7/8 Park Terrace, G3 is a hostel of superior standard that is open till 2 a.m. Open all year. You even get a free continental breakfast. Tel: 0141 332 3004

YMCA Scotland is at David Naismith Court, 33 Petershill Drive, Glasgow. This is a high rise in a slightly scary area. Tel: 0141 557 2355

Berkeley Globetrotters Hostel, 65 Berkeley Street, Charing Cross, G3 is open all year and costs £8. Tel: 0141 221 7880

B&B

3 King Edward Road (Mrs E. Anderson), G13, has rooms which start at £14 for a single or per person for a double. Tel: 0141 954 8033

Alamo Guest House, 46 Gray Street, G3 has good facilities, including some *en suite* bathrooms. Prices from £18 single, £16 double or twin per person. Tel: 0141 339 2395

North Ayrshire

Dalry

CAMPING

Craighead Caravan Site is close to the village centre near the A737. There are good facilities, although it caters mainly for caravans. Open April to October. Prices are £6 for caravans, £5 for tents (1996). Tel: 01294 835425

Irvine

CAMPING

Cunninghamhead Estate Caravan Park (J. Sim) is on the B769 north-east of Kilmarnock. Open April to September. Priced from £5 for a tent, from £6.50 for a caravan (1996). Tel: 01294 835425

Largs

CAMPING

South Whittleburn Farm (Mrs M. Watson), Brisbane Glen, Largs, is open April to October and has good facilities. Prices from £5 for tent or caravan (1996). Tel: 01475 675881

HOSTEL

Largs Tourist Hostel (Mr A. Mackinnon), 110 Irvine Road, Largs, is open all year. The hostel-type accommodation costs from £8 for a single. Tel: 01475 672851

B&B

Amberley (Mrs C. Inglis), 11 Auchenmaid Drive, is open all year. Prices from £12 per person (1996). Tel: 01475 675620

Skelmorlie

CAMPING

Mains Caravan Park (J. Stirrat), Skelmorlie Mains, Skelmorlie, is open March to October, and is actually on a working farm. Prices from £6 for tents, from £7 for caravans (1996). Tel: 01475 520794

ARRAN

CAMPING

Glen Rosa Farm, near Brodick. Basic amenities, cold water, no caravans. Tel: 01770 302380

HOSTELS

SYHA, Lochranza, is a standard hostel. Open end March to end October. Prices from £6.15–£7.35. Tel: 01770 830631.

SYHA, Whiting Bay, Shore Road, Brodick, is another standard hostel. Open March to October. Prices from £6.10–£7.20. Tel: 01770 700339

North High Corrie Croft, Arran Estate Trust, Douglas Park, Brodick, has bunkhouse accommodation from £5.20. Open all year. Tel: 01770 302203

CUMBRAE

B&B

Denmark Cottage (J. McCallum and L. Carruthers), 8 Ferry Road, Millport, is open all year. Prices from £13–£15.50 per person sharing, £15–£18 for singles. Tel: 01475 530958

College of the Holy Spirit, College St, Millport, offers accommodation with good facilities. Priced at £15 per person. Tel: 01475 530353

North Lanarkshire

Kilsyth

B&B

Mashobra (Mrs Dunlop), Coach Road, Kilsyth, is open all year and has rooms from £14–£15 single or £12.50–£13 for double or twin. Tel: 01236 822122

Motherwell

CAMPING

Strathclyde Country Park has excellent facilities for camping, with toilets, showers, laundry facilities, but above all a wealth of activities. Open all year. Pitches are from £4.50–£8.50 per night for two people plus tent/caravan/car. Tel: 01698 266155

Renfrewshire

Kilbarchan

CAMPING

Barnbrock Camping Site, Barnbrock Farm, Kilbarchan, has pitches from £5 per night for two people plus car/tent. No caravans. Tel: 01505 614791

Lochwinnoch

B&B

Garnock Lodge (Mrs V. Meechan), Boydstone Road, Loanhead, Lochwinnoch, does B&B from £15–£17.50 single or £15–£20 per person for double or twin rooms. Open all year. Tel: 01505 503690

South Ayrshire

Ayr

CAMPING

Crofthead Holiday Park, McNairston Road, by Ayr, is open Easter to October. It has good facilities. Prices range from £4.50 for tents to £6 for caravans with cars (1996). Tel: 01292 263516

HOSTEL

SYHA, 5 Craigweil Road, Ayr, is a standard hostel. Open 23 March to end October. Priced from £6–£7.10. Tel: 01292 262322

BUDGET

You can get accommodation at Wilson Hall (Carol Steel), SAC Auchincruive, Ayr, which is a halls of residence. Open around Easter, then July to September. Prices from £11 per person (1996). Tel: 01292 520331

B&B

Afton Lodge (M. Paxton), 10 Bath Place, Ayr, is open all year. Prices from £13–£15 per person, single or sharing (1996). Tel: 01292 611888

Kilkerran (M. Ferguson), 15 Prestwick Road, has very good facilities. Open all year. Priced from £13–£17 per person, single or sharing (1996). Tel: 01292 266477

Ballantrae

CAMPING

Laggan House Leisure Park, Ballantrae, near Girvan, is open March to October. It has excellent facilities. Priced from £5 for tents, to £7 for caravans (1996). Tel: 01465 831229

Barrhill

CAMPING

Windsor Holiday Park, Barrhill, is open March to October. Prices from £6 (1996). Tel: 01465 821355

Crosshill

CAMPING

Kilkerran Walled Garden Caravan and Camping Park, Kilkerran Estate, Crosshill, near Maybole, looks idyllic and has good amenities. Open April to October. Priced from £6 for a tent (1996). Tel: 01655 740323

Girvan

CAMPING

Bennane Hill Caravan Park, Lendalfoot, near Girvan, is open March to October. Prices from £7 (1996). Tel: 01465 891233

Carleton Caravan Park, Lendalfoot, is also open March to October. Prices from £4 for a tent only (1996). Tel: 01465 891215

B&B

Mrs Elsie Young, 7 The Avenue, Girvan, is open for B&B from April to September. Prices are £11.50 per person, single or sharing (1996). Tel: 01465 714852

Margaret Miller, 47 Vicarton Street, is open April to September. Priced from £13 per person sharing (1996). Tel: 01465 713569

Prestwick

CAMPING

Prestwick Holiday Park is one mile north of Prestwick, signposted off the A79. Prices from £5 for tents (1996). Facilities are excellent. Tel: 01292 479261

B&B

Knox (Mrs Janette Wardrope), 105 Ayr Road, is open all year. Prices from £13.50–£15.50 per person sharing (1996). Tel: 01292 478808

Tarbolton

CAMPING

Middlemuir Caravan Park, Tarbolton, near Ayr, is open March to October and has really good facilities. Prices from £5 for a tent, £7 for a caravan (1996). Tel: 01292 541647

Troon

CAMPING

St Meddans Caravan Site, Low St Meddans, Troon, is open March to October. Prices from £7 for a tent, £8 for a caravan (1996). Tel: 01292 312957

B&B

Tigh Dearg (Mrs N. Livingstone), 31 Victoria Drive, is open all year. Prices from £13 per person, single or sharing (1996). Tel: 01292 311552

Turnberry

B&B

High McGownston Farm (Mrs B. MacPherson), Turnberry, is open all year. Priced from £12.50 per person single or sharing (1996). Tel: 01655 331247

South Lanarkshire

Biggar

CAMPING

Biggar Caravan Site at Biggar Park is open April to October. It has facilities for caravans as well as tents. Caravans from £7–£9 per night. Tel: 01899 220319

HOSTEL

YMCA Scotland, Wiston Lodge, Biggar, is a YMCA National Council Residence. Phone ahead. Tel: 01899 850228

B&B

Walston Mansion Farmhouse (Mrs M. Kirby), Walston, by Biggar. You will pay £13.50–£15 per person at this B&B, which is open all year. There are plenty of facilities, too. Tel: 01899 810388

Crawford

CAMPING

Crawford Caravan and Camping Site at Murray Place, Carlisle Road, has pitches from £5 a night for two people plus car/tent or caravan. Open April to October. Tel: 01864 502258

Lanark

CAMPING

Newhouse Caravan and Camping Park, Ravenstruther, by Lanark, has pitches from £6–£7 per night for two people plus their car/caravan/tent. Open April to October. Tel: 01555 870228

Lesmahagow

CAMPING

Draffan Marshall Farm (Mrs J. Stewart), Blackwood, by Lesmahagow, has pitches for caravans or tents, from £4–£6 per night per pitch. Open April to October. Tel: 01555 860257

New Lanark

HOSTEL

SYHA, Wee Row, New Lanark, is a standard hostel with free continental breakfast for those staying. Open all year. Tel: 01555 666710

Strathaven

B&B

Elderslie (Mrs F. Taylor), Newton Road, Strathaven. Here you will pay from £15–£18 for a single and £15–£17 for a double/twin room, per person. Open all year. Tel: 01357 520649

West Dunbartonshire

Balloch

CAMPING

Tullichewan Holiday Park, Old Luss Road, Balloch, has excellent facilities. Open December to October. Prices from £5.50–£11 per pitch. Tel: 01389 759475

B&B

Mrs Gilfeather, 2 McLean Crescent, Balloch, is in easy walking distance of Loch Lomond and Balloch Park. Open all year. Priced from £13. Tel: 01389 753215

Loch Lomond

HOSTEL

SYHA, Arden, Alexandria, is a high standard hostel open till 2 a.m. Open March to end October. Tel: 01389 850226

THE EAST

East Lothian

Dirleton

CAMPING

Yellowcraig Caravan Club Site is at Dirleton, close to the sea and the amenities of North Berwick. No tents, but caravans cost £6.50–£9.50. Open April to September. Tel: 01620 850217

HOTEL

The Castle Inn, Dirleton, is an old coaching inn overlooking the green. Open all year. Prices from £15 for single, £18 for a person sharing. Tel: 01620 850221

Dunbar

B&B

Rosedene (Mrs Smith), 19a Belhaven Road, well placed for everything, at a great price. Only £10–£12.50 per person, £15 single. Open all year. Tel: 01368 862533

Haddington

B&B

The Farmhouse (Mrs A. Clark), Upper Bolton, Haddington, is a working farm three miles south of Haddington. Prices from £16.50 for a person sharing, £17 upwards for a single. Tel: 01620 810476

Longniddry

CAMPING

Gosford Gardens Caravan Club Site is in a lovely setting. Open April to October. Prices from £4.20–£15 for a caravan or a tent. Tel: 01875 870487

Musselburgh

B&B

Melville House (Mrs Bouglas), 103a North High Street, Musselburgh, is close to the Brunton Theatre. Prices from £14 per person sharing, £16–£18 for singles. Tel: 0131 665 6560

North Berwick

CAMPING

Rhodes Caravan Site, at Lime Grove, is close to the beach and is nice and grassy for a good pitch. Open mid-March to September. Tel: 01620 892197

Tantallon Caravan Park overlooks the golf course and the Firth of Forth. Prices from £6.50 for a caravan or tent, plus car, and they have caravans to let, too. Open March to October. Tel: 01620 893348

B&B

Beehive Cottage (Mrs Fife), 12 Kingston, North Berwick, is a country cottage! It has a garden and lovely views. B&B from £15 sharing. Tel: 01620 894785

HOTEL

The Belhaven Hotel, 28 Westgate, North Berwick, is close to the town centre, with sea views. Open all year. Prices from £16.50 for a person sharing, £18 upwards for singles. Tel: 01620 893009

Tranent

B&B

North Elphinstone Farmhouse, by Tranent, is in a quiet location, ten miles east of Edinburgh. Prices from £15–£17 per person, £16–£17 for singles. Tel: 01875 610329

City of Edinburgh

CAMPING

Mortonhall Caravan Park, 38 Mortonhall Gate, Frogston Road East, is close to the city bypass and just 15 minutes from the city centre. It is quite a pleasant location, fairly rural and near the Pentlands and all that they offer. Plenty of facilities. Open March to October. Pitches, for caravan or tent, plus car, cost from £7.75. Tel: 0131 664 1533

HOSTELS

SYHA, 7 Bruntsfield Crescent, EH10, is open February to December and is a high standard hostel open till 2 a.m. From £6.75–£9.15 for a person in a dormitory. Tel: 0131 447 2994

SYHA, 18 Eglinton Crescent, EH12, is another superior hostel open till 2 a.m., which also provides complimentary continental breakfast. Dormitory places cost £9.25–£11.60. Tel: 0131 337 1120

College Wynd Tourist Hotel, 205 Cowgate, costs only £12–£15 for a single. Tel: 0131 226 2353

Edinburgh Backpackers Hostel, 65 Cockburn Street, costs from £9.50 for a dormitory place, £15 for a person sharing a double room. Tel: 0131 220 1717

Annandale Hostel, Candlemaker Row, has private double rooms from £10–£12 per person per night. Tel: 0131 657 2525

Belford Hostel, Belford Church, 6–8 Douglas Gardens, is a historic church building. Costs are from £9 for the dormitory. Open 24 hours a day. Tel: 0131 225 6209

Backpackers Hostel – Royal Mile, 105 Royal Mile, is very central. Costs are £9.50–£9.90 per person in a dormitory. Tel: 0131 557 6120

Kinnaird Christian Hostel, 12 Coates Crescent, doesn't have a curfew, and encourages families. It has a range of charges, from £12 for the dormitory, £15 upwards for a double per person, £18 for a single. Tel: 0131 225 3608

Cowgate Tourist Hostel, 112 Cowgate, is open July to September. Prices from £9. Tel: 0131 226 2153

High Street Hostel, 8 Blackfriars Street, is open all year. It costs from £8.90. Tel: 0131 557 3984

Princes Street Hostel is at 5 West Register Street, and is open all year. Prices from £8. Tel: 0131 556 6894

B&B

St Colm's College, 23 Inverleith Terrace, is within shouting distance of the Botanics. Open all year. B&B per person costs from £16.50–£18.50. Tel: 0131 315 4854. (Many of the colleges and universities have accommodation in their halls of residence out of term-time. They aren't as cheap as traditional B&B establishments, so I haven't included them here. You can find out about them at the Tourist Information Centre.)

Aries Guest House, 5 Upper Gilmore Place, is in a quiet residential street, but close to the centre, too. Prices from £13–£22 per person. Tel: 0131 229 4669

Armadillo Guest House, 12 Gilmore Place, is close to the one above. Prices from £14 per person. Tel: 0131 229 6457

HOTEL

Victoria Hotel, 3 Forth Street, is bang in the city centre, but in a quiet(ish) street nonetheless. Prices from £18 per person. Tel: 0131 556 1616

Midlothian

Dalkeith

CAMPING

Fordel Caravan and Camping Park is in a woody spot. Open March to October. Prices from £6.50 for a tent, £8–£9 for a caravan. Tel: 0131 660 3921

B&B

Rathan House, 45 Eskbank Road, Eskbank, by Dalkeith, is a refurbished Victorian house. Prices from £18–£25 per person sharing, singles from £25. Tel: 0131 663 3291

Chalkieside Farm (Mrs Donald) is a working farmhouse on the A6124 near Cousland. Open all year. Prices from £14. Tel: 0131 663 1821

West Lothian

Bathgate

B&B

Tarrareoch Farm (Mrs F. Gibb), Armadale, near Bathgate, is open all year. Prices start at £12.50 per person sharing (1996). Tel: 01501 730404

Blackburn

CAMPING

Mosshall Farm, Blackburn, is close to the Bathgate Hills. Open all year. The price is good too: £4.50–£5.50 for a caravan or a tent. Tel: 01501 762318

Linlithgow

CAMPING

Loch House Farm Site is close to the loch itself. Open all year. Prices from £6 for a caravan, £4–£6 for a tent. Tel: 01506 842144

Beecraigs Caravan Park is open all year and costs £3.50–£4 for a tent (1996). Tel: 01506 844516

B&B

Belsyde Farm, Lanark Road, Linlithgow, is a farmhouse on a sheep farm beside the Union Canal. Good access to the M8/M9/M90. Prices from £16 for single, £16 for single person sharing a double. Tel: 01506 842098

Chantstoun (Mrs Martay), South Mains, Bathgate Hills, is on a working farm in a quiet location. Open all year. Prices from £15. Tel: 01506 811644

Philipstoun

B&B

Pardovan House (Mr and Mrs Baker), Philipstoun, by Linlithgow, is a stone-built house with gardens. Open April to September. Tel: 01506 834219

THE BORDERS

Dumfries and Galloway

Annan

B&B

'The Craig' (Mrs S. Anderson), 18 St John's Road, Annan, is open all year. Priced from £13.50–£14 per person single or sharing. Tel: 01461 204665

Auchenmalg

CAMPING

Cock Inn Caravan Park, Auchenmalg, is open March to October. Priced from £6.50–£8 for caravan/car, £6 for tent/car. Tel: 01581 500227

Beattock

CAMPING
Beattock House Hotel Caravan Park is open April to October. Priced at £6.50.
Tel: 01683 300403

Borgue

CAMPING
Brighouse Bay Holiday Park is open all year. There are great facilities,
including a pool. They also have caravans to let. Prices from £8.50–£11.25
caravans or tents. Tel: 01557 870267

Cairnryan

CAMPING
Cairnryan Caravan and Chalet Park is open April to October. Prices from
£4.50 for tents, £8.50 for caravans. Tel: 01581 200231

Castle Douglas

CAMPING
Lochside Caravan and Camping Site, Lochside Park, Castle Douglas, is open Easter
to late-October. Priced from £6.75–£8.25 per caravan/tent. Tel: 01556 502949
    Kirkstyle Farm (Mr and Mrs T. Edgar), Kirkpatrick Durham, near Castle
Douglas, is open April to October. Priced from £4–£6 for tents. Tel: 01556
650230

HOSTEL
SYHA, Kendoon, Dalry, Castle Douglas, is a simple hostel, Open mid-June to
October. Prices are seniors £4.40, juniors £3.65. Tel: 01786 891400

B&B
Woodlea (M.E. King), 37 Ernespie Road, Castle Douglas, is open all year.
Prices from £14–£15 per person, single or sharing. Tel: 01556 502247
    Blairinnie Farm (Mrs J. McMorran), Crossmichael, by Castle Douglas, is a
working hill farm. Open May to September. Priced from £14–£16 for a
person, single or sharing. Tel: 01556 670268

Creetown

CAMPING
Castle Cary Holiday Park, Creetown, is open all year. Priced from £7.80–£10.
Tel: 01671 820264

Crocketford

CAMPING
Park of Brandedleys, Crocketford, by Dumfries is open March to October.
With great facilities, it costs from £9–£13. Tel: 01556 690250
    Barnsoul Farm Park, Shawhead, by Dumfries is open Easter to October.
It costs £5–£8 per tent/caravan. Tel: 01387 730249

Dalbeattie

CAMPING

Islecroft Caravan and Camping Site, Mill Street, Dalbeattie, is open Easter to October. Priced from £5.25–£6.25 for tent or caravan. Tel: 01556 610012

Sandyhills Bay Leisure Park has a great beach and good facilities. Open April to October. Prices from £6.75–£9.95. Tel: 01557 870267

Drummore

CAMPING

New England Bay Caravan Club Site, Port Logan, by Stranraer, is open April to September. Priced at £4–£9 for a caravan or tent. Tel: 01776 860275

Dumfries

CAMPING

Beeswing Caravan Park, Drumjohn Moor, Kirkgunzeon, by Dumfries, is open March to October. Prices are £5–£6.80 for car/caravan, £5–£6.80 for car/tent, and £4–£5.80 for a tent. Tel: 01387 760242

Mouswald Park Caravan Site, Mouswald Place, Mouswald, by Dumfries, is open March to October. Prices from £6.50–£7. Tel: 01387 830226

B&B

17 Market Square (Mrs Adair) is open all year. Prices from £11–£13 single, £16–£20 twin/double. Tel: 01387 262820

Shambellie View (Mrs Burdekin), Wellgreen, Glencaple Road, is about one and a half miles from the town centre. Open all year. Prices from £14.50. Tel: 01387 269331

Ecclefechan

CAMPING

Cressfield Caravan Park has great facilities. Open all year. Prices from £6–£7.50 for caravans, £5 for a tent on its own. Tel: 01576 300702

Hoddom Castle Caravan Park, Hoddom, near Ecclefechan, is open Easter to October. It has good facilities too. Priced from £6.50–£10 for caravan or tent. Tel: 01576 300251

Gatehouse of Fleet

CAMPING

Auchenlarie Holiday Farm is open March to October. With good amenities, it is priced at £6–£10 for a car and caravan or tent. Tel: 01557 840251

Mossyard Caravan Park is on the estuary and is open April to October. Costs are £6–£7 for car plus tent or caravan, £5 for tent alone. Tel: 01557 840226

B&B

Newton Farm (Mrs E. Hamilton) is open April to October. Prices from £14–£15 per person, single or sharing. Tel: 01557 840234

Glenluce

CAMPING

Glenluce Caravan Park is open April to mid-October. Priced at £7.50–£8.50 for caravan and car, £6.50–£7.50 for tent and car. Tel: 01581 300412

Whitecairn Farm Caravan Park, Whitecairn, is open March to October. Priced from £6.50–£7.50 for car plus tent or caravan. Tel: 01581 300267

Glen Trool

CAMPING

Caldons Campsite, Forest Enterprise, is open April to September. Prices are just £6.20 for tent or caravan. Tel: 01671 840218

Glen Trool Holiday Park, Bargrennan, is open March to October. Prices start at £6.75. Tel: 01671 840280

Gretna

CAMPING

The Braids Caravan Park, Annan Road, is open March to October. Priced from £5 for tent alone. Tel: 01461 337409

B&B

The Braids (Mrs E. Copeland), Annan Road, is open all year. Priced at £15 per person. Tel: 01461 337409

Isle of Whithorn

CAMPING

Burrowhead Caravan and Chalet Park, Isle of Whithorn, is open March to October. Priced from £5–£6 for tents on their own. Tel: 01988 500252

Kippford

CAMPING

Kippford Caravan Park is open March to October. Prices are £5–£12 for car and tent, £9–£12 for car and caravan. Tel: 01556 620636

Kirkcudbright

CAMPING

Silvercraigs Caravan and Camping Site, Silvercraigs Road, is open Easter to late October. Prices from £6.25–£7.75 for caravans or tents. Tel: 01556 502521

Seaward Caravan Park has good facilities, and is open March to October. Prices from £6.95 for tents or caravans, they also have caravans to let. Tel: 01557 331079

HOTEL

Commercial Hotel is open all year. Prices from £15–£16 per person. Tel: 01557 330407

Kirkpatrick-Fleming

CAMPING

King Robert the Bruce's Cave, Cove Estate, Kirkpatrick-Fleming, is open all year. Prices are £5 for car/tent or car/caravan. Tel: 01461 800285

B&B

Georgefield (Mrs K. Scott), Kirkpatrick-Fleming, is open all year. Priced from £13 for single, £12 per person sharing. Tel: 01461 800226

Langholm

CAMPING

Ewes Water Caravan and Camping Park, Milntown, Langholm, is open April to September. Prices from £3 for a tent on its own. Tel: 013873 80386

Lockerbie

CAMPING

Halleaths Caravan Park is open March to November. Priced at £5.50 for tents and £7 for caravans. Tel: 01387 819630

Whiteshiels Caravan Park, near Lockerbie, is open March to November. Prices are £4–£5.50 for tents, £5.50 for caravans. Tel: 01387 380494

B&B

Castlehill Farm (Mrs Deamer), Tundergarth, near Lockerbie, is a breeding farm with home cooking. Open April to October. Priced from £15. Tel: 01576 710223

Moffat

CAMPING

Camping and Caravanning Club Site, Hammerland's Farm, is open from end March to early November. Prices are £9.20–£12.05 for tents or caravans. Tel: 01683 220436

B&B

Morlich House, Ballplay Road, is quiet and secluded. Open February to November. Prices from £14 single, £16–£18 per person sharing. Tel: 01683 220589

Seamore House (J. and J. Marchington), Academy Road, is in the centre of town. Open March to October. Tel: 01683 220404

Newton Stewart

HOSTEL

SYHA, Minnigaff, Newton Stewart, is a standard hostel. Open March to beginning October. Prices are seniors £5.75, juniors £4.70. Tel: 01671 402211

B&B

Dunbar House (Mr A. Cook), Creebridge, Minnigaff, Newton Stewart, is open May to October. Priced at £12.50–£14 per person, room only £11. Tel: 01671 402652

Palnackie

CAMPING

Barlochan Caravan Park has excellent facilities. Open April to October. Priced at £8.75–£9.45 for tents or caravans. Tel: 01557 870267

Penpont

CAMPING

Penpont (Floors) Caravan and Camping Park, near Thornhill, is open April to October. Priced from £6.50. Tel: 01848 330470

Portpatrick

CAMPING

Sunnymeade Caravan Park is open March to October. Prices from £7–£9 for a caravan, £7 for a tent. Tel: 01776 810293

Port William

CAMPING

West Bay Caravan Site is open March to October. Prices from £5. Tel: 01988 700367

B&B

Kenmara (Mrs J. Reid), 57 Main Street, is open April to October. Prices from £12.50–£13 per person. Tel: 01988 700469

Rockcliffe

CAMPING

Castle Point Caravan Site has excellent facilities and gorgeous sea views. Open March to October. Prices from £7–£9 for caravan or tent. Tel: 01556 630248

Stranraer

CAMPING

Sands of Luce Caravan Park, Sandhead, by Stranraer, is open mid-March to October. Priced at £6.50–£8 for tent or caravan. Tel: 01776 830456

B&B

The Old Manse (Ms Burns), Lewis Street, is open all year. Priced at £14 single, £13–£14 sharing, room only £12. Tel: 01776 702135

Talnotry

CAMPING

This site is a caravan and camping site again from the Forestry Commission. Find it on the A712, seven miles east of Newton Stewart. Open April to September. Prices are £5.50 for either car/caravan or car/tent. Tel: 01671 402420

Wanlockhead

HOSTEL
SYHA, Loftus Lodge, Wanlockhead, by Biggar, has standard accommodation. Open 21 March to 27 October. Prices are £5.75 for seniors, £4.70 for juniors. Tel: 01659 74252

Whithorn

B&B
Baltier Farm (Mrs E. Forsyth), Whithorn, is a house on a dairy farm with good views. Open March to November. Priced from £14. Tel: 01988 600241

Scottish Borders

Cockburnspath

CAMPING
Chesterfield Caravan Site, The Neuk is three miles from the beach. Open April to mid-October. Priced from £6. Tel: 01368 830459

Coldingham

CAMPING
Scoutscroft Caravan Site, Coldingham, is right by the coast. Open March to November. Prices from £6–£9. Tel: 01890 771338

HOSTEL
SYHA, Coldingham Sands, Coldingham, is a standard hostel. Open March to October. Tel: 01890 771298

Coldstream

CAMPING
Tweed Green Caravan and Camping Park, Abbey Road, overlooks the River Tweed. Open May to September. Priced at £7. Tel: 01890 883376

Duns

HOSTEL
SYHA, Abbey St Bathans, Duns, is a standard hostel. Open all year. Tel: 01361 840245

B&B
Cockburn Mill (Mrs A. Prentice), Duns, is a riverside farmhouse in a beautiful setting. There is even trout fishing available from the farm. Idyllic, with water coming from a hillside spring. From £17–£19 per person. Open March to November. Tel: 01361 882811

Ettrick Valley

CAMPING
Angecroft Caravan Park, Ettrick Valley, is open March to October. Priced from £4–£8.25. Tel: 01750 730657

Galashiels

B&B
Overlangshaw Farm (Sheila Bergius), Langshaw, Galashiels, is near the Southern Upland Way, only four miles from Galashiels and Melrose. Home cooking and wonderful views. Open all year. From £15–£18 per person. Tel: 01896 860244

Hawick

HOSTEL
SYHA, Snoot, Roberton, near Hawick, is a simple hostel. Open end March to October. Tel: 01450 880259

B&B
Wiltonburn Farm (Mrs Sheila Shell), Hawick, is a working farm in a valley two miles from Hawick. Open all year. From £15–£16 per person. Tel: 01450 372414

Innerleithen

CAMPING
Tweedside Caravan Park, Montgomery Street, is open April to October. Priced from £4–£6. Tel: 01896 831271

Jedburgh

CAMPING
Jedwater Caravan Park is on the banks of the River Jed, and it offers free fishing! Open April to October. Priced from £7–£9. Tel: 01835 840219

B&B
Mrs M. Crone, 15 Hartrigge Crescent, is in walking distance of the centre of town. Open all year. Prices from £13.50. Tel: 01835 862738

Kelso

CAMPING
Springwood Caravan Park, Springwood Estate, is open March to October. Priced from £8–£9. Tel: 01573 224033

HOSTEL
SYHA, Kirk Yetholm, near Kelso, is a standard hostel. Open March to October. Tel: 01573 420631

B&B
Cliftonhill Farm (Archie and Maggie Stewart), Kelso, is a traditional farmhouse with a river running through the farm for fishing (or swimming).

Home-made bread too. Two miles from Kelso. Open all year. From £15–£18 per person. Tel: 01573 226416

Morebattle Tofts (Mrs Debbie Playfair), Kelso, is a large eighteenth-century farmhouse in a gloriously beautiful setting. Open March to October. From £14–£16 per person. Tel: 01573 440364

Kielder (just over the border, but within easy reach for Scots!)

CAMPING
Kielder Campsite, Forest Enterprise, Earls Burn, Bellingham, Hexham is open Easter to end September. Prices from £4.50–£11. Tel: 01434 220756

Lauder

CAMPING
Thirlestane Castle Caravan and Camping Park, Thirlestane Castle, is in a great setting. Open April to October. Priced from £5–£6. Tel: 01578 722254

Melrose

CAMPING
Gibson Park Caravan Club Site, High Street, is adjacent to the main road close to the town centre. Open April to September. Prices from £6–£7. Tel: 01896 822969

HOSTEL
SYHA, Priorwood, Melrose, is a standard hostel. Open all year. Tel: 01896 822521

Peebles

CAMPING
Rosetta Caravan and Camping Park, Rosetta Road, is open April to October. Prices from £6–£9.50. Tel: 01721 720770

B&B
Lyne Farm (Mrs Arran Waddel), Peebles, is a large comfy farmhouse in a quiet, rural setting four miles west of Peebles on the A72. From £15–£17 per person. Tel: 01721 740255

St Abbs

B&B
Wilma Wilson, 7 Murrayfield, is a former fisherman's cottage close to the beach. Open all year. Priced from £14.50. Tel: 018907 71468

Selkirk

CAMPING
Victoria Caravan and Camping Park, Victoria Park, Buccleuch Road, is open April to October. Prices from £6. Tel: 01750 20897

HOSTEL
SYHA, Old Broadmeadows, Yarrowford, Selkirk, is a simple hostel. Open end March to October. Tel: 01750 76262

B&B
Queen's Head Inn (Mrs R. Paterson), 28 West Port, is central and open all year round. Prices from £12 per person sharing. Tel: 01750 21782

CENTRAL, TAYSIDE AND FIFE

Clackmannanshire

Alva

CAMPING
The Woods Caravan Club Site takes only caravans. Open end March to end October. Prices from £6–£7 per caravan. Tel: 01259 762802

Dollar

CAMPING
Riverside Caravan Park, Dollar, is a small sheltered park on the River Devon, with private fishing! Open April to September. Priced at £6–£11. Tel: 01259 742896

HOSTEL
SYHA, Glendevon, Dollar, is a simple hostel open end March to October. Tel: 01259 781206

Muckhart

B&B
Leys Farm (Mr and Mrs Wilson), Muckhart, is a modern working farmhouse in a lovely setting. Open April to September. Priced at £14. Tel: 01259 781313

Dundee City

HOSTELS/SELF CATERING
Mrs Ross, 10 Garland Place, is open end June to September. Priced at £10 per person. Tel: 01382 226808
    Mrs E. Keir, University of Abertay, Hillside Student Flats, Dalrymple Street, has two–eight-person flats to let out nightly from July to September. These cost £11.75 per night per person. Tel: 01382 308035

B&B
Auchenean (Margaret Laing), 177 Hamilton Street, Broughty Ferry, is open March to October. Prices from £14.50–£15.50. Tel: 01382 774782

Mo-Dhachaidh (Mrs M. MacPherson), 39 Step Row, is open all year. Priced at £12 per person, single or sharing. Tel: 01382 667436

Mr and Mrs Sill, 47 Shaftesbury Road, is open all year. Prices from £12.50. Tel: 01382 566598

HOTEL
Downfield Inn, 530 Strathmartine Road, is open all year. Priced at £15 per person. Tel: 01382 826633

The Tayview Hotel, 214 Broughty Ferry Road, is open all year, and is five minutes from the city centre. Priced from £15. Tel: 01382 451180

Falkirk

Falkirk

B&B
Ashbank, Main Street, Redding, by Falkirk, has views to the Ochils, and is five minutes from Falkirk. Open June to September. Prices are £13.50–£15. Tel: 01324 716649

Fife

Anstruther

HOSTEL
The Bunkhouse, West Pitkierie, near Anstruther, is open all year. Prices from £8.50. Tel: 01333 310768

B&B
Joyce and Tom Watson, 8 Melville Terrace, have a guest house open April to October. Prices from £12–£15 (1996). Tel: 01333 310453

Burntisland

B&B
Mr and Mrs P. Petrie, 5 Craigkennochie Terrace, is open all year. Prices from £14–£18 (1996). Tel: 01592 872091

Crail

CAMPING
Sauchope Links Caravan Park, Crail, is by the sea. It is open April to October. Prices from £9.90 for a tent or caravan. Tel: 01333 450460

Cupar

B&B
Mrs F. Stewart, 10 Holyburton Place, is open all year. Prices start at £13.50–£14.50 per person sharing. There is a single room supplement of £2.50–£3. (1996). Tel: 01334 652798

Dunfermline

CAMPING

Fordell Firs National Activity Centre (John Barnes), Hillend, Dunfermline, is open March to October. Prices are £3 for tents, £4–£7.60 for caravans. Tel: 01383 412704

Elie

CAMPING

Shell Bay Caravan Park is off the A917 a mile outside the village. Open March to October, the site has plenty of amenities. Prices from £7 per night for tents or £8.50 caravans. Tel: 01333 330283

B&B

Craigord (Mrs E. Lamond), 43 High Street, is open April to October. Priced at £14 (1996). Tel: 01333 330412

Falkland

HOSTEL

SYHA, Back Wynd, Falkland, is a simple hostel. Open March to October. Tel: 01337 857710

Glenrothes

B&B

Mr and Mrs H. Guy, 27 Duncan Road, is open all year. Prices from £12 (1996). Tel: 01592 756791

Kinghorn

CAMPING

Pettycur Caravan Park (Mary Davie) is open March to October and is close to a lovely beach. Prices from £8–£11 for tents or caravans. Tel: 01592 891420

Kirkcaldy

CAMPING

Dunnikier Caravan Park, Dunnikier Way, is within the Dunnikier estate. It has good facilities. Open March to January. Prices from £5 for tents, from £6.75 for caravans. Tel: 01592 267563

B&B

Elmsmere (Jess Moon), 49 Townsend Place, is open all year. Prices from £13–£15 (1996). Tel: 01592 269588

Ladybank

CAMPING

Annsmuir Caravan Park is open March to October. Prices are £7 per night for a tent, £8 for a touring caravan. Tel: 01337 830551

Leven

B&B
Forth Bay Guest House (Mrs P. Hamilton), Promenade, is open all year. Priced from £10–£17.50 per person (1996). Tel: 01333 423009

Lundin Links

CAMPING
Woodland Gardens Caravan and Camping Site (W. Neild), Blindwell Road, is open March to October, in a rural setting. Prices are set at £6.60 for tents or caravans. Tel: 01333 360319

Markinch

CAMPING
Balbirnie Park Caravan Club Site is open April to September. Prices from £6–£8 for caravans or tents. Tel: 01592 759130

Pittenweem

CAMPING
Grangemuir Woodland Park Caravan Site is nice and secluded. Open April to October. Prices are £8 for tents, £8.50 for caravans. Tel: 01333 311213

B&B
Mrs P. Vansittart, 27 James Street, offers minimal facilities, but at a price of £11–£15. Tel: 01333 311463

St Andrews

CAMPING
Cairnsmill Caravan Park (J. Kirkcaldy), Largo Road, is open April to October, and is just a mile from the town centre. It even has its own heated indoor pool! Prices from £4.50–£7 for tents, £9–£9.50 for caravans. Tel: 01334 473604

B&B
Maria Haston, 8 Nelson Street, has accommodation from £11–£12 per person per night (1996). Tel: 01334 473227

Ardmore (Mrs I. Methven), 1 Drumcarrow Road, is open all year. Prices per person from £12–£14 (1996). Tel: 01334 474574

St Monans

CAMPING
St Monans Caravan Park (D. Smith), Abbeyford Caravans, The Commons, St Monans, is at the edge of the village close to the beaches. Open March to October. Priced at £8 for a tent or caravan. Tel: 01333 730778

Tayport

CAMPING
Tayport Caravan Site, East Common, is open March to October. There is an

outdoor pool too. Priced at £7.80–£10.50 for tent or caravan.

Perth and Kinross

Aberfeldy

CAMPING
Aberfeldy Caravan Park, Dunkeld Road, has wonderful amenities. Open April to October. Prices from £7.50 per night, tent or caravan. Tel: 01887 820662

B&B
Ardtornish (Mrs M. Ross), Kenmore Street, is open all year, and is a non-smoking house. Prices from £15–£19. Tel: 01887 820629

Tom-na-Car (Mrs J. Hardie), Croftnamuick, is by Aberfeldy and open all year. Priced from £13–£20 per person. Tel: 01887 820335

Alyth

CAMPING
Nether Craig Caravan Park, Alyth, is in a really rural setting. Open mid-March to October. Prices from £5–£9 per pitch, tents and caravans. Tel: 01575 560204

Auchterarder

CAMPING
Auchterarder Caravan Park is in a beautiful setting. Open all year. Prices from £5 for tents or caravans. Tel: 01764 663119

Blair Atholl

CAMPING
The River Tilt Caravan Park is an award-winning site with facilities that include an indoor swimming pool and a gym! Open 22 March to 12 November. Priced from £4–£12 per night. They also have caravans to let. Tel: 01796 481467

B&B
Craigbeag (Mrs A. Graham), The Terrace, is open May to November. Prices from £12. Tel: 01796 481594

Blairgowrie

CAMPING
Blairgowrie Holiday Park, Hatton Road, has good facilities and caravans to let as well. Open all year. Prices from £6–£10 per night per pitch. Tel: 01250 872941

B&B
Millbank (Mrs A. Miller), Upper Mill Street, has good facilities and is open all year. Priced from £14–£20 per person. Tel: 01250 873304

Cargill

CAMPING
Beech Hedge Caravan Park is a small site that also has caravans to let. Open April to October. Prices from £9.50, caravans only. Tel: 01250 883249

Comrie

CAMPING
West Lodge Caravan Park has excellent facilities for caravans and tents, even caravans for hire. West Lodge is on the A85 a mile east of Comrie. Open Easter to end October. Priced from £6–£8 per night. Tel: 01764 670354

B&B
Bishopfauld Farm (Mrs C. Warton), Langside, by Comrie, has good facilities and is open all year. Prices from £14–£15. Tel: 01764 670384

Crieff

CAMPING
Thornhill Lodge Tenting Park is at Monzievaird, three miles west of Crieff on the A85. It is open Easter to October. Pitches cost £3–£5.50 per night, tents only. Tel: 01764 655382

HOSTEL
Braincroft Bunkhouse, Comrie Road, Crieff, is a converted farm steading in a rural area. A variety of bunkhouse accommodation, with breakfast available as well as other facilities. Cost per person per night was from £7–£8 (*en suite*) in 1996. Tel: 01764 670140

B&B
Ambleside (Mrs S. Donaldson), 3 Burrell Square, Crieff, is open all year. Priced from £14 for a single. Tel: 01764 652798

Dunkeld

B&B
Elwood Villa, Perth Road, Birnam, is open all year with good facilities. Prices from £15–£16 per person. Tel: 01350 727330

HOTEL
Atholl Arms Hotel, Tay Terrace, is packed with facilities and right beside the beautiful bridge and River Tay. Open all year. Prices from £25. Tel: 01350 727219

Glenshee

B&B
Glenkilrie, Blacklunans, Blairgowrie, is a family-run place on the A93 Braemar–Perth road. An old hill farm. Open January to March, then May to September. Prices are from £13.50–£15. Tel: 01250 882241

Kinloch Rannoch

CAMPING
Kilvrecht Caravan Park, Forest Enterprise, Inverpark, Dunkeld (for bookings) is open April to October. Priced at £5 per night. Tel: 01350 727284

Kinross

CAMPING
Gallowhill Farm Caravan Park, Gallowhill Road, is open April to October. Costs from £5–£8. Tel: 01577 862364

Perth

CAMPING
Cleeve Caravan Park, Glasgow Road, is sheltered and woody. Open April to October. Prices from £7.50 per night, tents or caravans. Tel: 01738 639521

HOSTEL
SYHA, Glasgow Road, is a standard hostel open end February to end October. Tel: 01738 623658

B&B
Marshall House (Mrs Gallacher), 6 Marshall Place, is open all year. Priced from £15 per person. Tel: 01738 442886
    Abbotsford, 23 James Street, is also open all year. Priced from £14 sharing, £15 single. Tel: 01738 635219

Pitlochry

CAMPING
Faskally Caravan Park also has caravans to let. Open April to October. Prices from £5.70, tents and caravans. Tel: 01796 472007

HOSTELS
SYHA, Knockard Road, is a standard hostel. Open all year. Tel: 01796 472308
    YMCA Scotland has a National Council Residence here at Bonskeid House. Phone ahead for help. Tel: 01796 473208

B&B
Tir Aluinn Guest House, 10 Higher Oakfield, is open all year. Priced at £13–£19 per person. Tel: 01796 472231
    Craig Dubh Cottage, Manse Road, Moulin, is a mile from Pitlochry at the end of a quiet country lane. Open mid-April to mid-October. Prices from £13.50. Tel: 01796 472058

Scone

CAMPING
Camping and Caravanning Club Site, Scone Palace Caravan Park, is open all year. Prices from £9.20 per night. Tel: 01738 552323

Stirling

Aberfoyle

CAMPING

Cobleland Campsite, Forest Enterprise, is on the banks of the River Forth in the Queen Elizabeth Forest Park. Open April to October. Priced at £7.90 per pitch, tents and caravans. Tel: 01877 382383

Blair Drummond

CAMPING

Blair Drummond Caravan Club Site, Cuthill Brae, is in a quiet rural area. Open March to January. Priced from £6–£9, caravans only. Tel: 01786 841208

Bridge of Allan

B&B

Mrs Skerry, 7 Mayne Avenue, is a central bungalow near the university. Open all year. Priced from £14. Tel: 01786 832178

Callander

CAMPING

Keltie Bridge Caravan Park is on the A84 between Doune and Callander. Open April to October. Prices from £5.50–£8.50. Tel: 01877 330811

B&B

Lenymede (Mr Green), Leny Road, Callander, is close to the River Teith. Open all year. Priced from £14–£16. Tel: 01877 330952

Crianlarich

HOSTEL

SYHA at Crianlarich is a standard hostel open February to end October. Prices from £6–£7.10. Tel: 01838 300260

Doune

B&B

Inverardoch Mains Farm (Mrs Joyce Anderson) overlooks the castle in its splendour on the River Teith. Find it on the B824. Open April to October. Priced from £17–£18. Tel: 01786 841268

Drymen

CAMPING

Cashel Campsite, Forestry Commission, Rowardennan, by Drymen, is in the Queen Elizabeth Forest Park, on the shores of Loch Lomond. Open April to October. Priced at £7.90 per night. Tel: 01360 870234

Easter Drumquhassle Farm (Mrs J. Cross), Drymen, is on the West

Highland Way. They have 'wooden wigwams'! Tents only, from £6. Open March to October. Tel: 01360 660893

HOSTEL

SYHA Rowardennan is near Drymen. This standard hostel is open end February to end October. Prices from £6–£7.10 per night. Tel: 01360 870259

B&B

Ceardach (Mrs Betty Robb), Gartness Road, Drymen, is a 300-year-old smiddy. Open all year. Prices start at £15. Tel: 01360 660596

Fintry

CAMPING

Balgair Castle Caravan Park, Overglinns, Fintry, is on the banks of the River Endrick. Open March to October. Price per night is £5.50–£8.95 for tents and caravans. Tel: 01360 860283.

Killin

CAMPING

The Shieling Accommodation, Aberfeldy Road, is very peaceful with good amenities. Priced at £6–£7 per tent (tents only). Open April to October. Tel: 01567 820334

HOSTEL

SYHA, Killin, is a standard hostel open mid-March to end October. Prices from £4.60–£5.60. Tel: 01567 820546

B&B

Fernbank (Mr and Mrs Holms), Main Street, has nice rooms and the best breakfast I've ever had in a B&B. (It was scambled egg with smoked salmon! You could even have chosen kidneys fit for a king!) Open all year. Prices from £14–£17.50. Tel: 01567 820511

Kippen

B&B

Hill of Arnmore Farm, Arnprior, Kippen, is open all year, and does a good breakfast. Priced at £15–£16. Tel: 01786 870225

Lochearnhead

CAMPING

Balquhidder Braes Caravan Park is in the midst of superb scenery. On the A84 between Callander and Lochearnhead. Open April to October. Priced at £6 per night. Tel: 01567 830293

Port of Menteith

B&B

Castle Rednock Farm (Mrs More) is a mile from the lake itself. Open in July and August. Prices are £13–£15 for single, £12 sharing. Tel: 01877 385276

Stirling

CAMPING
Auchenbowie Caravan Site, Auchenbowie, Stirling, is a peaceful site towards Denny, just on the A872. Open April to October. Costs from £5.50–£7 per pitch, for caravans and tents. Tel: 01324 822141

HOSTEL
SYHA, St John Street, Stirling, is a high standard hostel open till 2 a.m., which provides free continental breakfasts. Open all year. Prices are £9.20–£10.70. Tel: 01786 473442

B&B
Mrs Gillan, 13 Riverside Drive, Riverside, Stirling, is close to the town centre and riverside walks. Open May to September. Priced at £14. Tel: 01786 462292

Tioran (Mrs Agnes Thomson), 45 Douglas Terrace, is close to the Kings Park. Open April to October. Priced at £15.50–£16. Tel: 01786 464655

Strathyre

CAMPING
Immervoulin Caravan and Camping Park, Strathyre, is in a lovely setting by the River Balvaig. Fishing is available on Loch Lubnaig and the river! Open April to September. Priced from £5–£9. Tel: 01877 384285

Thornhill

CAMPING
Mains Farm Camping is near the village of Thornhill, with views to the Fintry Hills. Open April to October. Prices from £5–£6. Tel: 01786 850605

Tyndrum

CAMPING
Auchertye Farm has wooden wigwams and mountain views. Open all year. You will find it three miles north of Crianlarich on the A82. Prices are £5–£6 per night. Tents only. Tel: 01838 400251

GRAMPIAN

Aberdeen City

CAMPING
Marywell Park, Stonehaven Road, is a small quiet farm site a few minutes from the city centre. Open April to October. Prices from £6 for caravans and £5–£8 for tents. Tel: 01224 781973

Hazlehead Caravan Park and Campsite, Aberdeen Beach Leisure Centre,

Beach Promenade, has an attractive, sheltered site three miles from the city centre and four miles from the beach. Open April to September. Tents and caravans cost £7.05. Tel: 01224 647647

HOSTEL
SYHA, 8 Queen's Road, AB1, is a superior hostel, open daily till 2 a.m. Open February to December. Prices are £8.15 (over 18), £6.75 (under 18). Tel: 01224 646988

B&B
Allan Guest House, 56 Polmuir Road, is close to Duthie Park and Winter Gardens. It also serves a great breakfast, cooked to order. Excellent facilities in all the rooms, too. Open all year. Prices from £17 per person in a single or double. Tel: 01224 584484

Mrs M. Templeton, 263 Great Western Road, is in easy reach of the town centre. Open all year. Prices from £12–£14 per person in singles, £11–£12 per person sharing. Tel: 01224 588195

Aberdeenshire

Alford

B&B
Mrs Iris Henderson, 13 Montgarrie Road, offers a real home from home. Open March to October. Prices are £15 for single, £14 per person sharing. Tel: 019755 62159

Banchory

CAMPING
Silver Ladies Caravan Park, Strachan, Banchory, is a small park. Open April to October. Caravans cost from £5.50, tents cost from £4.10. Tel: 01330 822800

B&B
Knappach Toll Steading (Caroline Collen), Knappach, by Banchory, has home cooking and traditional hospitality to offer. Open all year. Prices from £12 single, £16.50 double. Tel: 01330 844425

HOTEL
Macbeth Arms Hotel is at 1 Station Square, Lumphanan, by Banchory. This is a small hotel open all day and all year. Prices from £16 single or sharing for B&B. Tel: 013398 83236

Banff

CAMPING
Banff Links Caravan Park, Banff Links, is a site right by a long sandy beach. Open April to September. Costs are £6.25 for caravans, £5.75 for tents. Tel: 01261 812228

Braemar

CAMPING
Invercauld Caravan Club Site, Glenshee Road, is to the south of the village. Open mid-December to September. Prices from £6 for caravans or tents. Tel: 013397 41373

HOSTEL
SYHA, Corrie Feragie, 21 Glenshee Road, is a standard hostel open end December to October. Tel: 01339 741659

Braemar Bunkhouse, 15 Mar Road, is open all year. Prices from £7. Tel: 01339 741242

B&B
Mayfield, 11 Chapel Brae, overlooks the Princess Royal Park. Open May to October. Prices are £15 for single or sharing per person. Tel: 013397 41238

Huntly

B&B
Strathlene (Mrs D. Ingram), McDonald Road, is close to the town centre. Open April to October. Prices are £13 single or per person sharing. Tel: 01466 792664

Inverey

HOSTEL
SYHA, Inverey, by Braemar, is a simple hostel open June to September.

Mintlaw

CAMPING
Aden Country Park, Mintlaw, has an award-winning caravan and camping site, with bags of facilities. Open April to October. Tel: 01771 623460

Sandend

CAMPING
Sandend Caravan Park, Sandend, by Portsoy, is a site near a sandy beach. Open April to October. Prices from £7.85 for caravans, £4–£5.80 for tents. Tel: 01261 842660

Stonehaven

CAMPING
Bookings can be made through the Aberdeenshire Council, Leisure and Recreation Dept, at Arduthie Road, Stonehaven. The site is near the sea with good facilities nearby. Open April to October. Pitches cost £6.50–£7.50 per night. Tel: 01569 762001/768224

B&B
Tewel Farm (Mrs E. Farquhar), Stonehaven, is on the Auchenblae road. This traditional farmhouse is on the outskirts of the town with great views. Open

all year. Prices vary: £10–£12 for room only, £16–£18 double per person (*en suite*), take your choice. Tel: 01569 762306

Strathdon

HOSTEL
Jenny's Bothy, Corgarff, Strathdon, is open all year. Prices from £7. Tel: 01975 651446/9

Tarland

CAMPING
Drummie Hill Caravan Park, Tarland, by Aboyne, is a quiet privately owned site. Luxury caravans to hire too. Open April to October. Tel: 013398 81388/81264

Tornaveen

HOSTEL
The Wolf's Hearth, The Steading, Tornaveen, by Torphins, is in a really rural location. Open all year. Prices from £8.50. Tel: 01339 883460

Angus

Arbroath

B&B
Maulesbank House (Mrs A. Rose), 11 Maul Street, is a small family-run guest house close to the bus and railway stations. B&B sharing costs £13.50–£16 per person per night. Open all year. Tel: 01241 870926

Seafar (Mrs Campbell), Dundee Road, Elliot, Arbroath, is a small guest house close to the beach. It costs from £13–£16.50 single or sharing, per person. Tel: 01241 431705

HOTEL
Inverpark Hotel, 42 Millgate Loan, Arboath, is a small licensed hotel near the town centre and harbour. Live entertainment at weekends, too! From £17.50 for a single for B&B, or £15 sharing. Open all year. Tel: 01241 873378

Brechin

B&B
The Post House (Mrs Gibb), Lethnot, Bridgend, Brechin, is a place with good food and home baking. Only £12.50 for single or sharing per person. Open November to July. Tel: 01356 660277

HOTEL
Northern Hotel, 2 Clerk Street, is full of facilities, all rooms have colour TV and a phone, tea-making stuff too. B&B costs £18–£28 for a single, £18–£24 sharing per person. Open all year. Tel: 01356 625505

Carnoustie

CAMPING
Woodlands Caravan Park, Carnoustie, is off the A92 in the grounds of the former Carnoustie House. Open April to October. Pitches from £6.30 per day, with tents costing £3.50–£4.65. Tel: 01241 853246

B&B
Balhousie Farm (Mrs E. Watson) is a secluded farmhouse off the A92. Ten minutes from Carnoustie. It costs from £15 for B&B per person. Open February to November. Tel: 01241 853533

Lochtybank (Mrs A. Malcolm), 20 High Street, is quiet but central and open January to November. B&B costs £16 for a single and £16 per person sharing. Tel: 01241 854849

HOTEL
Aboukir Hotel, 38 Ireland Street, is a small family hotel with prices from £18 single for B&B or £18 sharing per person. Open all year. Tel: 01241 852149

Forfar

CAMPING
Lochside Caravan Park, Forfar Country Park, is just off the A94 on the east shore of Forfar Loch. Open April to October. Caravans from £6.30–£7.55 per day, tents are £3.40–£4.65. Tel: 01307 468917

B&B
Glencoul House (Mrs R. Kirby), Justinhaugh, by Forfar, is an old stone farmhouse with good facilities. Prices from £14–£16 for a single or per person sharing. Open January to November. Tel: 01307 850248

Glenisla

HOTEL
Kirkside House Hotel, Kirkton of Glenisla, is an old manse by the River Isla. Open all year. Prices from £16–£17 single or £32–£34 for a shared room. Tel: 01575 582278

Kirriemuir

HOSTEL
SYHA, Glendoll, Clova, Kirriemuir, is a standard hostel open mid-March to end October. Tel: 01575 550236

B&B
Hillview (Mrs R. Keith), Main Road, Westmuir, by Kirriemuir, is a country cottage on the A926, with great views. Prices from £12.50 per person sharing. Open April to October. Tel: 01575 572548

Monifieth

CAMPING
Riverview Caravan Park, Riverview Drive, is a coastal site close to the town

centre. Open March to October, with good facilities. Prices £6.30 upwards for a caravan pitch, tents from £3.50–£4.65. Tel: 01241 853246

Montrose

CAMPING
South Links Caravan Park, Traill Drive, is near the town centre by the beach with pitch and putt and golf nearby. Open April to October. A pitch costs from £6.30 per day, with tents costing £3.50–£4.65. Tel: 01674 672026

B&B
Fairfield (Mrs M. Scott), 24 The Mall, is a detached Georgian house, nice and central for the town itself. Open all year. Prices are £16 for a single or £15 per person sharing. Tel: 01674 676386

West Ballochy Farm (Mrs M. Braes), by Montrose, is a farm guest house overlooking the wildlife centre and close to the House of Dun. Open all year. It costs £15–£17 single, £14–£16 per person sharing. Tel: 01674 810207

St Cyrus

CAMPING
East Bowstrips Caravan Park, St Cyrus near Montrose, is another quiet park near a beach. Caravans to hire too. Open April to October. Tents cost £3.50–£6.50 and caravans cost £6.50–£7.50 for pitches. Tel: 01674 850328

THE HIGHLANDS

Moray

Aberlour

B&B
Ferryview (Mrs L. Stuart), 129 High Street, is a small family guest house with B&B at £14 per person. Open all year. Tel: 01340 871335

Buckie

B&B
Mrs Elizabeth MacMillan, 81 High Street, is open all year. Prices from £12–£15 single or per person sharing. Tel: 01542 832367

Burghead

CAMPING
The campsite is run by the local authority, so bookings can be made through the Leisure Officer, Moray Council, Council Headquarters, High Street, Elgin.

The site is right by a sandy beach and great for kids. Open April to September. Prices from £6.80 for caravans and from £5.75 for tents. Tel: 01343 563403

Cullen

CAMPING
Cullen campsite is run by Moray Council, so the details, including prices and contact phone number, are the same as for *Burghead* (see above). This is another beautiful view place.

B&B
Torrach (Mrs A. Mair), 147 Seatown, Cullen, near Buckie, is a traditional house in the lower part of the village. Open April to October. Prices are £14 single, £12.50 per person sharing. Tel: 01542 840724

Elgin

HOSTEL
Elgin Saltire Independent Hostel, Pluscarden Road, is the booking centre for the bunkhouse which is about a mile from the city centre. Open all year. Prices are £6–£8.50 per person. Tel: 01343 550624

B&B
The Bungalow (Mr Ross), 7 New Elgin Road, Elgin, is a family-run guest house 15 minutes' walk from the town centre, five minutes from the station. Open all year. Prices from £13. Tel: 01343 542035

Findhorn

CAMPING
Findhorn Bay Caravan Park is a peaceful family site. Open April to October. Prices are £6 upwards for caravans, £4.50–£6 for tents. Tel: 01309 690203

Findochty

CAMPING
Findochty campsite is run by Moray Council, so the contact phone number is the same as for *Burghead* (see above). It is a little more expensive. This site is by the harbour.

Fochabers

B&B
Castlehill Farm (Mrs Alexia Shand), Blackdam, Fochabers, is a working farm with amazing views to Ben Aigan. Open March to October. Prices are £13–15 per person. Tel: 01343 820351

Forres

CAMPING
Riverview Leisure, Mundole Court, Forres, is on the A96. Fishing is available,

too. Open April to November. Cost is from £9 for caravans, £6 for tents. Tel: 01309 673932

B&B
Moss-side Farm, Rafford, by Forres, is a place with farmhouse baking and cooking. Open May to September. Prices are £13 for single or double, and £9 for room only accommodation. Tel: 01309 672954

Glenlivet

B&B
Roadside Cottage, Tomnavoulin, Glenlivet, Ballindalloch, has great views and lovely food. Open all year (except Xmas). Prices from £14–£17. Tel: 01807 590486

Keith

CAMPING
This is another Moray Council site, so contact as for *Burghead* (see above). Costs are £6.80 for caravans, £5.75 for tents. Open April to September. A quiet site.

B&B
T.A. Smith, 65 Mid Street, has a comfy B&B open all year. Prices from £12.50 single or per person sharing. Tel: 01542 882156

Lossiemouth

CAMPING
Details are the same as camping at *Keith* (see above). The site is near a long white sandy beach. Open April to September.

B&B
Letchworth Lodge (Mrs Anne Main), Dunbar Street, is a traditional kind of place. Close to the beach, too. Open all year. Prices from £14–£15.50. Tel: 01343 812132

Tomintoul

HOSTEL
SYHA, Main Street, is a simple hostel open mid-June to end September.

B&B
Findron Farm (Mrs Elma Turner), Braemar Road, is a farmhouse a mile from the village on the Braemar road. Open all year. Prices from £14–£17. Tel: 01807 580382

Highland Heartlands

Arisaig

CAMPING
Gorten Sands Caravan Site, Gorten Farm, Back of Keppock, is open April to September and costs from £6–£8 per night. Tel: 01687 450283

Aviemore

HOSTEL
SYHA, 25 Grampian Road, is a superior hostel open till 2 a.m. Open 22 December to end October. Tel: 01479 810345

Corrour

HOSTEL
SYHA, Loch Ossian, is at Corrour near Fort William. It is a simple hostel open March to end October. Tel: 01397 732207

Carrbridge

HOSTEL
Carrbridge Bunkhouse Hostel, Dalrachney House, is open all year. Prices from £5. Tel: 01479 841250

Drumnadrochit

HOSTEL
Loch Ness Backpackers Lodge, Coilte Farmhouse, East Lewiston, Drumnadrochit, is open all year. Priced from £8. Tel: 01456 450807

Fort Augustus

HOSTELS
The Abbey has accommodation for different pockets. There is a backpackers' lodge from £8 per night (self-catering) and other accommodation such as family rooms, twins and singles from £12 per person per night. Phone in advance to book where possible. Open April to October. Tel: 01320 366233

Bothy Bite Bunkhouse, Canal Side, Fort Augustus, is open all year and costs only £6.50. Tel: 01320 366710

Fort William

HOSTELS
Fort William Backpackers Hostel costs £8.50. Tel: 01397 700711

The Smiddy Lodge, Station Road, Corpach, by Fort William, is open all year and costs £7.50. Tel: 01397 772467

Inchree Bunkhouse Hostel, Onich, by Fort William, is open all year. Priced at £5.70–£8.50. Tel: 01855 821287

SYHA, Glen Nevis, near Fort William, is open December to 28 October. It is a high-standard hostel open till 2 a.m. nightly. Tel: 01397 702336

CAMPING
Glen Nevis Caravan and Camping Park, Glen Nevis, is open March to October. Prices range from £5–£10 per night. Tel: 01397 702191

B&B
Finnisgaig (Mrs A. Heger), Alma Road, is open all year. Prices from £13 (1996). Tel: 01397 702453

Foyers

HOSTEL
Foyers House has beds for £10. Open all year. Tel: 01456 486405

Glencoe

HOSTELS
SYHA, Ballachulish, is a standard hostel open all year. Tel: 01855 811219
Leacantuim Farm Bunkhouses, Glencoe, is open all year and costs from £6.
Tel: 01855 811256

B&B
An Darag (Mrs K. Rodger), Upper Carnoch, Glencoe, has great mountain
views. Prices from £15 (1996). Tel: 01855 811643

Glenmore

HOSTEL
SYHA, Loch Morlich, is at Glenmore, near Aviemore. Open mid-November
to end September. It is a standard hostel. Tel: 01479 961238

Inverness

HOSTEL
SYHA, 1 Old Edinburgh Road, is a high standard hostel open till 2 a.m. Open
February to December. Tel: 01463 231771
Inverness Student Hostel, 8 Culduthel Road, is open all year. Prices start at
£8.50. Tel: 01463 236556
The Bazpackers Backpackers Hostel is at 4 Culduthel Road. Open all year
and priced at £8–£12.50 for a double. Tel: 01463 717663

Kincraig

HOSTELS
Glen Feshie Hostel, Bacachroick, Glen Feshie, Kincraig, is open all year and
costs from £7 (including porridge!). Tel: 01540 651323
Kirkbeag Cabin, Kincraig, near Kingussie, is also open all year. Prices from
£8. Tel: 01540 651298

Kingussie

HOSTELS
Bothan Airigh, Insh, Kingussie, is open all year. Priced at £6. Tel: 01540 661051
The Laird's Bothy, High Street, Kingussie, is open all year and costs £7–£8.
Tel: 01540 661334

Kinlochleven

HOSTEL
West Highland Lodge, Hostel Brae, Kinlochleven, is open all year. Priced from
£6. Tel: 018554 831471

Knoydart

HOSTEL
Torrie Shieling, Torrie Cottage, Inverie, Knoydart, is open all year and costs £12–£15. Tel: 01687 462669

Loch Ness

HOSTEL
SYHA, Loch Ness, is at Glenmoriston and is a standard hostel open mid-March to end October. Tel: 01320 351274

Mallaig

HOSTEL
Sheena's Backpackers' Lodge, Harbour View, is open all year and costs from £6. Tel: 01687 462764

B&B
Jean Crocket, 1 Loch Nevis Crescent, is open June to September. Priced from £14 (1996). Tel: 01687 462171

Newtonmore

HOSTEL
Newtonmore Independent Hostel, Craigellachie, Main Street, is open all year. Prices from £6.22. Tel: 01540 673360

B&B
'Craigellachie House' (Mrs K. Main), Main Street – the same place as the hostel marked above also has bed and breakfast. It is a no-smoking establishment. Tel: 01540 673360

Roybridge

HOSTELS
The Grey Corrie Lodge, Roybridge, is open all year. It costs £8–£9.50. Tel: 01397 712236
   Aite Cruinnichidh, is at 1 Achluachrach, by Roybridge, and is open all year. Prices from £7. Tel: 01397 712315

Spean Bridge

HOSTEL
SYHA, Loch Lochy, is at South Laggan and is a standard hostel open mid-March to end October. Tel: 01809 501239

Strathglass

HOSTELS
Cougie Lodge, Tomich, is open April to October. Prices are £6 and £8.50. Tel: 01456 415399

SYHA, Allt Beithe, Glen Affric, Cannich, is a simple hostel open mid-March to end October. Tel: 01456 415244

Glen Affric Backpackers Hostel, Chairein Lodge, Cannich, is open all year and costs £4.80. Tel: 01456 415263

The Northern Highlands

Achiltibuie

HOSTEL
SYHA, Achininver, Achiltibuie, by Ullapool, is a simple hostel open mid-June to October. Tel: 01854 622254

Balintore

HOSTEL
The Stables, Balintore Hotel, East Street, is open March to October and costs £6. Tel: 01862 832219

Culrain

HOSTEL
SYHA, Carbisdale Castle, Culrain, is a large, beautiful hostel building of a superior standard with free continental breakfast too! They are going to be refurbishing the castle over the next year or two. Open February to end October (shut 6–15 June). Tel: 01549 421232

Diabaig

HOSTEL
SYHA, Craig, Diabaig, Achnasheen, is a simple hostel open mid-June to October.

Durness

HOSTEL
SYHA, Smoo, Lairg, is a simple hostel, open mid-June to October. Tel: 01971 511244

Gairloch

HOSTELS
SYHA, Carn Dearg, Gairloch, is a standard hostel open mid-June to October. Tel: 01445 712219

Rubha Reidh Lighthouse, Melvaig, Gairloch, is open all year and costs £7. Tel: 01445 771263

Badachro Bunkhouse, Badachro, Gairloch, is also open all year and costs from £7–£9. Tel: 01445 741291

Achtercairn Hostel, Gairloch Sands Apartments, Gairloch, is open March to November, and costs £6. Tel: 01445 712131

Garve

HOSTEL
Sail Mhor Croft Hostel, Camusnagaul, Dundonnel, Garve, is open all year (except Christmas and New Year). Priced at £7. Tel: 01854 633224

Glenshiel

HOSTEL
SYHA, Ratagan is at Glenshiel, Kyle. This standard hostel is open April to end October. Tel: 01599 511243

Helmsdale

HOSTEL
SYHA, Helmsdale, is a simple hostel open mid-March to October. Tel: 01431 821577

John o' Groats

HOSTEL
SYHA, Canisbay, near Wick, is a standard hostel open end March to end October. Tel: 01955 611424

Lairg

HOSTELS
SYHA, Achmelvich, Recharn, Lairg, is a simple hostel open end March to October. Tel: 01571 844480

Assynt Field Centre, Inchnadamph Lodge, Inchnadamph, by Lairg, costs £8.50 upwards. Tel: 01571 822218

Rogart Station

HOSTEL
Rogart Railway Carriage is at Rogart Station! Open Easter to October, they give a discount to bike/train users. Prices from £8. Tel: 01408 641343

Strathcarron

HOSTEL
Achnashellach Hostel, Craig, Achnashellach, Strathcarron, is open all year. Costs are £6.30–£7. Tel: 01520 766232

Strathpeffer

HOSTEL
SYHA, Strathpeffer, is a standard hostel that is open end February to end October. Tel: 01997 421532

Thurso

HOSTEL
Thurso Youth Club, Old Mill, Millbank, Thurso, offers accommodation from July to August. The cost is £8. Tel: 01847 892964

Tongue

HOSTEL
SYHA, by Lairg, is a standard hostel that is open mid-March to end September. Tel: 01847 611301

Torridon

HOSTEL
SYHA, Achnasheen, Torridon, is a standard hostel open February to end October. Tel: 01445 791284

Ullapool

HOSTELS
SYHA, Shore Street, is a standard hostel open mid-March to end October. Tel: 01854 612254
   West House, West Argyle Street, is open all year and costs £7.50-£10. Tel: 01854 613126

Unapool

HOSTEL
Kylesku Lodges, Kylesku, by Unapool, offers beds for £8, Easter to October. Tel: 01971 502003

ISLANDS

The Inner Hebrides

SKYE

HOSTELS
SYHA, Armadale, Ardvasar, Sleat, is a standard hostel open mid-March to October. Tel: 01471 844260
   SYHA, Broadford, is open end February to December. It is a standard hostel. Tel: 01471 822442
   SYHA, Glenbrittle, Carbost, is another standard hostel open mid-March to October. Tel: 01478 640278
   Glenhinnisdal Bunk House, Glenhinnisdal, is open all year and costs £6.50. Tel: 01876 500480

SYHA Kyleakin is a high standard hostel open all year. It stays open till 2 a.m. each night. Tel: 01599 534585

Skye Backpackers Hostel, Benmhor, Kyleakin, is open all year, priced at £8.50–£10. Tel: 01599 534510

Fossil Bothy Hostel, 13 Lower Breakish, is open April to November and costs £6.50. Tel: 01471 822644

Lealt Falls Hostel, 1 and 2 Tote, North Scorrybreck, is open March to January, and costs £7.50. Tel: 01470 562363

Croft Bunkhouse and Bothy – Backpackers Hostels, 7 Portnalong, is open all year. Priced at £5.50. Tel: 01478 640254

Skyewalker Independent Hostel, The Old School, Portnalong, is open all year and costs £6. Tel: 01478 640250

SYHA, Uig, is a standard hostel open mid-March to end October. Tel: 01854 612254

Portree Backpackers, 2 Douglas Row, Portree, is open all year and costs £7.50. Tel: 01478 613332

Portree Backpackers Hostel, 6 Woodpark, Portree, is open all year as well. It costs £8.50–£9.50. Tel: 01478 613641

Portree Independent Hostel, Old Post Office, The Green, Portree, costs £7.50. Tel: 01478 613737

Sleat Bunkhouse, The Glebe, Kilmore, Sleat, is open all year and costs £6 or £5 depending on the season. Tel: 01471 844440

Dun Flodigarry Hostel, by Staffin, is open all year and costs £7–£8. Tel: 01470 552212

RAASAY

HOSTEL

SYHA, Creachan Cottage is a simple hostel open mid-June to October. Tel: 01478 660240

MULL

CAMPING

Newdale Campsite, by Tobermory, is on the B8073 to Dervaig, a mile from Tobermory. Call at the house when you arrive. Priced at only £2 per night for a pitch, caravan or tent. Tel: 01688 302306

Balmeanach Park (Alex MacFadyen), Fishnish. From Craignure take the A849 for five miles. Open March to October. Priced at £7 per pitch per night. Tel: 01680 300342

HOSTELS

SYHA, Main Street, Tobermory, is a simple hostel that is open mid-March to end September. Tel: 01688 302481

Mr and Mrs Williams, Arle, Aros, have budget accommodation in a bunkhouse-type arrangement. Priced at £10 upwards per night. Open all year. Tel: 01680 300343

B&B

Clachan House (Mrs P. Appleby), Loch Don, Craignure, is good and central. Open all year. Prices from £12.50–£15 per person. Tel: 01680 812439

Gowanbrae (Mr and Mrs Halcrow), Bunessan, is a beautiful, welcoming place. The landlady really saved our bacon some years ago, and this is an unambivalent thanks for that. Open all year. Priced at £16–£17 per person. Tel: 01681 700436

Mrs MacLachlan, 31 Bentalla Crescent, Salen, has a good central spot, close to buses too. Open April to September. Priced at £15 for a single, £13.50 sharing. Tel: 01680 300419

Kengharair Farm, Dervaig, is an old hillside farmhouse only five miles from Calgary beach. Priced at £15–£16 for a single, £14–£15 sharing. Tel: 01688 400251

Tom A Mhuillin (Mrs F. MacLean), Salen Road, Tobermory, is just five minutes' walk from the main street and harbour. Open all year. Prices from £14. Tel: 01688 302164

IONA

B&B

Cruachan (Mrs M.I. Morrison) is just half a mile from the ferry overlooking the Sound of Iona. Open March to October. Priced from £15–£18. Tel: 01681 700523

COLL

CAMPING

Mrs Graham at Garden House has a small campsite. Prices per night are £4–£5. Open April to October. Tel: 01879 230374

B&B

Roy Barrie, Taigh Solas, Arinagour, Isle of Coll, is idyllic, as you would expect. Open all year. Priced from £16–£18 sharing. Tel: 01879 230333

Garden House (Mrs Pat Graham) is a farmhouse at the end of the island surrounded by the nature reserve. Move over Katie Morag. Open all year. Priced at £15 per person. Tel: 01879 230374 (see Camping above!)

TIREE

B&B

Mr W. Campbell, 26 Balephetrish, is just 50 yards from the sea. Glorious views. Open April to October. Priced from £14–£15 per person. Tel: 01879 220334

ISLAY

CAMPING

Kintra Farm Site, The Oa, Port Ellen, is open April to September. Prices from £4.80–£6.50 per night for tents or caravans. Tel: 01496 302051

Craigens (Mr and Mrs Archibald), Gruinart, is open April to October. It is in a remote spot, from Bridgend take the B847 to Black Rock, then right on the B8017 to Gruinart. Cost is only £2.50 per night. Tel: 01496 850256

HOSTELS

SYHA, Port Charlotte, is open March to end October. It is a standard grade hostel. Prices from £4.60–£5.60. Tel: 01496 850385

Kintra Farm (Mrs McTaggart), Kintra Beach, Port Ellen, has budget accommodation, priced from £5.50–£7.50 per bunk per night. Open all year. Tel: 01496 302051

B&B
Meadowside (Kate McAffer), Birch Drive, Bowmore, is a good location. Open all year. Priced from £15–£16.50 for singles, £13.50–£15.50 for sharing. Tel: 01496 810479

Anchorage (Mrs A. MacDonald), Bruichladdich, is on the shores of Lochindaal. Open all year. Prices from £14–£16. Tel: 01496 850540

The Bothy (Mick Stuart), 91 Lennox Street, Port Ellen, will even supply you with a bike! Open all year. Prices from £14–£16 for sharing, £15–£17 single. Tel: 01496 302391

HOTEL
Loch Gruinart House, Gruinart, Bridgend, is a family-run place next to an RSPB reserve. Open all year. Prices from £17 per person. Tel: 01496 850212

JURA

B&B
Craighouse (Isabell Miller), Knockrome, is a croft overlooking the bay, with good access to the Paps of Jura. Open all year. Prices from £12.50–£17. Tel: 01496 820311

GIGHA

B&B
Of course, first you need to make your way over, but it will be worthwhile! Post Office House (Mrs McSporran), Isle of Gigha, will make you at home. Glorious. Open all year. Prices from £16–£17 for singles, £17 for double/twin. Tel: 01583 505251

COLONSAY

B&B
Seaview (Mr and Mrs Lawson), Isle of Colonsay, is a croft close to the standing stones of Kilchattan. Open April to October. Priced at £21. Tel: 01951 200315

MUCK

HOSTEL
Isle of Muck Bunkhouse, Port Mor, is open all year, priced at £8.50. Tel: 01687 462042

The Western Isles

BARRA

B&B
Ravenscroft (Mrs M. MacKechnie), Nasg (Nask), is open April to

September. Prices from £13.50–£15. Tel: 01871 810574

HOSTEL
Breibhig (Brevig), Barra Hostel, is one of SYHA's simple hostels, which is open all year.

BENBECULA

HOSTEL
Bunkhouse (Mr R. Millar), 22 Balivanich, is open all year. Prices are £5–£9 per person per night. Tel: 01870 602522

B&B
'Culla Bay View' (Mrs M. Macdonald), 11 Aird, Balivanich, is a working croft near a sandy beach. Open all year. Priced at £15–£17 for B&B per person, from £10–£12 for room only. Tel: 01870 602201

BERNERAY

HOSTEL
Berneray (Bhearnaraigh) is a simple hostel open all year. It has just 16 beds. The warden is Annie Mackillop. (Run by the Gatcliff Hebridean Hostel Trust.)

B&B
Mrs Mairi Macinnes, 1 Borve, is open all year. Priced at £15. Tel: 01876 540253

HARRIS

HOSTELS
Rhenigidale (Reinigeadal) is open all year, and is classed as a simple hostel. Warden Marion MacInnes lives in the house nearest the shore. (This is a Gatcliff Hebridean Hostel Trust place.)

SYHA, Kyles, Stockinish, is a simple hostel open end March to October.

Drinishader Hostel, 8 Drinishader, is open all year and costs £7. Tel: 01859 511255

B&B
Post Office House (Mrs C. Mackay), Amhuinnsuidhe, is open April to October. Priced at £15, room only £9. Tel: 01859 560207

34 Taobh Tuath, Northton, is open all year and has home produce and Highland cattle. Priced at £14, or room only for £12.

Mrs P. Macsween, Suil-Na-Mara, Isle of Scalpay, is open all year. Priced at £14–£15, or £10–£11 for room only. Tel: 01859 540278

LEWIS

CAMPING
Shawbost Caravan Site (Eilean Fraoich Camp Site), North Shawbost, is on the A858. Open May to October. Prices from £4–£7.50 per day. Tel: 01851 710504

Laxdale Holiday Park, 6 Laxdale Lane, is close to Stornoway. Open April to October. Prices from £6–£8.50. Tel: 01851 703234

HOSTELS

Garenin, Carloway, is a simple hostel open all year, run by the Gatcliff Hebridean Hostels Trust. Get access from Mrs Pat Macgregor at 3 Uraghag.

SYHA, Ravenspoint, Kershader, South Lochs, is a standard hostel open all year. Prices from £5.85–£6.95 per person per night. Tel: 01851 880236

Galston Farm Bunkhouse, South Galson, Ness, is on the coastal route ten miles from Butt of Lewis. Open all year. Priced at £8. Tel: 01851 850492

Stornoway Backpackers Hostel, 47 Keith Street, Stornoway, has male and female dormitories. Open March to November (in winter by arrangement only). Priced at £8.50 per night. Tel: 01851 703628

B&B

Mrs B. Macdonald, 41 Gearraidh Ghuirm (41 Upper Coll), is ten minutes from Stornoway beside Coll sands. Priced at £12 per person. Open April to October. Tel: 01851 820478

Mrs J. Macleod, 131 Bakers Road, Laxdale, has views over Stornoway. Open all year. Tel: 01851 702858

Mrs J. Buchanan, 3 Cairisiadar (Carishader), Uig, is open all year. Priced at £13, or £8 for room only. Tel: 01851 672252

NORTH UIST

HOSTELS

SYHA Lochmaddy is at Ostram House and is a standard hostel open mid-June to end September. Tel: 01876 500368

Uist Outdoor Centre, Cearn Dusgaidh, Lochmaddy, is open all year and costs £8. Tel: 01876 500480

B&B

Mrs Joan MacDonald, 14 Hougharry, is on the Balranald Bird Reserve, and has great views. Open April to October. Priced from £13 or room only for £10. Tel: 01876 510279

SOUTH UIST

HOSTEL

Howmore (Tobhamor), South Uist, is a simple hostel that is open all year. The warden Betty Macdonald lives at Ben More House, the house at the main road junction. (A Gatcliff Hebridean Hostel Trust hostel.)

B&B

'Reineval' (Miss M. Maclean), Gearraidh Bhailteas (Milton), is open all year. Prices from £12.50–£13.50, with room only at £8–£10. Tel: 01878 710320

Orkney

MAINLAND

CAMPING

Eviedale Centre, Dale Farm, Evie, is beside the A966 north of the village, part of the Eviedale complex. Price per night £5. Open April to September. Tel: 01856 751270

Pickaquoy Caravan and Camping Site, Orkney Islands Council, is on the outskirts of Kirkwall, off the A965. Open mid-May to mid-September. Prices from £4.85–£6 for caravans, £3.15–£4.50 for tents. Tel: 01856 873535

Ness Point Caravan and Camping Site, Orkney Islands Council, is on the southern side of town. Open 10 May to 13 September. Prices from £4.85–£6 for caravans, £3.15–£4.50 for tents. Tel: 01856 873535

HOSTELS

SYHA, Old Scapa Road, Kirkwall, is a standard hostel, open 22 March to end October. Tel: 01856 872243

SYHA, Hellihole Road, Stromness, is a standard hostel, open end February to end October. Priced at £4.70–£5.75. Tel: 01856 850589

Brown's Hostel, 45/47 Victoria Street, Stromness, is open all year and costs £7.50. Tel: 01856 850661

Evie Hostel (Mrs Sabiston), Flaws, Evie, is near the Rousay Ferry. Priced from £5 per night. Tel: 01856 751208

Eviedale Centre Bothy, Evie, is a small hostel, priced at £4.50 per bunk per night. Open April to September. Tel: 01856 751270

B&B

Heathfield Farmhouse (Mrs M. Hourie), St Ola, Kirkwall, is on a 500-acre working farm. Prices from £15–£17. Tel: 01856 872378

Millbrig (Mrs S. Harvey), Rendall, uses home and local produce. Priced at £12 per person. Tel: 01856 761254

HOTEL

Royal Hotel, Stromness, is central. Prices from £15–£25 per person. Tel: 01856 850342

BIRSAY

HOSTEL

Birsay Hostel, Orkney Island Council, Kirkwall – this is the contact for booking/information. Price per night is £5.40–£5.75. Tel: 01856 873535

BURRAY

B&B

Garisle (Mr and Mrs Reeves) is close to a beach. Priced from £12.50–£15. Tel: 01856 731269

EDAY

HOSTEL

SYHA, Eday, Loudon Bay, is a simple hostel open mid-March to October. Tel: 01857 622283

HOY

HOSTELS

SYHA, Rackwick, Hoy, is a standard hostel open mid-March to September. Priced from £5.40–£5.75. Tel: 01856 873535

SYHA, Hoy, is a standard hostel that is open mid-June to mid-September. Priced from £5.40–£5.75. Tel: 01856 873535

NORTH RONALDSAY

HOSTEL AND B&B
North Ronaldsay Bird Observatory has solar-powered accommodation! Priced from £16.20 for single or sharing, per person for B&B. They also have hostel accommodation, from £10–£12 per night. Tel: 01857 633200

PAPA WESTRAY

HOSTEL
SYHA is at Beltane House and is a standard hostel open all year. Priced at £6.95. Tel: 01857 644267

ROUSAY

HOSTEL
Rousay Hostel (Mrs C. Rae), Trumland Farm, is close to the pier. There is also a campsite. Open all year. Prices from £2.50–£8 per night. Tel: 01856 821252

SANDAY

B&B
Kettlefield Hotel has good food on offer. Priced at £15 per person, single or sharing. Tel: 01857 600217

SOUTH RONALDSAY

HOSTEL
Wheems Bothy, Wheems, Eastside, is open April to end September. Priced at £5, this includes organic food. Tel: 01856 831537

WESTRAY

B&B
Sand o' Gill (Mrs Groat) is near the village of Pierowall. Priced at £13 per person. Tel: 01857 677374

Shetland

MAINLAND

CAMPING
Shetland has a great attitude to 'wild' camping – simply find the local landowner (usually the nearest cottage or croft) and they will normally oblige. Sometimes they can tell you of better spots than the one you have chosen! If you would prefer some 'facilities', there are a few sites on

Shetland, all of which are listed below. (Note no camping allowed on Noss or Fair Isle or the Tresta Links on Fetlar.)

Clickimin Caravan and Camp Site, Lochside, Lerwick, is open May to September. Priced from £4–£9 per night. Tel: 01595 741000

Levenwick Campsite, Levenwick, South Mainland, overlooks the bay. Open April to September. Priced from £5–£6.50 per night. Tel: 01950 422207

Valleyfield Camp Site, Brae, North Mainland, is open May to September. The prices are £6–£7.50 per pitch. Tel: 01806 522563

BODS

A bod (or barn) is very basic, like a bothy, and you need to have with you all the kind of things you would need in a tent. All the bods listed need to be booked in advance through Shetland Islands Tourism in Lerwick (Tel: 01595 693434.)

Voe House, Walls, West Mainland, is open April to October. Price per person per night is £3. Tel: 01595 693434

The Sail Loft, Voe, Delting, North Mainland, is open April to October. £3 a night again. Tel: 01595 693434

'Johnny Notions', Hamnavoe, Eshaness, North Mainland, is open from April to October and costs £3 per person per night. Tel: 01595 693434

Betty Mouat's Cottage, Scatness, Dunrossness, overlooks Fitful Head. Open April to October, and £3 per person per night. Tel: 01595 693434

HOSTELS

SYHA is at Isleburgh House, King Harald Street, Lerwick, and is open April to end September. It is a standard hostel. Prices from £5.85 (junior) and £6.95 (adult).Tel: 01595 692114

Cunningsburgh Village Club (Mr M. Smith), Aith, Cunningsburgh, is a youth centre hostel. Open June to August. Prices from £3.50–£4.50 per night. Tel: 01950 477777

Aith Camping Barn (Miss C. Anderson), Wirlegert, Aith, is in the village at the head of Aith Voe. Open June to August. Price per night is £4. Tel: 01595 810327

B&B

Orblaa (Mrs J. Hutchison), 3 Twaegoes Road, Lerwick, overlooks the entrance to the harbour. Prices from £15–£16 single or sharing. Tel: 01595 693417

Solbrekke (Mrs J. Stove), Sandwick, South Mainland, costs just £12–£14 single or sharing. Tel: 01950 431410

Skeo Green (Mrs B. Ford), Lunning, Vidlin, North Mainland, is in a remote location. Prices are £14 per person. Tel: 01806 577302

HOTEL

The Old Manse, 9 Commercial Street, Lerwick, is actually Lerwick's oldest inhabited house, built in 1685! Prices from £18–£20 for single or sharing, per person. Tel: 01595 696301

FETLAR

CAMPING

The Garths Campsite (Mr N. Boxall), Gord, overlooks Tresta Beach. Open May to September. Priced from £3.60–£6.60. Tel: 01957 733227

B&B

The Glebe (Mr P. Kelly) is a listed building overlooking Papil Water. Priced from £13–£15 single or sharing. Tel: 01957 733242

UNST

HOSTEL

Gardiesfauld Hostel, Uyeasound, is in an idyllic situation by the sea. Open May to September. Price per night is £6.95 for adults, £5.85 for children. Tel: 01957 755298

WHALSAY

BOD

The Grieve House, Sodom, was the home of Hugh MacDiarmid whilst he lived in Shetland. Open April to October. Priced at £3 per person per night. Tel: 01595 693434

YELL

BOD

Windhouse Lodge, Mid Yell, is near the A968. Open April to October, priced at £3 per person per night. Tel: 01595 693434

B&B

Post Office, (Mrs M. Tulloch), Gutcher, is beside the Unst/Fetlar ferry terminal. Priced at £14 for single or double. Tel: 01957 744201

TRAVEL

The only way to travel for nothing is to walk, or to cycle if you have your own bike.

Scotland has some of the finest long-distance walks in the world – the West Highland Way and the Southern Upland Way. Naturally, these thunderingly long walks can be taken in sections, often gentle or mildly strenuous ones, frequently with a pub and a railway station or bus stop at the other end. The section of the West Highland Way that runs along the banks of Loch Lomond is a delightful example of this. There are also many pleasant recreational walks waiting to be taken through all the landscapes of Scotland. In fact, there are so many paths and tracks, criss-crossing the countryside and even the urban areas, that no book could ever list them all. I haven't attempted to do so. In fact, I have completely steered away from 'walks' in this travel section. It is almost a philosophical thing. To walk is free. To step outside a door, anywhere in the country and take a few steps costs you absolutely zero. So where would you draw a line? If you need information on those long hike-type walks, there are books especially for you, written by people with far more pairs of those thick itchy woolly hiking socks than my family might possess in a lifetime. (Together with the usual free leaflets from your ubiquitous Tourist Information Centres.) If, on the other hand, you are on the look-out for a bit of a stroll, maybe with a little undefined 'something' to go with it (like chips and vinegar: none of us know quite why the vinegar is needed, but you won't like them without it), then look through the Days Out section. Days Out has all manner of parks, gardens, beaches and woodland for you to stretch your legs in.

Now, if cycling is your preferred mode of transport, you might find some ideas here. There are other guides specifically for cyclists, which go through the many cycle routes in great detail; but here you will find plenty of suggested bike hire places, too. Hiring a bike will cost you from £5 to £10 per day for a regular bike, and more for a mountain bike. No shoestring stuff I grant you.

Bus or coach (for longer trips) is usually the next cheapest way to get anywhere. The bus networks go further into rural parts than the trains, and will immerse you in the real Scotland. Please don't look to this book for information about 'tours'; these are never particularly cheap (although some specialist backpacker ones are beginning to operate from the central belt). If these are your scene, then look into it further at your local Tourist Information Service. Some hostelling groups run buses that can be useful, for example from one hostel to the next. For the adventurous there is even a postbus service which runs on various routes throughout the Highlands (and some islands); you could get to know intimately the local postmen (or women)! There are many different bus companies (or operators) across Scotland, the result of deregulation of the bus system, so planning ahead is wise. And always ask for any special fare information, as deals change often.

Trains are wonderful. Much quicker than buses, and let's be honest, more comfortable. The cost, however, can be offputting; so if you decide to go by train, remember to look at all the special ticket deals that are available, and try to book in advance wherever you can. Absolutely not on a shoestring.

Ferries can be an integral part of your journey, particularly if travelling to any of the islands, or to the beauty of Ardnamurchan, the Mull of Kintyre, or the Cowal peninsula. The best thing about ferries is the physical reminder that you are crossing from one place to another, from one state of mind to another. The Connel ferry can change your life. You step on board a city-bound bundle of frayed humanity and step off the other side enriched and revitalised. Better than an hour's reflexology any day. As usual, there are cheap ways, and expensive ways of crossing. Get over to Mull, for example, via Lochaline, which is cheap and regular. Make sure you know the ferry times and the *last ferry times* too, because an unexpected overnight stay is not what you want if you are on a budget. In other words, call a few of the numbers listed here a little in advance, so that you know what you are doing beforehand.

What more can I say? Travelling in Scotland is an integral part of the experience. Immerse yourself!

THE WEST

Argyll and Bute

Cycling

Hire yourself two-wheeled self-propelled transport from one of a number of little outlets. Try for instance, Calder Brothers in Bridge Street, Rothesay, Tel: 01700 504477 (£5 per day, £7.50 per day for mountain bikes); DM Automarine at The Pier, Lochgoilhead, Tel: 01301 703432/703249 (for mountain bikes); Highland Stores in Argyll Street, Dunoon, Tel: 01369 702001; or WM Montgomery and Sons, Strachur Filling Station, Tel: 01369 860227.

A nice little homespun leaflet details cycle routes on the Isle of Bute, and as all routes begin and end at the Tourist Information Centre in Rothesay's Victoria Street you can go in and pick up a leaflet!

Bus

Take a bus to Argyll from Glasgow's Buchanan Bus Station (see Glasgow below). Scottish Citylink, for example, operate the only coach service to Inveraray, Tel: 0990 505050. Local buses are operated by Western Scottish Buses. Get timetable and fare information before you travel, Tel: 01563 522551. On the Isle of Bute too, the service is run by Stagecoach Western Scottish, with plenty of routes to choose from.

Train

Travel from Glasgow Central to stations which include: Arrochar, Dalmally, Taynuilt, Connel and Oban. Strathclyde Passenger Transport are responsible for promoting travel throughout the area, Tel: 0141 332 6811.

Ferries

For Bute (Rothesay) sail from Wemyss Bay (Caledonian MacBrayne, Tel: 01475 520521). For Dunoon sail from Gourock (Caledonian MacBrayne, Tel: 01475 650100), or for Hunter's Quay near Dunoon, sail from McInroy's Point (Western Ferries, Dunoon, Tel: 01369 704452). The truly adventurous could take the ferry from Ardrossan to Brodick on Arran, and then from Lochranza to Claonig in the north of Kintyre. Alternatively, go a little overland and take the short ferry crossing from Portavadie to Tarbert (Caledonian MacBrayne, Tel: 01475 650100).

Ayrshire

Cycling

You can get hold of a bike in Ayr from AMG Cycles in Dalblair Road, Tel: 01292 287580.

Irvine is a good base for cycle paths. Look for the brochure called 'Glasgow and Clyde Coast Cycle Routes', which you should be able to pick up at a local Tourist Information Centre. It is free and has a great map. There is a local section, entitled 'Guide to the Paisley to Irvine and Ardrossan Section' which is helpful.

Train
Take the train from Glasgow Central to many destinations in Ayrshire including Ardrossan, Saltcoats and Stevenston, Irvine, Largs, Kilwinning, Kilmarnock, Auchinleck, New Cumnock, and south to Ayr, Prestwick, Troon, Maybole and Girvan. Contact the National Rail Enquiry Line for timetable and fare details. Always check out any special deals that are available. Tel: 0345 484950 (24 hours)

ARRAN
Cycling
If you are on Arran, why not hire yourself a bike? There are plenty of places to choose from, such as Brodick Boat and Cycle Hire, Tel: 01771 302388; Brodick Cycles, Tel: 01771 302460; Spinning Wheels in Corrie, Tel: 01770 810660; and Whiting Bay Cycle Hire, Tel: 01770 700382.

Ferries
The ferry to Arran leaves from Ardrossan and takes just 55 minutes to reach Brodick. In summer you can sail from Claonaig on the Kintyre peninsula to Lochranza in the north of the island – a ten-minute crossing. Both these routes are run by Caledonian MacBrayne, Tel: 01475 650100.

CUMBRAE
Cycling
Cumbrae also lends itself to bike hire. Try: AT Morton, Mount Stuart Street, Millport, Tel: 01475 530478; FVG Maples and Son, Guildford Street, Millport, Tel: 01475 530444 (who also hire out buggies, tandems and even adult trikes!); or Bremners Cycle Hire at Cardiff Street, Millport, Tel: 01475 530309/530707.

Ferry
To get across to Cumbrae, take a ferry from Largs. These leave every 15 minutes and buses connect to take you on to Millport.

East Dunbartonshire
Cycling
You can hire a bike from Discount Bike Hire, Auchinairn, Bishopbriggs, Tel: 0141 762 1616.

City of Glasgow
All roads lead here, as well as all railway lines! You will have no problems

getting around in Glasgow, or getting from Glasgow to almost any other destination of your choice! To be sure though, remember to find out as much as you can in advance, and compare prices (particularly between bus/coach and rail) before you go. An excellent source of route-planning help (including timetables) and price information is the Travel Centre, St Enoch Square, Glasgow, Tel: 0141 226 4826. Ask them for a Visitors Transport Guide, with a map and information about every transport service provider; it will give you far more information than you will ever need, but a sense of well-being, too.

Cycling

There are a series of cycle paths in the Glasgow area. Try out the *Glasgow/Loch Lomond Cycleway*, which takes you from the centre of Glasgow to Killin in the heart of the Highlands. The route starts at the Scottish Exhibition and Conference Centre (SECC) on the banks of the Clyde, then takes in Clydebank and Dumbarton before heading up the Vale of Leven to Balloch on the banks of Loch Lomond. The route can then link you into forest routes around Aberfoyle (via Drymen in the Campsie Hills), and on to Callander for the Central Highland Way route that heads north to Strathyre and Killin via Glen Ogle.

Other cycle paths worth looking at are the *Clyde Coast Cycle Routes*, which go from Bells Bridge at the SECC in Glasgow through the parks of the city, following the old Paisley and Ardrossan Canal (now a railway line!) and the White Cart River. The trail goes on to Greenock, Irvine and Ardrossan.

The heroic amongst you might even be interested in the *Glasgow to Edinburgh Cycleway* which incorporates the Clyde Walkway, Airdrie to Bathgate Railway Path, Livingston Paths Network and Lothian Cycle Routes. The middle section through the Central Scotland Forest has interesting sculpture along the way. For further details on any of these cycle routes, and others, contact Sustrans Scotland, 53 Cochrane Street, Glasgow G1 1HL, Tel: 0141 552 8241. There is also a snazzy brochure called 'Glasgow and Clyde Coast Cycle Routes', which you should be able to pick up at a local Tourist Information Centre. It is free and has a great map.

Hire a bike from West End Cycles, Chancellor Street, Partick, Tel: 0141 357 1344.

Bus

Many bus and coach links run from Glasgow's Buchanan Bus Station in Killermont Street. Local services are operated mostly by Strathclyde Passenger Transport. Express coach services operated by National Express and Scottish Citylink can take you all over Britain from here, at a reasonable price. Always ask about concessions and special tickets. For information on coach services, Tel: 0990 505050 (8 a.m. to 8 p.m. daily). To enquire about local services, Tel: 0141 332 7133. Skye-Ways Travel operate daily services from Glasgow to Skye, Inverness and the Outer Hebrides in modern luxury coaches. Tel: 01599 534328 (Kyle of Lochalsh) or 01463 710119 (Inverness)

There are other Strathclyde Passenger Transport Travel Information Centres at St Enoch Square, Tel: 0141 226 4826; and Hillhead Travel Centre on Byres Road, Tel: 0141 333 3673.

Train

Roughly speaking, Glasgow Queen Street Station serves the East, whilst Glasgow Central Station serves the West. So head for Queen Street Station for trains to Edinburgh (every half-hour), Aberdeen, Elgin and Inverness. Glasgow Central can take you to Ayr, Oban, Fort William, Gourock, and south to Manchester, Birmingham and London. As before, ask for details of special fares, which change all the time. National Rail Enquiry Line, Tel: 0345 484950 (24 hours). If you are travelling locally, via ScotRail or Strathclyde Transport, then watch out for cheap fares in the form of 'Roundabout' tickets, which allow train and underground travel for one day. There are over 100 stations in the Greater Glasgow and Clyde Valley area!

Underground
Yes, Glasgow has an efficient and economic underground system. You can use special tickets on the 'Clockwork Orange' or even choose to follow the 'Underground Heritage Trail' to visit the city's main attractions.

Inverclyde

Bus
Travel by coach and bus in this area is easy. Contact Scottish Citylink at Buchanan Bus Station in Glasgow for detailed information. Tel: 0990 505050

Train
Regular train services from Glasgow link the stations at Port Glasgow, Greenock and Gourock and Wemyss Bay (a particularly beautiful station). Strathclyde Transport offer special ticket deals such as the 'Day Tripper Ticket', so be sure to find out about any bargains. If you need train help, call the National Rail Enquiry Line (local call rate) on 0345 212282/0345 484950.

Ferries
Sail from Gourock to the Cowal peninsula all year with Caledonian MacBrayne; there are also summer-season pleasure cruises from Gourock to Tighnabruaich, Kyles of Bute, Arran, etc., but these are more expensive. Tel: 01475 650100

Alternatively, you can take a ferry with Western Ferries from McInroy's Point, a mile west of Gourock. This car and passenger service sails to the Cowal peninsula all year. Tel: 01369 704452

It is also possible to sail from Princes Pier in Greenock, across the Clyde to Kilcreggan and Helensburgh. This service is operated by the Clyde Marine Motoring Company. Tel: 01475 721281

Wemyss Bay is the place for sailings to the Isle of Bute, with Caledonian MacBrayne. Tel: 01475 520521

North Lanarkshire

This is another area close enough to Glasgow to benefit from the extensive travel network of the city.

Bus and train
Cumbernauld Bus Station has a Strathclyde Passenger Transport Travel Information Centre, where you can enquire about local tickets, long-distance coach bookings, day and extended tour bookings, and generally get information on the timetables. Tel: 01236 733731. Some local buses are run

out of Wishaw by Hutchisons Coaches, Tel: 01698 372132.

Get the answer to your rail travel query by calling 0345 212282 (24 hours).

Renfrewshire

There are excellent transport links in this region, not a surprise really as Paisley also boasts Glasgow Airport on its doorstep.

Cycling

Some brilliant cycle routes link Inverclyde with Renfrewshire, and Renfrewshire with Glasgow. The *Glasgow–Paisley Cycle Route* runs from the Scottish Exhibition and Conference Centre, through the parks of Glasgow before following the old Paisley and Ardrossan Canal and the White Cart River. Try instead the *Paisley–Greenock Cycle Route*, which follows an old railway line through Elderslie, Kilbarchan, Bridge of Weir, Kilmacolm and Port Glasgow to Octavia Park in Greenock. There is even sculpture along the way! Another route is the *Paisley–Irvine Cycle Route*, which uses the old Lochwinnoch railway loop and minor roads to reach Irvine. Further details on any of these cycle routes can be had from Sustrans Scotland, 53 Cochrane Street, Glasgow, Tel: 0141 552 8241. The Paisley–Irvine route is part of the larger Glasgow and Clyde Coast Cycle Routes, and there are some superb leaflets available from Tourist Information Centres on the route itself – good simple maps and little extras, too.

Hire yourself a set of wheels from Discount Bike Hire, Unit 16, Phoenix Retail Park in Linwood, Tel: 0141 889 9111.

Bus and train

Served in the main by Strathclyde Transport, so make the most of special tickets such as 'Roundabout' tickets, which allow unlimited train and underground travel for a day. If you call in at Strathclyde Passenger Transport offices at the Travel Centre, Gilmour Street Station, County Square, Paisley (Tel: 0141 848 6313), you can pick up details on the range of fast frequent local rail services and the range of tickets for bus, rail and underground too. They even have information on coach links and prices.

Find out about rail services by calling 0345 212282 (24 hours).

South Lanarkshire

South Lanarkshire is also an area close enough to Glasgow to benefit from an excellent transport network.

Cycling

If you feel the need, why not hire yourself a bike? You can get one from MGB Ralton Cycles at Avon Street, Hamilton, Tel: 01698 284926.

Bus and train

Head for Strathclyde Passenger Transport to get details on local rail services, as well as facts on the range of bargain tickets for leisure travel on rail, bus and underground. This travel centre is at Hamilton Bus Station, Tel: 01698 281926. Another Strathclyde Passenger Transport Travel Information Centre is located at the bus station in East Kilbride, Tel: 01355 236502.

Get the answer to your rail travel query by calling 0345 212282 (24 hours).

THE EAST

East Lothian

Bus

The area enjoys good travel links of all kinds as a result of its closeness to the capital. For information on the local network, call 0131 225 3858.

Train

The mainline London–Edinburgh service calls at Dunbar. There are also regular services from Edinburgh to Wallyford, Musselburgh, Prestonpans, Longniddry, Drem and North Berwick. Further train information can be obtained by calling 0131 556 2451.

City of Edinburgh

Cycling

There are a number of places in the city from which to hire a bike. Try Corstorphine Cycles, at 9 Featherhall Ave, Edinburgh, Tel: 0131 334 2748; or Sandy Gilchrist Cycles, 1 Cadzow Place, Abbeyhill, Edinburgh, Tel: 0131 652 1760.

Bus

There are excellent fast coach and bus links from Edinburgh to cities all over Scotland and the rest of the UK. The bus station at St Andrew Square caters for Scottish Citylink and National Express coaches. Some other services leave from Waverley Bridge, near the train station. Local travel is made easy by Lothian Regional Transport (the maroon and white buses) as well as other small local operators (Midland Bluebird, Fife Omnibuses, etc.). Wherever you want to go, there should be a bus to get you there. Lothian Regional Transport have a helpful Touristcard ticket which, at £10 for an adult and £5 for a child, allows two days' unlimited travel, and includes the 'Edinburgh Classic Tour' bus trip, which is well worth a try. The Touristcard also gives you discounts at a number of the attractions around the city which have an entrance fee (such as the Camera Obscura, the Zoo and the Edinburgh Crystal Centre). Get information from the LRT Travel Shop at Waverley Bridge, Tel: 0131 555 6363, or the LRT Travel Shop at 27 Hanover Street, Tel: 0131 554 4494. Another good ticket they offer is the Day Saver Ticket, at £2.20 for adults, £1.50 for children. This ticket gives unlimited travel in Edinburgh and the Lothians that day, and you can simply buy it on the first bus you board.

Train

If you need train help, call the National Rail Enquiry Line (local call rate) on 0345 212282/0345 484950. Edinburgh's mainline station is Waverley, and from here you can go north to Inverness (and further), as well as south to London and even Weymouth and Plymouth. As ever, check out the cheapest fare deals, and shop around as there are now several operators.

Midlothian

Cycling
You could do worse than to hire yourself a couple of wheels. Try the Dalkeith Bike Shed at Tait Street, Dalkeith, Tel: 0131 654 1170.

West Lothian

Cycling
Hire a pair of wheels for the day from Roving Cyclepaths, at 13 Greendykes Road, Broxburn, Tel: 01506 852330.

Bus
Midland Bluebird is the operator in the Linlithgow/Bo'ness area, and there is a bus travel centre in Linlithgow High Street. You can also call the Bluebird Busline on 01324 613777/623901.

Train
There are regular services linking West Lothian with Edinburgh, as well as Glasgow, Perth, Stirling, Inverness and beyond. Linlithgow (and Polmont) is well served by a fast service, and trains from Edinburgh to Glasgow Central will take you to the likes of Kirknewton and Livingston. A helpful train number is 0141 332 9811.

Canal
You will recall that I waxed lyrical about the canal boat trips on the Union Canal at Linlithgow in the Days Out section. Flick back for a change!

THE BORDERS

Dumfries and Galloway

Cycling
You can hire bicycles from Ace Cycles in Castle Douglas, Tel: 01556 504542; or Grierson and Graham in Dumfries, Tel: 01387 259483.

Cycleways and trails can be found in Mabie Forest. Get into the wilds, too, at various Forest Enterprise mountain-bike trails – Kirroughtree and Glen Trool (Tel: 01671 402420), Clatteringshaws (Tel: 01556 503626).

Train
Plenty of places to choose from here, from Kirkconnel, Sanquhar, Lockerbie and Dumfries, to Stranraer. Good access from Edinburgh and Glasgow, as well as from London and stations on the West Coast line (now run by Richard Branson's Virgin organisation). If you need train help, call the National Rail Enquiry Line (local call rate) on 0345 212282/0345 484950.

Ferries
Sail from Stranraer (Cairnryan) to Larne in Ireland with P&O European Ferries, Tel: 01581 200276. Alternatively, take the Stena Line and sail from

Stranraer to Belfast; these ferries go from the Ferry Terminal, Port Rodie, Stranraer, Tel: 0990 707070. There is plenty of competition on this route, which is also operated by Seacat Scotland, from the West Pier, Stranraer, Tel: 0345 523523.

Scottish Borders

Cycling

There are plenty of wonderful places for cycling in the Borders. The *Tweed Cycleway* is a 90-mile signposted route on generally quiet public roads from Biggar to Berwick-upon-Tweed. Border Forests have miles of waymarked routes for novices and the experienced. Borders Tourist Information have a series of leaflets on cycling and mountain-biking. So, why not hire yourself a bike and pedal your way round the beautiful Borders (if your stamina is up to it)? Try Hawick Cycle Centre at Bridge Street in Hawick, Tel: 01450 373352. There are great mountain-bike trails in the nearby Craik Forest. George Pennel Cycles in the High Street, Peebles, also hires out bikes, Tel: 01721 720844. Scottish Border Trails hire out bikes at three locations, Glentress, Peebles; Bowhill Estate, Selkirk; and Craik Forest, near Hawick, Tel: 01721 720336.

Bus

Buses are superb for cheap easy access to the Borders. The local company is Lowland Omnibuses, and they have special explorer tickets (the Reiver Rover and Waverley Wanderer) to get you around economically with unlimited travel either on a daily or a weekly basis. Collect your information from the bus people at any of the following: Berwick (Tel: 01289 307461), Galashiels (Tel: 01896 752237), Hawick (Tel: 01450 372784), Kelso (Tel: 01573 224141), and Peebles (Tel: 01721 720181). (If you are heading for the Borders from Edinburgh, aim for the bus station at St Andrew Square.)

Train

Try working your way north from Berwick-upon-Tweed. The Borders isn't really served by the rail network, so think laterally! (For example, take the bus!)

CENTRAL, TAYSIDE AND FIFE

Dundee City

Bus

The local service operator is Strathtay Scottish Omnibuses Ltd, whom you can contact at the Seagate Bus Station, Tel: 01382 228345. Remember to ask about concessionary fares and special tickets and deals. Tayside Public Transport are another operator, who can be contacted at East Dock Street, Tel: 01382 201121.

Train

There are sleeper services to Dundee from London King's Cross.

The station at Dundee is on a fairly busy main link both to mainline stations in the Central Belt (Edinburgh to Glasgow), and for local services. The station, called Taybridge Station, is down near the Discovery Centre, on Union Street, Tel: 01382 228046.

Falkirk

Trains

Falkirk has two stations, Falkirk High and Falkirk Grahamston. Falkirk High takes trains on the Edinburgh–Glasgow route, whilst Falkirk Grahamston serves the routes to Stirling, Perth and beyond. Nearby Polmont is another busy station, on the Edinburgh–Glasgow main line. If you need information, call the National Rail Enquiry Line (local call rate) on 0345 212282/0345 484950.

Fife

Cycling

Why not get hold of a pair of wheels? Try the Dalkeith Bike Shop at 68 Chambers Street, Dunfermline, Tel: 01383 620708.

Bus

From St Andrews the main operator is Fife Scottish Omnibuses, who run out of the bus station on City Road. There are express links from here to Glasgow, Edinburgh and Dundee, as well as local routes throughout Fife, Tel: 01334 474328. For more detailed information on local routes, contact the bus station in Kirkcaldy, in Hill Street, Tel: 01592 642394, or Leven Bus Depot at Aberhill, Tel: 01333 426038. Another bus centre is in Glenrothes, Tel: 01592 610686.

Train

There are stations in many towns in Fife, including Inverkeithing, Aberdour, Burntisland, Glenrothes (with Thornton), Kinghorn, Kirkcaldy, Markinch, Ladybank and Leuchars. You can get local information from the station at Kirkcaldy, Tel: 01592 204771. (The main station to get across the Rail Bridge to Fife is Edinburgh Waverley.)

Perth and Kinross

Detailed timetables, area guides and price information on public transport in the area can be obtained from Perth and Kinross Council, Tel: 0345 413883 (local call rate), or write to the Public Transport Unit, Perth and Kinross Council, Business Park, Whitefriars Crescent, Perth PH2 0ZA.

I'm not giving you much information in this section about walks or walking – I figure that we all know this is free anyway! However, there is a lovely brochure of Pitlochry walks that is free, and has a good map to boot.

Cycling

Bikes can be hired throughout Perthshire. One example is Crieff Cycle Centre at Leadenflower Road, Crieff, Tel: 01764 652599. For local details, contact the nearest Tourist Information Centre.

Bus

The main towns, for example Blairgowrie, Crieff, Kinross and Pitlochry, are served by hourly bus or coach services. Perth has many routes in and round about, from the main bus station in Leonard Street or the local service bus station at Mill Street. Pitlochry has express coach links to Perth, Inverness and beyond, as well as local services, Tel: 01796 472290. Most rural villages have public transport services, some via school-bus services. Dunkeld, for example, benefits from regular services to Perth, Pitlochry and Aberfeldy, Tel: 01738 629339 for bus enquiries. There are even 11 postbus routes, so you could find yourself sharing your journey with parcels and letters, and enjoy the experience of getting to know postmen (and women). There is one postbus which travels along Loch Rannoch from Pitlochry to Rannoch Station.

Train

Through either Edinburgh or Glasgow there are links to the south from Perthshire. The famous Highland Line has stations at Gleneagles (close to Auchterarder), Perth, Birnam (for Dunkeld), Pitlochry and Blair Atholl. On the scenic West Highland Line you can travel to the remoteness of Rannoch. Local Rail Enquiry Line: 01738 637117.

Stirling

Cycling

You can hire bikes from New Heights at Barnton Street, Stirling, Tel: 01786 450809. A little further afield, in Aberfoyle for example, and you can choose from On Track Bikes, Tel: 01877 382858; or Forest Cycle Centre, Main Street, Aberfoyle, Tel: 01877 382802.

Bus

From Stirling you can take a fast bus to Glasgow and then virtually anywhere in the western world. Pretty fast buses also operate to Falkirk, whilst the extremely fast ones will zoom you off to Inverness, Dundee, or Aberdeen, via Dunblane, Auchterarder, Perth and the like. Investigate with Scottish Citylink. Local services are operated by Bluebird, and these run up to the Trossachs or towards Denny, Alloa and the hillfoot villages or the Campsie Hills.

Train

Stirling is a mainline station, with sleepers to London, the lot. Travel from here to either Edinburgh or Glasgow, or head north to Perth and many stations to Inverness. I once saw the royal train parked here! There are local stations at Bridge of Allan and Dunblane. For rail information contact the National Rail Enquiry Line (local call rate) on 0345 212282/0345 484950.

GRAMPIAN

Aberdeen

Cycling
Walk or cycle the *Deeside (former) Railway Line* from Duthie Park to Peterculter. It's only six miles. Hire a two-wheeled friend from Reid's Cycles in Broom Hill Road, Aberdeen, Tel: 01224 586974; or Aberdeen Cycle Centre in King Street, Tel: 01224 644542.

Bus
Aberdeen is served by long-distance coaches from almost all parts of England, Wales and Scotland. For information, call either Scottish Citylink on 0141 332 9191 or National Express on 0990 808080.

For local information on buses in Aberdeen and the immediate area call the Grampian Busline on 01224 633333.

Train
Aberdeen has direct services from London King's Cross, Edinburgh, Glasgow, north Scotland and most points in between. Services from London include sleepers. ScotRail passenger enquiries: 01224 594222.

Aberdeenshire

Cycling
There are some glorious cycle routes in Aberdeenshire. You could try out the *Bunzeach Cycle Route* at Old Semeil, Bellabeg, Strathdon. These are a series of waymarked trails through the forest which are good for family mountain-biking. Tel: 01466 794161. *Gartly Ski Trail and Mountain Bike Route* is at Gartly by Huntly, Tel: 01466 794161. *Pitfichie Cycle Route* starts at Tilly-fourie, Monymusk. Waymarked mountain-bike trails lead to some spectacular views. Tel: 01466 794161.

Hire the machine of your dreams from BG Cycles, The Barn, Aboyne, Tel: 013398 85355; or from Cycling World, Cross Street, Fraserburgh, Tel: 01346 513355.

Walkers might be more comfy on one of many scenic walks in the region, which include the *Formartine and Buchan Way*, which runs from Dyce to Mintlaw along the course of the old railway line. (I know, I said I wasn't going to talk about walking. I lied.)

Bus
Bluebird operate services throughout the Grampian Highlands area, Tel: 01224 212226. All but a few remote parts of the area have regular bus or postbus services. For information on the postbus phenomenon, call 0131 228 7407.

Train
Trains run regularly between Aberdeen and Inverness, calling at Dyce, Inverurie, Huntly, Keith, Elgin and Forres. Stonehaven and Portlethen are also on the main railway line. To flesh out the detail, call ScotRail passenger enquiries on 01224 594222.

Angus

Cycling

Hire that bike for your outing from Clan Green Ltd, in Ferry Street, Montrose, Tel: 01674 77199.

Bus

The services throughout Angus are reasonably regular, but as ever, call and organise yourself first. You can ask about any fare deals then, and you might even be pleasantly surprised! At Arbroath the bus station is in Catherine Street, Tel: 01241 870646.

Strathtay Scottish Omnibuses operate throughout Angus (as they do in Dundee) and you can contact them at Brechin Bus Station for details on services to Montrose, Edzell, Aberdeen and Dundee. There are usually timetables at bus stops and (of course and thank goodness) local Tourist Information Centres. Call Brechin Bus Station, Tel: 01674 672855. Forfar Bus Station is at Prior Road, Tel: 01307 463144. Kirriemuir Bus Station is at The Square, Tel: 01382 228054. Montrose Bus Station is at Rossie Island, Tel: 01674 672855.

Train

Remember those sleeper services from London's King's Cross, which stop at Dundee early in the morning? Well, if you stay on the train a few more minutes then you can alight at Arbroath or Montrose.

ScotRail services run the local trains in the region. Call in advance to find out about the regularity of the service and the fares. Arbroath Railway Station is at Keptie Street, Tel: 01382 228046. For Montrose Railway Station, call 01382 228046.

THE HIGHLANDS

Moray

Cycling

Moray is covered by the excellent 'Bike Speyside' brochure produced by Aviemore and Speyside Tourist Board in association with Moray Council. The guide covers plenty of cycle routes, both off and on road, as well as giving suggestions for bike hire and repair places, and even B&Bs!

Bus

Almost every town and village in Moray is served by regular buses. Bear in mind though that some services are infrequent and a few do not run in the local school holidays, so advance planning is the key! Local timetables are available from Tourist Information Centres. Good local services are provided by Bluebird, which operates from Elgin to Burghead, Lossiemouth, via Baxters at Fochabers to Buckie, Banff and Macduff and also to Keith, Huntly and Aberdeen. They also operate south of Elgin to Aberlour and Dufftown and east to Forres, Brodie, Nairn and Inverness. For information, call Elgin 544222.

Train

Elgin is at the end of the line from Glasgow Queen Street, which also takes in stations such as Nairn. There is also a service from Aberdeen to Inverness which passes through Moray. For information call the National Rail Enquiry Line on 0345 484950.

Highland Heartlands

Cycling

If you can stand the pace, then perhaps hiring a bike might appeal? Try Off Beat Bikes in the High Street, Fort William, Tel: 01397 704008; alternatively, try Aviemore Mountain Bikes at the Mountain Bike Centre, Tel: Aviemore 811007. I would take lots of Kendal Mint Cake if I were you. Get in touch with the Aviemore and Spey Valley Tourist Board, who publish an excellent booklet, 'Bike Speyside', with details of a number of off-road trails and many road routes to follow. There is also a digest of cycle hire, spares and repairs shops. Well done Aviemore and Speyside Tourist Board!

Bus

Nationwide coach services run to Fort William and Inverness from Glasgow and Edinburgh. Highland Country Buses Ltd is the local bus service in Lochaber, running a service to Oban and Inverness. The main bus station is at Farraline Park, Inverness, Tel: 01463 233371. Other operators include Oban and District Buses, Tel: 01631 562856; Scottish Citylink, Tel: 0990 505050; and Gaelic Bus, Tel: 01855 811229. Skye-Ways Travel link Inverness and the Outer Hebrides in modern luxury coaches, Tel: 01463 710119. Bluebird operate services in the Grampian Highlands area, Tel: 01224 212226. All but a few remote parts of the area have regular bus or postbus services, Tel: 0131 228 7407.

Train

The train to Inverness is a journey that you will never forget. I once saw a huge stag and his female friends in the sunset near Drumochter – magical. Travel with ScotRail from either side of the central belt, and main stops in between. The trains are fairly regular on these routes. Of course the other line (the West Highland Line) to Fort William and Oban, or to Kyle of Lochalsh, is equally legendary. Plan your trip in advance and ask about the special fares from ScotRail, like the Freedom of Scotland Travelpass, or a ScotRail Rover Ticket. For rail information, Tel: 0141 332 9811/0141 204 2844. Fort William and Lochaber also have one of the world's most scenic steam-train journeys, on the Jacobite Steam Train from Fort William to Mallaig.

Ferries

From Mallaig you can take the ferry to Armadale (Skye), Lochboisdale (North Uist), Castlebay (Barra), Rum, Eigg, Muck and Canna. Go to Kilchoan on the Ardnamurchan peninsula to take a ferry to Tobermory (Mull). The cheapest Mull crossing is the shortest, from Lochaline to Fishnish. The local office is in Mallaig, but for enquiries contact the big Caledonian MacBrayne line on 01475 650100.

The Northern Highlands

Cycling

Hire the bike you need from the Bicycle Bothy, Ar-Dachaidh, Badnellan, Brora, Tel: 01408 621658; or from Kyle Cycles, Old Plock Road, Kyle of Lochalsh, Tel: 01599 4842.

Bus

There are fast frequent coach services to Thurso from Edinburgh and Glasgow. Call Scottish Citylink/National Express on 0141 332 9191. Local bus services are regular and reliable, but not always frequent! In Caithness you will do well to explore with Highland Country Buses, who are based at Lovers Lane, Thurso, Tel: 01847 893123. If in doubt, pick up timetables at the Tourist Information Centres.

Train

The northern line from Inverness to Wick and Thurso is one of the world's most beautiful railway journeys. The train splits in two at Georgemas Junction, so make sure you are on the right part! Inverness is a mainline station, so from there you can travel to all major cities in the UK. There is also a daily sleeper service to London. For train information, call 0345 484950.

Ferries

Ferries for Orkney sail from Scrabster (P&O, Tel: 01856 850655) and John o' Groats (passengers only, Tel: 01955 611353).

ISLANDS

The Inner Hebrides and The Western Isles

Don't be put off travelling to the Inner Hebrides or the Western Isles by the ferries. In most cases the crossings are fairly quick and not expensive, particularly if you are travelling on foot or with a bike. Take a tip, though, and plan a little ahead – call the ferries in question and find out the time of the last sailings if you are going to be late, and compare prices and distances by examining a map of your intended journey. Remember to ask about any special fare deals that may be on offer, like Island Hopscotch and Island Rover from Caledonian MacBrayne. Island Hopscotch fares are good if you intend using more than one crossing, and over 20 combinations of routes are offered – good savings, especially if you are travelling by car. Island Rover tickets give unlimited travel with or without a car for a period of either eight or 15 days. Tel: 01475 650100 for general enquiries. You need to allow for little extras, like the tides and the weather, so find out in advance of any delays by calling the travel operators. This is all part of the fun of your trip!

If you need any help with planning your route or getting the cheapest crossings, call the helpful folk at the Western Isles Tourist Board in Stornoway on 01851 703088. A Skye and Western Isles travel guide is available from the Tourist Information service detailing bus, air and ferry timetables, which at only 75 pence could be a good investment.

Getting to the ferry ports by bus or rail isn't too tricky. Regular buses head for Ullapool, Uig (Skye), Oban and Mallaig from central Scotland. Try Scottish Citylink (Tel: 0990 505050) or Skye-Ways Express Coaches if you are travelling from either Glasgow or Inverness (Tel: 01599 534328). Macdonald Coaches also cover the Inverness/Ullapool route (Tel: 01851 706267 or 820367). If you are feeling a bit more flush, then take the train to Oban, Mallaig or Kyle of Lochalsh from Glasgow.

The Inner Hebrides

SKYE, RAASAY, RUM, EIGG, MUCK AND CANNA

Bus

Skye-Ways Travel operate daily services between Glasgow and Skye, also linking Inverness and the Outer Hebrides in modern luxury coaches. Tel: 01599 534328 (Kyle of Lochalsh) or 01463 710119 (Inverness)

Ferries

From Mallaig you can take the ferry to Armadale (Skye). Call the Caledonian MacBrayne line on 01475 650100. Of course, none of this ferry business is necessary now there is a bridge at Kyle of Lochalsh! (Beware tolls.)

To get across to Harris from Skye, take the ferry from Uig. You guessed it, it's CalMac again, Tel: 0990 650000.

Raasay is reached from Skye, via the ferry at Sconser.

MULL AND IONA

Bus

One local operator is Bowman's Coaches of Craignure.

Ferries

Go to Kilchoan on the Ardnamurchan peninsula to take a ferry to Tobermory (Mull). The cheapest Mull crossing is the shortest, from Lochaline to Fishnish. The local office for these crossings is in Mallaig, but for enquiries contact the big Caledonian MacBrayne line on 01475 650100

Take the ferry from Phionnfort in Mull to Iona. A very quick crossing, and extremely regular too. Operated by Caledonian MacBrayne, Tel: 01475 650100

The islands of Rum, Eigg, Muck and Canna are all served by Caledonian MacBrayne from Mallaig, Tel: 01475 650100. An alternative is to take a trip with Hebridean Cruises from Arisaig. They sail to Eigg, Rum and Muck (£13, £13 and £17 in 1996), Tel: 01687 450224.

COLL AND TIREE

Ferries

The Caledonian MacBrayne service to these islands operates from Oban. Tel: 01475 650100

ISLAY, JURA, GIGHA AND COLONSAY

Ferries

For Islay the obvious ferry service is from Kintyre, near Tarbert, sailing to Port Ellen with Caledonian MacBrayne. Tel: 01475 650100

Jura is reached from Islay via a short crossing at Port Askaig.

Gigha is a ferry ride from Tayinloan in Kintyre.

Colonsay is served by the same service as Islay. You can also reach the island by CalMac ferry from Oban. The port on Colonsay is Scalasaig.

The Western Isles

BARRA

Cycles

Hire yourself a bike from Barra Cycle Hire at 29 St Brendan's Road, Isle of Barra. Tel: 01871 810284

Bus

Buses go from Castlebay to Northbay and the airport, then Eoligarry (W32) Monday to Saturday. The W33 also goes between Castlebay and Vatersay.

Ferries

Get to Barra from Oban and Mallaig, sailing to Castlebay, Tel: 01475 650000. Linked by ferry (Eoligarry) with South Uist (Ludag), Tel: 01878 720233. You can also take the Caledonian MacBrayne ferry on certain days of the week between Castlebay (Barra) and Lochbiosdale (South Uist), Tel: 01475 650000.

ERISKAY

Ferry

Connected by ferry with South Uist, Tel: 01878 720261.

HARRIS

Cycles

For bike hire contact DM MacKenzie at Pier Road, Tarbert, Tel: 01859 502271.

Bus

On schooldays you can get from Tarbert to Maaruig and Rhenigidale on a W11. Try the W12 (on schooldays and Tuesdays and Fridays outside term-time) from Tarbert to Ardhasaig, Amhuinnsuidhe and Hushinish. A useful bus going between Leverburgh and Tarbert from Mondays to Saturdays (via Rodel, Manish, Stockinish, Scadabay and Drinishader) is the W13. Bus from Tarbert to Kyles Scalpay for the Scalpay ferry, again on schooldays or Tuesdays and Fridays outside term-time.

Ferries

Get to Harris (Tarbert) from Skye (Uig), with Caledonian MacBrayne. Harris is also connected to North Uist by Caledonian MacBrayne, Tel: 01475 650000. Car ferries connect Harris with Scalpay too, Tel: 01859 540266.

LEWIS

Cycles

To hire your bike, try Alex Dan's Cycle Centre at 67 Kenneth Street in Stornoway, Tel: 01851 704025.

Bus

Travel from Stornoway to Barvas, Borve, Dell and Port of Ness (W1), to Arnol, Shawbost, Carloway, Callanish, Garynahine and back to Stornoway (W2). With the W3 you can explore Great Bernera, with the W4 take in Uig district and Brenish. Tolsta, Back, Coll, Tong, Stornoway, Knock, Swordale, Shulishader and Portnaguran are served by the W5 and you can get from Stornoway to Leurbost and Ranish on the W8. Go to Lemreway, Gravir, Kershader and Balallan from Stornoway on the W9 and head out to Leverburgh pier (for the Harris ferry) on a W10.

Ferries

Get over to Lewis from Ullapool. The crossing takes two and a half hours, and there are no sailings on Sunday. (You are always as well to check, if you intend making any crossings on a Sunday.) Tel: 0990 650000

NORTH UIST

Bus

North Uist is linked with South Uist by the W17, which plys from Otternish to Lochmaddy, Clachan, Balivanich, Lionacleit, Creagorry, Howmore, Daliburgh and Lochboisdale to Ludag. From Lochmaddy take the W18 to Sollas, Tigharry, Bayhead and Clachan, or the W19 to Otternish for the Berneray/Harris ferries. These buses run from Monday to Saturday. The W20 travels from Sidinish to Locheport and then Clachan, and there is the W21 for Baleshare Island. The W22 is the Grimsay Island service. Benbecula is served by the W26 and W27.

Ferry

Sail six days a week from North Uist (Otternish) to Harris (Leverburgh) with Caledonian MacBrayne, Tel: 01475 650100. The local CalMac office is at Lochmaddy, Tel: 01876 500337.

SOUTH UIST

Bus

Take the handy W17 to travel up the island to North Uist (see above). The W29 plys between Lochboisdale and South Glendale, linking with Ludag Pier for the Eriskay/Barra ferries. Try the W30 for Askernish and Daliburgh from Lochboisdale, whilst the W31 goes from South Lochboisdale to Lochboisdale, both these buses are on schooldays and alternate days in the holidays.

Ferry

You can cross to South Uist from Oban and Mallaig, Tel: 01876 500337 – local office in Lochboisdale (Caledonian MacBrayne, bookings, Tel: 01475 650000). Services tend to focus on alternate days, so do check out that there is a sailing on your day of travel. Sail from here to Eriskay, Tel: 01878

720261; likewise to (or from) Harris, Tel: 01475 650000 (Caledonian MacBrayne). For sailings to Barra, see in the Barra entry above (the main Mallaig/Oban service sails back and forth to Barra via South Uist).

Orkney

Bus

Take the bus to Orkney from Inverness Bus Station, stance number ten at 2.20 p.m. every day from the beginning of May to 7 September. The Orkney Bus leaves Kirkwall every day at 9 a.m. and arrives in Inverness at 1.45 p.m., Tel: 01955 611353.

Scottish Citylink/National Express services link London, Glasgow, Edinburgh, Stirling, Perth, Inverness, Wick, Thurso and Scrabster for the Orkney ferry. For full details, contact Scottish Citylink, Tel: 0900 505050, or National Express, Tel: 0990 808080.

JD Peace coaches operate a service from Kirkwall bus station that connects with the Hoy ferry. Rosie Coaches run connecting services to Tingwall for the ferry to Rousay, Egilsay and Wyre from Kirkwall via Finstown.

Causeway Coaches run from Kirkwall to St Margaret's Hope.

Ferries

Ferries for Orkney sail from Scrabster to Stromness (P&O, Tel: 01856 850655) – with ferries from Aberdeen calling at Shetland too, and John o' Groats to Burwick in summer only (passengers and bikes only, Tel: 01955 611353). A free bus meets the afternoon train from Thurso at approximately 2.30 p.m., and connects with the 4 p.m. (or 6 p.m.) ferry from Scrabster to Orkney. The Orkney Bus direct express coach from Inverness at 2.20 p.m. meets the 6 p.m. ferry. There are bus connections between Burwick and Kirkwall for all ferry sailings.

HOY, FLOTTA AND GRAEMSAY

Sailing from Houton, Orphir to Lyness in Hoy, calling at Flotta. The journey takes 35 minutes. To book, Tel: 01856 811397. Another ferry, for passengers only, sails from Stromness Pier to Moaness, North Hoy, calling at Graemsay. To book, Tel: 01856 872044.

Prices for ferries to Hoy, Graemsay, Flotta, Rousay, Egilsay and Wyre cost from £1.05, to £4.20 for return adult fare, depending on the type of ticket you buy. A car will cost £12.60 return.

ROUSAY, EGILSAY AND WYRE

Ferries sail from Tingwall, Evie. To book, call 01856 751360. Sailing time is about 20 minutes.

SHAPINSAY

Take the ferry to Shapinsay from Kirkwall. Sailing time is about 20 minutes. To book, call 01856 872044.

EDAY

Take the ferry from Kirkwall, sailing time is about one hour and 15 minutes. To book, call 01856 872044.

The cost for crossings to Eday, Stronsay, Sanday, Westray, Papa Westray and North Ronaldsay are from £2.10 to £8.40 adult return, depending on your ticket. Cars are more costly, expect to pay around £18.90 return.

STRONSAY

Sailings are regular from Kirkwall, taking about an hour and 35 minutes. To book, call 01856 872044.

SANDAY

Sail from Kirkwall again, the time taken will be around one hour and 25 minutes. To book, call 01856 872044.

WESTRAY

Regular ro-ro ferries from Kirkwall to Rapness take around one hour and 25 minutes. To book, call 01856 872044.

PAPA WESTRAY

Reach Papa Westray on the small boat service from Pierowall, Westray.

NORTH RONALDSAY

This is the most remote of the islands. There is a weekly lift on/lift off ferry service from Kirkwall. Sailing time is about two hours and 30 minutes. To book, call 01856 872494.

Shetland

A tip for organising your travel to Shetland: an Inter-Island Transport Timetable is published by Shetland Islands Council, and contains details of all air, sea and road services. It has full details and schedules for over 30 services. Get hold of a copy from Shetland Islands Tourism for just 75 pence. Under a quid and probably a valuable spend! Now, I'm not telling you about travelling to Shetland by air, as my guess is that if you've bought this book, you would rather *not* pay the air fare prices. The same applies in the section on Orkney and the Isles. Of course you can fly if you want to, but a sea voyage really sets you up for an 'island' experience.

Ferries

P&O Scottish Ferries provide a passenger and vehicle ferry service almost daily between Aberdeen and Lerwick. The service goes twice-weekly via Orkney during the summer, so you can make the most of your precious holiday time. Leave from Aberdeen or Lerwick around 6 p.m. and arrive at the other end at about 8 a.m. the following morning. You can reckon on sailing from around £50 per person. Remember to try for any special fare deals and concessions. (Not on a shoestring, I agree.) For further information contact P&O Scottish Ferries, PO Box 5, Jamieson's Quay,

Aberdeen AB9 8DL, Tel: 01224 572615.

Once on Shetland you will find that there are excellent passenger and drive on/drive off car ferry links with most of the islands from Mainland, and the passenger fares are not so pricey. The islands of Unst, Yell, Whalsay, Fetlar, Out Skerries and Bressay are served by drive on/drive off ferries which make up to 22 crossings a day on the busiest routes. Advance booking or at least enquiry is recommended, as usual. Passenger and cargo vessels serve the islands of Fair Isle (from Grutness, South Mainland), Foula (from Scalloway or Walls, West Mainland), and Papa Stour (from West Burrafirth). These are scheduled services and they are only once or twice a week, so sort yourself out well in advance. Basically – contact the Shetlands Tourist Board to get a copy of the Travel Timetables, and to pick their brains.

Bus

There are some public bus routes on the islands, again check the details before you go. If I were you, I'd take my bike. Few hills and cheaper than a car by far.

INDEX